CROCHET
Wishes and Wonders™

Interim Editorial Director
Janet Tipton Perrin

Product Development Manager
Fran Rohus

Production/Photography Director
Ange Van Arman

Editorial
Senior Editor: Jennifer Christiansen McClain
Editor: Sharon Lothrop
Associate Editors: Lyne Pickens, Jana Robertson,
Trudy Atteberry
Copy Editor: Salway Sabri

Book Design
Minette Collins Smith

Production
Production Manager: Jean Schrecengost
Production Coordinator: Glenda Chamberlain
Color Specialist: Betty Holmes

Photography
Photography Manager: Scott Campbell
Photogapher: Keith Godfrey
Photo Stylist: Martha Coquat

Product Design
Product Development Coordinator: Deborah Hamburg
Publications Coordinator: Janet Birch

Business
CEO: John Robinson
Vice President/Marketing: Greg Deily

Sincerest thanks to all the designers and other professionals
whose dedication has made this book possible.
Special thanks to David Norris and Kaye Stafford
of Quebecor Printing Book Group, Kingsport, Tennessee.

Library of Congress Cataloging-in-Publication Data
ISBN: 1-57367-112-6
First Printing: 2000
Library of Congress Catalog Card Number: 99-75969
Published and Distributed by
The Needlecraft Shop, LLC, Big Sandy, Texas 75755
Printed in the United States of America.

We would like to express our appreciation to Gallo Pewter Sculptures for the permission to
use the "Friendship Faeries" images shown throughout this book. You may purchase
"Friendship Faeries" by calling 1-800-554-2556 or by writing to Gallo Pewter Sculptures,
P. O. Box 1996, Green Cover Springs, FL 32043

Dear Friend,

Ever since I can remember, I've been fascinated by the wonders of crochet. It's so magical! With just a little imagination and a wave of my hook, I can transform a single strand of thread into a delicate doily or a silky ball of mohair into a sumptuously soft afghan right before my eyes. Just as an artist brings canvas and oil together to create a masterpiece, a tiny hook is all I need to unlock a treasure chest of handcrafted beauty.

In a world where so many things are mass-produced, this ageless, mystical craft offers a unique perspective on how to make our world a better place. With each new item I stitch, the sense of accomplishment never wanes. Filling my world with crochet is not only a way to enhance my surroundings, but also a way of expressing my personal style and creativity. Even the highest-priced catalogs and stores can't supply me with the custom-made look I can create with my hook.

But, making the world brighter for others is also a benefit of this wonderful craft. Presenting someone with a lovingly handmade gift lets them know they're thought of enough to deserve a piece of your heart, wrapped within each stitch. Crocheted mementos for any occasion become heartfelt reminders of life's joy, however large or small.

Are the wonders of crochet real? Ask anyone who knows the exhilaration of completing, or receiving, a prized project. Can we wish for more ideas and time in which to indulge our love of the art? Most certainly! Well, we can't provide the time, but we can promise the projects. Begin fulfilling your crochet fantasies today with the spellbinding selection you'll find in Wishes & Wonders. The results are sure to be miraculous!

Magically yours,

Jennifer

Jennifer Christiansen McClain

Contents

Confident glances in the mirror, gracious compliments
from friends, that boost of pride you get from
wearing something new. Fashion Magic turns your hook into
a wondrous wand of personal crochet creativity.

Chapter One

Fashion Magic

Darling Dress

Design by
Carol Smith

Finished Sizes:

Instructions given fit infant's size 9-12 mos.; changes for 18-24 mos. are in [ ].

Materials:

- ★ 7½ [8½] oz. baby blue pompadour baby sport yarn
- ★ 1¾ [2] yds. white/pastels pleated and gathered 2½" ruffle
- ★ 8 [8½] yds. blue ⅜" satin ribbon
- ★ 1½ yds. pink ⅞" satin ribbon
- ★ One pink ⅝" satin ribbon rose with leaves
- ★ 3 white ⁹⁄₁₆" shank buttons
- ★ White sewing thread
- ★ Sewing needle
- ★ H crochet hook or size needed to obtain gauge.

Gauge:

7 dc = 2"; 8 dc rows worked in pattern = 5".

Skill Level:

Average

Dress

Row 1: Starting at **bodice**, ch 68 [74], dc in 4th ch from hook, dc in next 8 [9] chs, (2 dc, ch 1, 2 dc) in next ch, dc in next 12 [13] chs, (2 dc, ch 1, 2 dc) in next ch, dc in next 18 [20] chs, (2 dc, ch 1, 2 dc) in next ch, dc in next 12 [13] chs, (2 dc, ch 1, 2 dc) in next ch, dc in last 10 [11] chs, turn (78 dc, 4 ch-1 sps) [84 dc, 4 ch-1 sps].

NOTE: Work all even-numbered rows or rnds in **front lps** only. Work all odd-numbered rows or rnds in **back lps** only.

Rows 2-4: Ch 3, dc in each st across with (2 dc, ch 1, 2 dc) in each ch sp, turn, ending with 126 dc and 4 ch-1 sps [132 dc and 4 ch-1 sps] in last rnd.

Rnd 5: Working in rnds, for **skirt**, ch 3, dc in next 17 [18] sts, dc in next ch sp; for **armhole**, skip next 28 [29] sts; dc in next ch sp, dc in next 34 [36] sts, dc in next ch sp; for **armhole**, skip next 28 [29] sts; dc in next ch sp, dc in last 18 [19] sts, join with sl st in top of ch-3, **turn** (74 dc) [78 dc].

Rnd 6: Ch 4, skip next st, (dc in next st, ch 1, skip next st) around, join with sl st in 3rd ch of ch-4, **turn** (37 dc, 37 ch-1 sps) [39 dc, 39 ch-1 sps].

Rnd 7: Ch 3, dc in each ch and in each st around, join with sl st in top of ch-3, **turn** (74 dc) [78 dc].

Rnd 8: Ch 3, dc in same st, 2 dc in each st around, join, **turn** (148) [156].

Rnd 9: Ch 3, dc in each st around, join, **turn.**

Rnd 10: Repeat rnd 6 (74 dc, 74 ch-1 sps) [78 dc, 78 ch-1 sps].

Rnds 11-13: Ch 4, skip next ch sp, (dc in next st, ch 1, skip next ch sp) around, join, **turn.**

Rnd 14: Repeat rnd 7 (148 dc) [156 dc].

Rnds 15-20 [15-22]: Ch 3, dc in each st around, join, **turn.**

Rnd 21 [23]: Ch 1, sc in first st, ch 4, (sc in next st, ch 4) around, join with sl st in first sc, fasten off.

Armhole Trim

Working around one armhole, join with sc in first ch sp at underarm, ch 4, (sc in next st, ch 4) across to last ch sp, sc in last ch sp, fasten off.

Repeat on other armhole.

Finishing

1: Cut 2 pieces of blue ribbon each 20" [21"] long. Starting on one side of back opening, leaving ½" end, weave one piece under 2 sts and over 2 sts across row 1 to center front leaving long end. Fold end on back to wrong side and tack in place. With remaining piece, repeat on other side. Tie long ends into a bow at front.

2: Cut 2 pieces of blue ribbon each 10" long. Starting at underarm, weave one piece under and over every 2 sts across skipped sts on row 4 to opposite side of underarm. Fold ends to wrong side and tack in place. With remaining piece, repeat on other armhole.

3: Cut 4 pieces of blue ribbon each 45½" [46½"] long. Starting at center back, weave through ch sps on rnd 10. Tack ends together. Repeat on rnds 11-13.

4: Cut 45½" [46½"] piece of blue ribbon. Starting at center back, weave one piece under and over every 2 sts on rnd 20 [22]. Tack ends together.

5: Starting at center front, weave pink ribbon through ch sps on rnd 6, tie ends into a bow.

6: Sew rose to bow on row 1.

7: Cut 10" piece of ruffle. Sew bound edge to wrong side of armhole over skipped sts on row 4. Fold outer corners of ruffle down to wrong side and sew in place. Repeat on other armhole.

8: Starting at center back, overlapping ends 1", sew bound edge of remaining ruffle to wrong side of rnd 19 [21]; trim excess and tack ends together.

9: Sew buttons to ends of rows/rnd 1, 3 and 5 on right back using ends of rows on left back for buttonholes. ✪

Spring Flowers Gloves

Design by Shirley Patterson

Finished Sizes & Gauges:

Girl's Small, No. 5 steel hook, 8 dc = 1"; 17 dc rnds = 4". Medium, No. 4 steel hook, 15 dc = 2"; 4 dc rnds = 1". Large, No. 3 steel hook, 7 dc = 1"; 15 dc rnds = 4".

Materials:

★ Size-10 bedspread cotton:
   350 yds. Main Color (MC)
   25 yds. each green and desired flower color
★ Thin elastic to fit around both wrists
★ Steel crochet hook needed to obtain Size & Gauge given above

Skill Level:

Average

Right Glove

Little Finger

Rnd 1: With MC, ch 4, 11 dc in 4th ch from hook, join with sl st in top of ch-3 (12 dc).

Rnds 2-9: Ch 3, dc in each st around, join. At end of last rnd, fasten off.

Ring Finger

Rnd 1: With MC, ch 4, 15 dc in 4th ch from hook, join with sl st in top of ch-3 (16 dc).

Rnds 2-11: Ch 3, dc in each st around, join. At end of last rnd, fasten off.

Middle Finger

Rnd 1: With MC, ch 4, 15 dc in 4th ch from hook, join with sl st in top of ch-3 (16 dc).

Rnds 2-13: Ch 3, dc in each st around, join. At end of last rnd, fasten off.

Index Finger

Work same as Ring Finger. At end of last rnd, **do not** fasten off.

Palm

Rnd 1: Ch 1, sc in each of first 3 sts, sc next 2 sts tog, sc in each of next 3 sts leaving remaining sts unworked, sc in each of first 3 sts on Middle Finger, sc next 2 sts tog, sc in each of next 3 sts leaving remaining sts unworked, sc in each of first 3 sts on Ring Finger, sc next 2 sts tog, sc in each of next 3 sts leaving remaining sts unworked, sc in first st on Little Finger, sc next 2 sts tog, sc in last 9 sts, sc in 8 unworked sts on each of last 3 Fingers, join with sl st in first sc (56 sc).

Rnds 2-8: Ch 3, dc in each st around, join.

Row 9: Working in rows, ch 3, dc in each of next 2 sts, 2 dc in next st, dc in next 5 sts, 2 dc in next st, dc in next 11 sts, 2 dc in next st, dc in next 4 sts, 2 dc in next st, dc in next 21 sts leaving remaining sts unworked for **thumb opening,** turn (52).

Row 10: Ch 3, dc in each st across, turn.

Rnd 11: Working in rnds, ch 3, dc in each st across, ch 8, join with sl st in top of ch-3 (52 dc, 8 chs).

Rnd 12: Ch 3, dc in next 51 sts, (dc next 2 chs tog) 4 times, join (56 dc).

Rnd 13: Ch 3, dc in next 51 sts, (dc next 2 sts tog) 2 times, join (54).

Rnds 14-16: Ch 3, dc in each st around, join.

Rnd 17: Ch 1, sc in first 8 sts, 2 sc in next st, (sc in next 8 sts, 2 sc in next st) around, join with sl st in first sc (60 sc).

NOTE: Cut elastic in half. Knot ends of one piece together.

Rnd 18: Working around elastic (see illustration), ch 1, sc in each st around, join, fasten off.

SC AROUND ELASTIC

Thumb

Rnd 1: With last rnd towards you, join MC with sl st in first ch on rnd 11 of Palm, ch 3, dc in next 7 chs, 2 dc in end of each of next 3 rows, (dc next 2 sts tog) 4 times, 2 dc in end of each of next 3 rows, join with sl st in top of ch-3 (24 dc).

Rnd 2: Ch 3, dc in next st, dc next 2 sts tog, (dc in each of next 2 sts, dc next 2 sts tog) around, join (18).

Rnd 3: Ch 3, dc in each st around, join.

Rnd 4: Ch 3, dc in next 6 sts, dc next 2 sts tog, dc in next 7 sts, dc last 2 sts tog, join (16).

Rnds 5-9: Ch 3, dc in each st around, join. At end of last rnd, leaving 6" end for gathering, fasten off.

Weave end through sts on last rnd, pull tight to gather, secure.

Left Glove

Fingers

Work same as Right Glove's Little Finger, Ring Finger, Middle Finger and Index Finger.

Palm

Rnds 1-8: Repeat same rnds of Right Glove's Palm. At end of last rnd, fasten off.

Row 9: Working in rows, skip first 8 sts, join MC with sl st in next st, ch 3, dc in each of next 2 sts, 2 dc in next st, dc in next 5 sts, 2 dc in next st, dc in next 11 sts, 2 dc in next st, dc in next 4 sts, 2 dc in

Continued on page 15

Wonderfully Warm

Design by
Carol Smith

Finished Sizes:

Instructions given fit lady's size 36"-38" bust; changes for 42"-44" and 46"-48" are in [ ].

Materials:

★ 68 [70, 72] oz. variegated chunky yarn
★ 6 brown ⅞" flat buttons
★ Tapestry needle
★ K crochet hook or size needed to obtain gauge

Gauge:

9 pattern sts = 4"; 7 dc pattern rows = 6"; 3 ribbing sts = 1"; 3 hdc post st ribbing rows = 1"; 2 dc post st ribbing rows = 1¼".

Skill Level:

Advanced

Sweater

Bottom Ribbing

Row 1: Ch 12, dc in 4th ch from hook, dc in each ch across, turn (10 dc).

NOTE: For **double crochet front post (dc-fp,** see page 159), yo, insert hook from front to back around post of next st, yo, draw lp through, (yo, draw through 2 lps on hook) 2 times.

Rows 2-61 [2-69, 2-77]: Ch 3, dc-fp around each st across, turn. At end of last row, fasten off.

Body

Row 1: Working in ends of rows across Bottom Ribbing, join with sl st in first row, ch 3, dc in same row, (dc in next row, 2 dc in next row) across, turn (92 dc) [104 dc, 116 dc].

NOTES: For **treble crochet front post (tr-fp),** yo 2 times, insert hook from front to back around post of next st, yo, draw lp through, (yo, draw through 2 lps on hook) 3 times.

For **treble crochet back post (tr-bp),** yo 2 times, insert hook from back to front around post of next st, yo, draw lp through, (yo, draw through 2 lps on hook) 3 times.

Row 2: Ch 3, dc in next st, (tr-fp around next st, dc in each of next 2 sts) across, turn (62 dc, 30 tr-fp) [70 dc, 34 tr-fp; 78 dc, 38 tr-fp].

Row 3: Ch 3, dc in next st, (tr-bp around next st, dc in each of next 2 sts) across, turn.

NOTES: For **double treble crochet front post (dtr-fp),** yo 3 times, insert hook from front to back around designated st, yo, draw lp through, (yo, draw

through 2 lps on hook) 4 times.

For **cable,** skip next post st and next 2 dc, dtr-fp around next post st, dc in 2nd and 3rd skipped dc, dtr-fp around first skipped post st.

Row 4: Ch 3, dc in next st, (cable, dc in each of next 2 sts) across, turn (32 dc, 15 cables) [36 dc, 17 cables; 40 dc, 19 cables].

NOTE: Pattern is established in rows 3 and 4.

Rows 5-19 [5-21, 5-21]: Work in pattern.

NOTES: For **ending decrease (end dec),** dc last 2 sts tog.

For **beginning decrease (beg dec),** ch 2, dc in next st. Beginning ch-2 will not be used or counted as a st.

Row 20 [22, 22]: For **right front,** work in pattern across first 21 [24, 27] sts, end dec leaving remaining sts unworked, turn (22 sts) [25 sts, 28 sts].

NOTES: If there is not enough sts to work next cable at beginning of row after working decrease, dc in each st across to next cable pattern.

If there are 8 sts or less at end of row after last cable pattern before end dec, dc in each st across to last 2 sts, dc last 2 sts tog.

If there are 7 sts or less at end of row after last cable worked, dc in each st across.

Row 21 [23, 23]: Beg dec, work in pattern across, turn (21) [24, 27].

Row 22 [24, 24]: Work in pattern across to last 2 sts, end dec, turn (20) [23, 26].

Rows 23-24: For **size 36"-38" only,** repeat rows 21 and 22 (19, 18).

Row 25: Work in pattern.

Row 26: Beg dec, work in pattern across, turn (17).

Row 27: Work in pattern across to last 3 sts, end dec leaving last st unworked, turn (15).

Row 28: Sl st in each of first 2 sts, beg dec, work in pattern across, turn (13).

Row 29: Repeat row 27 (11).

Row 30: Beg dec, work in pattern, turn (10).

Row 31: Ch 1, sc in each of first 2 sts, hdc in each of next 3 sts, dc in last 5 sts, turn, fasten off.

Row [25, 25]: For **sizes 42"-44" and 46"-48" only,** beg dec, work in pattern across, turn [22, 25] sts.

Row [26, 26]: Beg dec, work in pattern across to last 2 sts, end dec, turn [20, 23].

Row [27, 27]: Beg dec, work in pattern across to last 3 sts, end dec leaving last st unworked, turn [17, 20].

Continued on next page

Fashion Magic
13

Wonderfully Warm

Continued from page 13

Row [28]: For **size 42"-44" only,** sl st in each of first 2 sts, beg dec, work in pattern across, turn [15].

Row [29]: Work in pattern across to last 3 sts, end dec leaving last st unworked, turn [13].

Row [30]: Sl st in each of first 2 sts, beg dec, work in pattern across, turn [11].

Rows [31-32]: Work in pattern.

Row [33]: Ch 1, sc in each of first 3 sts, hdc in each of next 3 sts, dc in last 5 sts, turn, fasten off.

Row [28]: For **size 46"-48" only,** sl st in each of first 2 sts, beg dec, work in pattern across to last 2 sts, end dec, turn [17].

Row [29]: Beg dec, work in pattern across to last 3 sts, end dec leaving last st unworked, turn [14].

Row [30]: Sl st in each of first 2 sts, beg dec, work in pattern across, turn [12].

Row [31]: Work in pattern.

Row [32]: Ch 3, dc in next 5 sts, hdc in each of next 3 sts, sc in each of last 3 sts, turn.

Row [33]: Ch 1, sc in each of first 3 sts, hdc in each of next 3 sts, dc in last 6 sts, turn, fasten off.

Row 20 [22, 22]: For **back and all sizes,** join with sl st in next unworked st on row 19 [21, 21], beg dec, work in pattern across next 42 [48, 54] sts, end dec leaving remaining sts unworked, turn (44 sts) [50 sts, 56 sts].

Rows 21-24 [23-27, 23-28]: Beg dec, work in pattern across to last 2 sts, end dec, turn, ending with 36 [40, 44] sts in last row, turn.

Rows 25-29 [28-31, 29-31]: Work in pattern.

Row 30 [32, 32]: For **first shoulder,** work in pattern across first 10 [11, 12] sts leaving remaining sts unworked, turn (10) [11, 12].

Row 31 [33, 33]: Work in pattern, fasten off.

Row 20 [22, 22]: For **left front,** join with sl st in next unworked st on row 19 [21, 21], beg dec, work in pattern across, turn (22) [25, 28].

Row 21 [23, 23]: Work in pattern across to last 2 sts, end dec, turn (21) [24, 27].

Row 22 [24, 24]: Beg dec, work in pattern across, turn (20) [23, 26].

Rows 23-24: For **size 36"-38" only,** repeat rows 21 and 22 (19, 18).

Row 25: Work in pattern.

Row 26: Work in pattern across to last 2 sts, end dec, turn (17).

Row 27: Sl st in each of first 2 sts, beg dec, work in pattern across, turn (15).

Row 28: Work in pattern across to last 3 sts, end dec leaving last st unworked, turn (13).

Row 29: Repeat row 27 (11).

Row 30: Repeat row 26.

Row 31: Ch 1, sc in each of first 2 sts, hdc in each of next 3 sts, dc in last 5 sts, turn, fasten off.

Row [25, 25]: For **sizes 42"-44" and 46"-48" only,** work in pattern across to last 2 sts, end dec, turn [22, 25] sts.

Row [26, 26]: Beg dec, work in pattern across to last 2 sts, end dec, turn [20, 23].

Row [27, 27]: Sl st in each of first 2 sts, beg dec, work in pattern across to last 2 sts, end dec, turn [17, 20].

Row [28]: For **size 42"-44" only,** work in pattern across to last 3 sts, end dec leaving last st unworked, turn [15].

Row [29]: Sl st in each of first 2 sts, beg dec, work in pattern across, turn [13].

Row [30]: Work in pattern across to last 3 sts, end dec leaving last st unworked, turn [11].

Rows [31-32]: Work in pattern.

Row [33]: Ch 3, dc in next 4 sts, hdc in each of next 3 sts, sc in each of last 3 sts, turn, fasten off.

Row [28]: For **size 46"-48" only,** beg dec, work in pattern across to last 3 sts, end dec leaving on last st unworked, turn [17].

Row [29]: Sl st in each of first 2 sts, beg dec, work in pattern across to last 2 sts, end dec, turn [14].

Row [30]: Work in pattern across to last 3 sts, end dec leaving last st unworked, turn [12].

Rows [31-32]: Work in pattern.

Row [33]: Ch 3, dc in next 5 sts, hdc in each of next 3 sts, sc in each of last 3 sts, turn, fasten off.

For **all sizes,** sew shoulder seams.

Edging

Working in sts and in ends of rows around outer edge of Body, with right side of work facing you, join with sc in first st on Bottom Ribbing, sc in next 9 sts, 2 sc in each row across Right Front; working across Back, 2 sc in each of next 2 rows, sc in next 16 [18, 20] sts, 2 sc in each of next 2 rows, 2 sc in each row across Left Front, sc in last 10 sts on Bottom Ribbing, fasten off.

Collar

Row 1: Ch 14, dc in 4th ch from hook, dc in each ch across, turn (12 dc).

Rows 2-78 [2-92, 2-96]: Ch 3, dc-fp around each st across, turn.

For **edging,** ch 1, sc in first 11 sts, 3 sc in last st; working in ends of rows, (sc in next row, 2 sc in next row) across; working in starting ch on opposite side of row 1, 3 sc in first ch, sc in each ch across, fasten off.

Matching center of unworked long edge on Collar to center back st on neckline of Body, easing to fit, sew unworked long edge to **back lps** of sts across Edging.

Sew buttons evenly spaced across Edging on Left

Front using corresponding ends of rows on Right Front for buttonholes.

Sleeve (make 2)
Ribbing
Row 1: Ch 11, hdc in 3rd ch from hook, hdc in each ch across, turn (10 hdc).

NOTE: For **half double crochet front post (hdc-fp),** yo, insert hook from front to back around post of next st, yo, draw lp through, yo, draw through all 3 lps on hook.

Rows 2-25 [2-27, 2-29]: Ch 2, hdc-fp around each st across, turn. At end of last row, **do not** turn or fasten off.

Arm
Row 1: For **size 38"-40" only,** working in ends of rows across Ribbing, ch 3, dc in next row, (2 dc in next st, dc in last 21 sts, turn (52).

next row, dc in next row) across to last 2 rows, dc in each of last 2 rows, turn (32 dc).

Row [1]: For **size 42"-44" only,** working in ends of rows across Ribbing, ch 3, dc in each of next 3 rows, 2 dc in next row, (dc in next row, 2 dc in next row) across to last 2 rows, dc in each of last 2 rows, turn (38 dc).

Row [1]: For **size 46"-48" only,** working in ends of rows across Ribbing, ch 3, (dc in each of next 2 rows, 2 dc in next row) across to last row, dc in last row, turn (38 dc).

Rows 2-4: Repeat same rows of Body on page 13.

Rows 5-14: Work in pattern.

Rows 15-26: Beg dec, work in pattern across to last 2 sts, end dec, turn. At end of last row, fasten off.

Matching center of last row on Sleeve to shoulder seam, easing to fit, sew Sleeve to Body.

Sew ends of rows on Sleeve together. ✰

Spring Flower Gloves

Continued from page 11
next st, dc in last 21 sts, turn (52).

Rnds 10-18: Repeat same rnds of Right Glove's Palm on page 11.

Thumb
Work same as Right Glove's Thumb.

Cuffs
Rnd 1: Join green with sc in first st on last rnd of Palm on one Glove, sc in each st around, join with sl st in first sc (60 sc).

Rnd 2: Ch 6, (dc in next st, ch 3) around, join with sl st in 3rd ch of ch-6 (60 ch-3 sps).

Rnd 3: Sl st in first ch sp, ch 1, (sc, hdc, 2 dc, hdc, sc) in same sp and in each of next 2 ch sps, *[insert hook in next ch sp, yo, draw lp through, skip next 5 ch sps; holding skipped ch sps to the front, insert hook in next ch sp, yo, draw lp through ch sp and through both lps on hook], (sc, hdc, 2 dc, hdc, sc) in each of next 3 ch sps; repeat from * 4 more times; repeat between [ ], join with sl st in first sc, fasten off (6 groups of 5 skipped ch-3 sps).

First Flower
With right side of work facing you and fingers pointing up, working in one group of 5 skipped ch sps on rnd 2 of Cuff, join flower color with sc in top center ch sp, (hdc, 3 dc, hdc, sc) in same sp, (sc, hdc, 3 dc, hdc, sc) in each of last 4 ch sps, join with sl st in first sc, fasten off.

Second Flower
With right side of work facing you, working in next group of 5 skipped ch sps to the left, join flower color with sc in top center ch sp, (hdc, 3 dc, hdc, sc) in same sp, (sc, hdc, 3 dc, hdc, sc) in each of next 3 ch sps, (sc, hdc, dc) in last ch sp; for **joining dc,** yo, insert hook in same sp, yo, draw lp through, yo, draw through 2 lps on hook, insert hook in center dc on 2nd petal of last Flower made, yo, draw lp through dc and through 2 lps on hook, (dc, hdc, sc) in same sp on this Flower, join with sl st in first sc, fasten off.

Repeat Second Flower 3 more times for a total of 5 Flowers.

Sixth Flower
Working in last group of 5 skipped ch sps on rnd 2 of Cuff, join flower color with sc in top center ch sp, (hdc, 3 dc, hdc, sc) in same sp, (sc, hdc, dc) in next ch sp; for **joining dc,** yo, insert hook in same sp, yo, draw lp through, yo, draw through 2 lps on hook, insert hook in center dc of 5th petal on First Flower, yo, draw lp through dc and through 2 lps on hook, (dc, hdc, sc) in same sp on this Flower, (sc, hdc, 3 dc, hdc, sc) in each of next 2 ch sps, (sc, hdc, dc) in last ch sp; for **joining dc,** yo, insert hook in same sp, yo, draw lp through, yo, draw through 2 lps on hook, insert hook in center dc on 2nd petal of last Flower made, yo, draw lp through dc and through 2 lps on hook, (dc, hdc, sc) in same sp on this Flower, join with sl st in first sc, fasten off.

Repeat Cuff on other Glove. ✰

Summertime Accessories

Design by
Dot Drake

Finished Sizes:

Bag is 11" deep not including Handles. Cap is girl's one size fits all.

Materials:

★ !00% cotton worsted-weight yarn:
    11 oz. white
    1½ oz. yellow
★ 122 crystal 6-mm x 8-mm pony beads
★ F and G crochet hooks or size needed to obtain gauge

Gauge:

With **G** hook, 4 dc = 1"; 7 dc rows = 4".

Skill Level:

Average

Notes:

Use G hook unless otherwise stated.
Back of sts is right side of work.

Bag

Rnd 1: With white, ch 6, sl st in first ch to form ring, ch 3, 15 dc in ring, join with sl st in top of ch-3 (16 dc).

NOTE: Back of rnd 1 is right side of work.

Rnd 2: Ch 3, dc in same st, 2 dc in each st around, join (32).

Rnd 3: Ch 3, 2 dc in next st, (dc in next st, 2 dc in next st) around, join (48).

Rnd 4: Ch 3, dc in same st, dc in each of next 2 sts, (2 dc in next st, dc in each of next 2 sts) around, join (64).

Rnd 5: Ch 3, dc in each of next 2 sts, 2 dc in next st, (dc in each of next 3 sts, 2 dc in next st) around, join, fasten off (80).

Rnd 6: Working this rnd in **back lps** only, join yellow with sl st in first st, sl st in each st around, join with sl st in first sl st, fasten off.

Rnd 7: Working in **front lps** of rnd 5, join white with sl st in first st, ch 3, dc in each st around, join with sl st in top of ch-3.

Rnd 8: Ch 3, dc in each st around, join, fasten off.

NOTE: Thread 40 beads onto yellow, push back along yarn until needed.

Rnd 9: With F hook, join yellow with sc in first st, sc in next st, pull up one bead, (sc in each of next 2 sts, pull up one bead) around, join with sl st in first sc, fasten off.

Rnd 10: With G hook, join white with sl st in first st, ch 3, dc in each st around, join with sl st in top of ch-3.

NOTES: For **beginning V-stitch (beg V-st)**, ch 4, dc in same st or sp.

For **V-stitch (V-st)**, (dc, ch 1, dc) in next st or ch sp.

For **shell**, (3 dc, ch 2, dc) in next st or ch sp.

For **reverse shell (rev shell)**, (dc, ch 2, 3 dc) in next st.

Rnd 11: Beg V-st, skip next 3 sts, shell in next st, ch 1, skip next 3 sts, (V-st in next st, skip next 3 sts, shell in next st, ch 1, skip next 3 sts) around, join with sl st in 3rd ch of ch-4 (10 shells, 10 V-sts).

Rnd 12: Sl st in ch sp of first V-st, beg V-st, ch 1, rev shell in ch sp of next shell, (V-st in ch sp of next V-st, ch 1, rev shell in ch sp of next shell) around, join.

Rnd 13: Sl st in first V-st, beg V-st, shell in next rev shell, ch 1, (V-st in next V-st, shell in next rev shell, ch 1) around, join.

Rnds 14-18: Repeat rnds 12 and 13 alternately ending with rnd 12.

Rnd 19: Skipping ch-1 sps between rev shells and V-sts, ch 1, sc in each st and in each ch-2 sp around, join with sl st in first sc (80 sc).

Rnd 20: Ch 3, dc in each st around, join with sl st in top of ch-3, fasten off.

NOTE: Thread 40 beads onto yellow, push back along yarn until needed.

Rnds 21-22: Repeat rnds 9 and 10.

Rnd 23: Ch 4, skip next st, (dc in next st, ch 1, skip next st) around, join with sl st in 3rd ch of ch-4 (40 dc, 40 ch-1 sps).

Rnd 24: Ch 3, dc in each st and in each ch sp around, join with sl st in top of ch-3, fasten off (80 dc). Turn Bag right side out.

Rnd 25: With F hook, join yellow with sl st in first st, sl st in each st around, join with sl st in first st, fasten off.

Handle (make 2)

For **corded single crochet**, leaving 3" end, ch 2, sc in 2nd ch from hook; turn last st made to left so back of sc is facing you; sc in strand on left side of st (see illustration 1); *turn last st made to left; sc in parallel strands on left side of st (see illustration 2); repeat from * until piece measures 21", leaving 3" end, fasten off.

CORDED SC

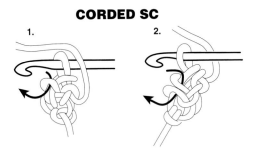

Starting on one side of rnd 23, weave one Handle through ch sps to opposite side. Pull ends of Handle even. Repeat with other Handle on opposite

Continued on page 19

Starlight

Design by
Maria Nagy

Finished Size:

21" x 68½".

Materials:

★ 24 oz. black with glitter twist worsted-weight yarn
★ H crochet hook or size needed to obtain gauge

Gauge:

3 dc and 1 shell = 2¼"; 3 dc rows = 2".

Skill Level:

Average

Shawl

NOTE: For **shell,** 5 dc in next st or ch.

Row 1: Ch 69, dc in 4th ch from hook, dc in next ch, (skip next 2 chs, shell in next ch, skip next 2 chs, dc in each of next 3 chs) across, turn (27 dc, 8 shells).

Rows 2-97: Ch 3, dc in each of next 2 sts, (shell in 3rd dc of next shell, skip next 2 sts of same shell, dc in each of next 3 sts) across, turn.

Rnd 98: For **border,** working in rnds, ch 1, sc in first st, ch 2, skip next st, sc in next st, *(ch 2, skip next 2 sts, sc in next st) 2 times, ch 2, skip next st, sc in next st; repeat from * across; working in ends of rows, ch 2, (sc in next row, ch 2) across; working in starting ch on opposite side of row 1, sc in first ch, ch 2, skip next ch, sc in next ch, [(ch 2, skip next 2 chs, sc in next ch) 2 times, ch 2, skip next ch, sc in next ch]; repeat between [ ] across; working in ends of rows, ch 2, (sc in next row, ch 2) across, join with sl st in first sc (246 ch sps).

NOTE: For **double treble crochet (dtr),** yo 3 times, insert hook in next st, yo, draw lp through, (yo, draw through 2 lps on hook) 4 times.

Rnd 99: Sl st in first ch sp, ch 6, dtr in same sp, (ch 1, dtr in same sp) 5 times, *ch 1, skip next ch sp, sc in next ch sp, ch 1, skip next ch sp, dtr in next ch sp, (ch 1, dtr in same sp) 6 times; repeat from * 36 more times, ch 2, skip next ch sp, sc in next ch sp, (ch 3, sc in next ch sp) 94 times, ch 2, skip last ch sp, join with sl st in 5th ch of ch-6 (302 ch-1 sps, 94 ch-3 sps, 2 ch-2 sps).

NOTE: For **picot,** ch 3, sc in 3rd ch from hook.

Rnd 100: Sl st in first ch-1 sp, ch 1, sc in same sp, (picot, sc in next ch-1 sp) 5 times, *sc in each of next 3 ch-1 sps, (picot, sc in next ch-1 sp) 5 times; repeat from * 36 more times, sc in next ch-2 sp, sc in next ch-3 sp, (ch 3, sc in next ch-3 sp) 93 times, sc in last ch-2 sp, join with sl st in first sc, fasten off.☆

Summertime Accessories

Continued from page 17

side of Bag.

Run 3" ends of both Handles on one side of Bag through one bead. Tie ends into a knot to secure, trim. Repeat on other side.

Hat

Rnds 1-5: Repeat same rnds of Bag on page 17. At end of last rnd, **do not** fasten off.

Rnds 6-9: Ch 3, dc in each st around, join.

NOTE: Thread 40 beads onto yellow, push back along yarn until needed.

Rnd 10: With F hook, join yellow with sc in first st, sc in next st, pull up one bead, (sc in each of next 2 sts, pull up one bead) around, join with sl st in first sc, fasten off.

Rnd 11: With G hook, join white with sl st in first st, ch 3, dc in each st around, join with sl st in top of ch-3.

Rnd 12: Ch 3, dc in each st around, join.

Rnd 13: Ch 3, dc in same st, dc in next 7 sts, (2 dc in next st, dc in next 7 sts) around, join (90).

Rnd 14: Ch 3, dc in each st around, join.

Rnd 15: With F hook, ch 3, dc in each st around, join, fasten off.

Rnd 16: With F hook, join yellow with sl st in first st, sl st in each st around, join with sl st in first sl st, fasten off. Turn Hat right side out.☆

Hidden Secrets

Design by
Lena Chamberlain

Finished Size:

Fits ladies up to size 16.

Materials:

* ★ 12 oz. gold worsted-weight yarn
* ★ Two ¾" Velcro® circles
* ★ 2½" square piece of cardboard
* ★ White sewing thread
* ★ Sewing and tapestry needles
* ★ F and H crochet hooks or sizes needed to obtain gauges

Gauges:

With **F** hook, 9 sc = 2". With **H** hook, 7 sc = 2"; 8 V-sts = 6½"; 9 sc **back lp** rows = 2"; 6 V-st rows = 3½".

Skill Level:

Average

Note:

Use H hook unless otherwise stated.

Dickie

Neck Ribbing

Row 1: Ch 14, sc in 2nd ch from hook, sc in each ch across, turn (13 sc).

Rows 2-49: Working these rows in **back lps** only, ch 1, sc in each st across, turn. At end of last row, fasten off.

Matching sts, sew first and last rows together.

Body

NOTES: For **beginning V-stitch (beg V-st),** ch 4, dc in same sp.

For **V-stitch (V-st),** (dc, ch 1, dc) in next ch sp.

Rnd 1: Working in ends of rows around Neck Ribbing, join with sl st in first row, beg V-st, V-st in next 14 rows, skip next row, (V-st in next 15 rows, skip next row) 2 times, skip last row, join with sl st in 3rd ch of ch-4 (26 V-sts).

Rnd 2: Sl st in first ch sp, beg V-st, V-st in ch sp of each of next 2 V-sts, V-st in sp between last V-st and next V-st, (V-st in next 4 V-sts, V-st in sp between last V-st and next V-st) 5 times, V-st in ch sp of each of last 3 sts, join (32).

Rnds 3-6: Sl st in first ch sp, beg V-st, V-st in each V-st around, join.

Row 7: For **back,** working in rows, sl st in first ch sp, beg V-st, V-st in next 9 V-sts leaving remaining sts unworked, turn (10 V-sts).

Row 8: Ch 3, dc in next ch sp, V-st in next 8 V-sts, skip next st, dc in next ch sp, dc in 3rd ch of last ch-4, turn (8 V-sts, 4 dc).

Rows 9-16: Ch 3, dc in next st, V-st in next 8 V-sts, dc in each of last 2 sts, turn. At end of last row,

fasten off.

Row 7: Skip next 6 unworked V-sts on rnd 6; for **front,** join with sl st in next V-st, beg V-st, V-st in next 9 V-sts leaving remaining sts unworked, turn.

Rows 8-16: Repeat same rows of back.

Side Straps

Row 1: For **first Strap,** working in ends of rows 15 and 16 on back of Body, join with sc in row 15, sc in same row, 2 sc in row 16, turn (4 sc).

Rows 2-30 or to desired length to fit around to front: Ch 1, sc in each st across, turn. At end of last row, fasten off.

Row 1: For **second Strap,** working on opposite ends of rows 15 and 16, join with sc in row 16, sc in same row, 2 sc in row 15, turn.

Rows 2-30 or to desired length to fit around to front: Ch 1, sc in each st across, turn. At end of last row, fasten off.

Sew one side of each piece of Velcro® to end of each Strap on right side. Sew remaining side of each piece of Velcro® to each bottom corner of Body on wrong side. Attach Straps to front of Body.

Cuff (make 2)

Row 1: Ch 12, sc in 2nd ch from hook, sc in each ch across, turn (11 sc).

Rows 2-24: Working these rows in **back lps** only, ch 1, sc in each st across, turn. At end of last row, fasten off.

Matching sts, sew first and last rows together through **back lps.**

Hat

Row 1: With H hook, ch 30; with F hook, ch 7, sc in 2nd ch from hook, sc in next 6 chs; with H hook, sc in last 30 chs, turn (36 sc).

Row 2: Ch 1, sc in first 30 sts leaving remaining sts unworked, turn (30).

Row 3: Ch 1, sc in each st across, turn.

Row 4: Ch 1, sc in first 30 sts; with F hook, sc in last 6 unworked sts 3 rows below, turn (36).

Row 5: Ch 1, sc in first 6 sts; with H hook, sc in last 30 sts, turn.

Rows 6-72: Repeat rows 2-5 consecutively, ending with row 4. At end of last row, leaving 8" end, fasten off.

Weave 8" end through ends of rows, pull tight to gather, secure.

Pom-Pom

Wrap yarn around cardboard 100 times, slide loops off cardboard; tie separate strand around middle of all loops. Cut loops. Trim ends. Sew to top of Hat. ☆

Snips 'n' Spice

Design by
Carol Carlile

Finished Sizes:

Instructions given fit child's size 6; changes for sizes 8 and 10 are in [ ].

Materials:

★ 12 [14, 16] oz. green worsted-weight yarn
★ 6 novelty ½" shank buttons
★ Tapestry needle
★ G and H crochet hooks or sizes needed to obtain gauges

Gauges:

With **G hook**, 4 sts = 1"; 4 sc **back lp** rows = 1". With **H hook**, 13 dc = 4"; 4 dc rows = 2".

Skill Level:

Average

Back Waist Ribbing

Row 1: With G hook, ch 11, sc in 2nd ch from hook, sc in each ch across, turn (10 sc).

Rows 2-44 [2-48, 2-52]: Working these rows in **back lps** only, ch 1, sc in each st across, turn. At end of last row, **do not** turn or fasten off.

Body

Row 1: Working in ends of rows across Back Waist Ribbing, with H hook, ch 3, dc in same row, dc in each row across to last row, 2 dc in last row, turn (46 dc) [50 dc, 54 dc].

Rows 2-12 [2-16, 2-18]: Ch 3, dc in each st across, turn. At end of last row, fasten off.

Row 13 [17, 19]: For **sleeve**, with G hook, ch 51 [55, 57]; with H hook, join with dc in first st on last row, dc in each st across; for **sleeve**, with G hook, ch 52 [56, 58], turn.

Row 14 [18, 20]: For **cuff**, sc in 2nd ch from hook, sc in next 9 chs, hdc in each of next 2 chs; with H hook, dc in each ch and in each st across to last 12 chs; for **cuff**, with G hook, hdc in each of next 2 chs, sc in last 10 chs, turn (148 sts) [160 sts, 168 sts].

Rows 15-21 [19-25, 21-29]: Working in **back lps**, ch 1, sc in first 10 sts, hdc in each of next 2 sts; with H hook, working in **both lps**, dc in each st across to last 12 sts; working in **back lps**, with G hook, hdc in each of next 2 sts, sc in last 10 sts, turn.

Row 22 [26, 30]: Working in **back lps**, ch 1, sc in first 10 sts, hdc in each of next 2 sts; with H hook, working in **both lps**, dc in next 54 [60, 64] sts; for

neck shaping, hdc in next 16 sts; dc in next 54 [60, 64] sts; working in **back lps**, with G hook, hdc in each of next 2 sts, sc in last 10 sts, turn.

Row 23 [27, 31]: For **first side**, working in **back lps**, ch 1, sc in first 10 sts, hdc in each of next 2 sts; with H hook, working in **both lps**, dc in next 54 [60, 64] sts leaving remaining sts unworked, turn (66) [72, 76].

Row 24 [28, 32]: Ch 3, dc in next 53 [59, 63] sts; with G hook, working in **back lps**, hdc in each of next 2 sts, sc in last 10 sts, turn.

Row 25 [29, 33]: Working in **back lps**, ch 1, sc in first 10 sts, hdc in each of next 2 sts; with H hook, working in **both lps**, dc in each st across to last st, 2 dc in last st, turn (67) [73, 77].

Row 26 [30, 34]: Ch 3, dc in same st, dc in each st across to last 12 sts; with G hook, working in **back lps**, hdc in each of next 2 sts, sc in last 10 sts, turn (68) [74, 78].

Rows 27-30 [31-34, 35-38]: Repeat rows 25 and 26 [29 and 30, 33 and 34] alternately, ending with 72 [78, 82] sts in last row.

Row 31 [35, 39]: Working in **back lps**, ch 1, sc in first 10 sts, hdc in each of next 2 sts; with H hook, working in **both lps**, dc in each st across, turn.

Row 32 [36, 40]: Ch 3, dc in each st across to last 12 sts; with G hook, working in **back lps**, hdc in each of next 2 sts, sc in last 10 sts, turn.

Rows 33-35 [37-39, 41-45]: Repeat rows 31 and 32 [35 and 36, 39 and 40] alternately, ending with row 31 [35, 39].

Row 36 [40, 46]: Ch 3, dc in next 20 [22, 24] sts leaving remaining sts unworked, turn (21 dc) [23 dc, 25 dc].

Rows 37-48 [41-56, 47-64]: Ch 3, dc in each st across, turn. At end of last row, fasten off.

Row 23 [27, 31]: For **second side**, skip next 16 unworked sts on row 22 [26, 30], with H hook, join with sl st in next st, ch 3, dc in each st across to last 12 sts; with G hook, working in **back lps**, hdc in each of next 2 sts, sc in last 10 sts, turn (66) [72, 76].

Row 24 [28, 32]: Working in **back lps**, ch 1, sc in first 10 sts, hdc in each of next 2 sts; with H hook, working in **both lps**, dc in each st across, turn.

Row 25 [29, 33]: Ch 3, dc in same st, dc in each st across to last 12 sts; with G hook, working in **back lps**, hdc in each of next 2 sts, sc in last 10 sts, turn (67) [73, 77].

Row 26 [30, 34]: Working in **back lps**, ch 1, sc in first 10 sts, hdc in each of next 2 sts; with H hook,

Continued on next page

working in **both lps,** dc in each st across to last st, 2 dc in last st, turn (68) [74, 78].

Rows 27-30 [31-34, 35-38]: Repeat rows 25 and 26 [29 and 30, 33 and 34] of second side alternately, ending with 72 [78, 82] sts in last row.

Row 31 [35, 39]: Ch 3, dc in each st across to last 12 sts; with G hook, working in **back lps,** hdc in each of next 2 sts, sc in last 10 sts, turn.

Row 32 [36, 40]: Working in **back lps,** ch 1, sc in first 10 sts, hdc in each of next 2 sts; with H hook, working in **both lps,** dc in each st across, turn.

Rows 33-35 [37-39, 41-45]: Repeat rows 31 and 32 [35 and 36, 39 and 40] of second side alternately, ending with row 31 [35, 39]. At end of last row, fasten off.

Row 36 [40, 46]: Skip first 51 [55, 57] sts, with H hook, join with sl st in next st, ch 3, dc in each st across, turn (21 dc) [23 dc, 25 dc].

Rows 37-48 [41-56, 47-64]: Ch 3, dc in each st across, turn. At end of last row, fasten off.

First Front Waist Ribbing

Row 1: Working on last row of first side on Body, with wrong side of last row facing you, with G hook, join with sl st in first st, ch 11, sc in 2nd ch from hook, sc in each ch across, sl st in each of next 2 sts on Body, turn (10 sc).

Row 2: Working the following rows in **back lps** only, ch 1, skip sl sts, sc in each st across, turn.

Row 3: Ch 1, sc in each st across, sl st in each of next 2 sts on Body, turn.

Rows 4-20 [4-22, 4-24]: Repeat rows 2 and 3 alternately, ending with row 2. At end of last row, fasten off.

Second Front Waist Ribbing

Row 1: Working on last row of second side on Body, with right side of last row facing you, with G hook, join with sl st in first st, ch 11, sc in 2nd ch from hook, sc in each ch across, sl st in each of next 2 sts on Body, turn (10 sc).

Rows 2-20 [2-22, 2-24]: Repeat same rows of Left Front Ribbing.

Matching sts and ends of rows, sew side and sleeve seams.

Neck Trim

Row 1: With right side of work facing you, with G hook, join with sl st in end of row 30 [34, 38], ch 3, dc in end of same row, 2 dc in end of next 7 rows, dc in next worked st on row 22 [26, 30], dc in next 16 sts, dc in next worked st, 2 dc in end of next 8 rows, turn (50 dc).

NOTES: For **front post stitch (fp,** see page 159), yo, insert hook from front to back around post of next st, yo, draw lp through, (yo, draw through 2 lps on hook) 2 times.

For **back post stitch (bp,** see page 159), yo, insert hook from back to front around post of next st, yo, draw lp through, (yo, draw through 2 lps on hook) 2 times.

Row 2: Ch 3, (fp around next st, bp around next st) across to last st, dc in last st, fasten off.

Button Placket

Row 1: Working in ends of rows across first front of Body, with wrong side facing you, with G hook, join with sc in row 31 [35, 39], sc in same row, 2 sc in each of next 17 [21, 25] rows, sc in last 10 sts, turn (46 sc) [54 sc, 62 sc].

Rows 2-5: Ch 1, sc in each st across, turn. At end of last row, fasten off.

Buttonhole Placket

Row 1: Working in ends of rows across second front of Body, with right side facing you, with G hook, join with sc in row 31 [35, 39], sc in same row, 2 sc in each of next 17 [21, 25] rows, sc in last 10 sts, turn (46 sc) [54 sc, 62 sc].

Row 2: Ch 1, sc in each st across, turn.

Row 3: Ch 1, sc in each of first 2 [1, 3] sts; for **buttonhole,** ch 1, skip next st; *sc in next 7 [9, 10] sts; for **buttonhole,** ch 1, skip next st; repeat from * 4 more times, sc in each of last 3 [2, 3] sts, turn (6 buttonholes).

Row 4: Ch 1, sc in each st and in each ch-1 sp across, turn.

Row 5: Ch 1, sc in each st across, fasten off.

Sew buttons to row 3 of Button Placket opposite buttonholes. ✿

Girl's Night Out

Design by
Darla Sims

Red Rounded Bag

Finished Size:
6½" x 7½" not including strap.

Materials:
★ 2¾ oz. red worsted-weight chenille yarn
★ 1½" gold shank button
★ Tapestry needle
★ G and H crochet hooks or size needed to obtain gauge

Gauge:
With **H hook**, 7 sc = 2"; 7 sc rows = 2".

Skill Level:
Average

Note:
Use H hook unless otherwise stated.

Side (make 2)

Row 1: Ch 18, sc in 2nd ch from hook, sc in each ch across, turn (17 sc).

NOTE: For **puff stitch (puff st)**, yo, insert hook in next st, yo, draw lp through, (yo, insert hook in same st, yo, draw lp through) 2 times, yo, draw through all 7 lps on hook.

Row 2: Ch 1, 2 sc in first st, sc in each of next 3 sts, (puff st in next st, sc in each of next 3 sts) across to last st, 2 sc in last st, turn (19 sts).

Row 3: Ch 1, 2 sc in first st, sc in each st across to last st, 2 sc in last st, turn (21).

Rows 4-5: Repeat rows 2 and 3 (23, 25).

Row 6: Ch 1, sc in first 4 sts, puff st in next st, (sc in each of next 3 sts, puff st in next st) across to last 4 sts, sc in last 4 sts, turn.

Row 7: Ch 1, sc in each st across, turn.

Row 8: Ch 1, sc in each of first 2 sts, puff st in next st, (sc in each of next 3 sts, puff st in next st) across to last 2 sts, sc in each of last 2 sts, turn.

Row 9: Repeat row 7.

Rows 10-14: Repeat rows 6-9 consecutively, ending with row 6.

Row 15: Ch 1, sc first 2 sts tog, sc in each st across to last 2 sts, sc last 2 sts tog, turn (23).

Row 16: Ch 1, sc in first st, puff st in next st, (sc in each of next 3 sts, puff st in next st) across to last st, sc in last st, turn.

Row 17: Repeat row 15 (21).

Row 18: Repeat row 8.

Row 19: Repeat row 15 (19).

Row 20: Ch 1, sc in each of first 3 sts, (puff st in next st, sc in each of next 3 sts) across, turn.

Row 21: Repeat row 15 (17). At end of last row on first Side, fasten off. At end of last row on second Side, **do not** fasten off.

Flap

Row 1: Ch 1, sc in first 4 sts, puff st in next st, (sc in each of next 3 sts, puff st in next st) across to last 4 sts, sc in last 4 sts, turn.

Row 2: Ch 1, 2 sc in first st, sc in each st across to last st, 2 sc in last st, turn (19 sc).

Row 3: Ch 1, sc in each of first 3 sts, (puff st in next st, sc in each of next 3 sts) across, turn.

Row 4: Ch 1, sc in each st across, turn.

Row 5: Ch 1, sc in first st, puff st in next st, (sc in each of next 3 sts, puff st in next st) across to last st, sc in last st, turn.

Row 6: Ch 1, sc in each st across, turn.

Row 7: Repeat row 3.

Row 8: Ch 1, sc first 2 sts tog, sc in each st across to last 2 sts, sc last 2 sts tog, turn (17).

Row 9: Ch 1, sc first 2 sts tog, sc in each of next 2 sts, puff st in next st, (sc in each of next 3 sts, puff st in next st) across to last 4 sts, sc in each of next 2 sts, sc last 2 sts tog, turn (15 sts).

Row 10: Ch 1, sc first 3 sts tog, sc in next 9 sts, sc last 3 sts tog, turn (11).

Row 11: Ch 1, sc first 3 sts tog, puff st in next st, sc in each of next 3 sts, puff st in next st, sc last 3 sts tog, turn, **do not** fasten off.

For **edging**, working around outer edge, with G hook, sc in each st and in end of each row around with 2 sc in each bottom corner, join with sl st in first sc, fasten off.

For **edging on first Side**, working around outer edge, with G hook, join with sc in first st on last row, sc in each st and in end of each row around with 2 sc in each corner, join with sl st in first sc, fasten off.

Holding Sides wrong sides together, working through both thicknesses, matching sts, using Backstitch (see page 159), sew posts of sts on sides and bottom together.

For **strap,** with G hook, join with sl st in end of first row on Flap, ch 135 or to desired length, sl st in opposite end of same row, sl st in each ch across to joining, sl st in joining sl st, fasten off.

Sew button to center front of Flap over rnd 10.

Teal Bag

Finished Size:
6" x 7¾" not including chain.

Materials:
★ 2¾ oz. teal worsted-weight chenille yarn
★ 1¾" gold shank button
★ 47" gold 5-mm chain
★ Tapestry needle
★ F and G crochet hooks or size needed to obtain gauge

Gauge:

With **G hook**, 4 sc = 1"; 4 slanted shell rows = 1½"; 4 sc rows = 1".

Skill Level:

Average

Note:

Use G hook unless otherwise stated.

Front

Row 1: Ch 30, sc in 2nd ch from hook, sc in each ch across, turn (29 sc).

NOTE: For **slanted shell (sl shell),** (sc, 3 dc) in next st.

Rows 2-13: Ch 1, sl shell in first st, skip next 3 sts, (sl shell in next st, skip next 3 sts) across to last st, sc in last st, turn (7 shells, 1 sc). At end of last row, fasten off.

Back

Rows 1-13: Repeat same rows of Front. At end of last row, **do not** fasten off.

Rows 14-15: Ch 1, sc in each st across, turn. At end of last row, fasten off.

Flap

Row 1: Ch 2, 3 sc in 2nd ch from hook, turn (3 sc).

Row 2: Ch 1, 2 sc in first st, sc in next st, 2 sc in last st, turn (5).

Rows 3-6: Ch 1, 2 sc in first st, sc in each st across to last st, 2 sc in last st, turn, ending with 13 sc in last row.

Row 7: Ch 1, 2 sc in first st, sc in each of next 3 sts; for **buttonhole,** ch 5, skip next 5 sts; sc in each of next 3 sts, 2 sc in last st, turn (10 sc, 1 ch-5 sp).

Row 8: Ch 1, 2 sc in first st, sc in each st and 5 sc in ch-5 sp across to last st, 2 sc in last st, turn (17 sc).

Rows 9-14: Repeat row 3, ending with 29 sc in last row.

Row 15: Ch 1, sc in each st across, fasten off.

Hold Flap and Back wrong sides together, matching sts, working through both thicknesses, with Flap towards you, join with sc in first st on last row, sc in each st across, fasten off.

Edging

Rnd 1: Working around outer edge of Back and Flap, with right side facing you, with F hook, join with sc in any st, sc in each st and in end of each row around with 2 sc in each corner, join with sl st in first sc.

Rnd 2: Ch 1, working from left to right, **reverse sc** (see page 159) in each st around, join, fasten off.

Repeat Edging on Front.

Hold Front and Back wrong sides together, matching sts, working through both thicknesses, using Backstitch (see page 159), sew posts of sts on sides and bottom together.

Sew button to center front of row 10 on Front.

Sew one end of each chain to each end on first row of Flap.

Stained Glass Bag

Finished Size:

6½" x 9" not including chain.

Materials:

★ Worsted-weight chenille yarn:
   2¾ oz. black
   1½ oz. each teal and mulberry
★ 1½" gold shank button
★ 45" gold 5-mm gold chain
★ Tapestry needle
★ G and H crochet hooks or size needed to obtain gauge

Gauge:

With **H hook**, 7 sc = 2"; 3 sc rows and 1 dc row = 1¼"; 7 sc rows = 2".

Skill Level:

Average

Note:

Use H hook unless otherwise stated.

Bag

Row 1: With black, ch 33, dc in 4th ch from hook, dc in each ch across, turn, fasten off (31 dc).

Row 2: Join teal with sc in first st, sc in each st across, turn.

Row 3: Ch 1, sc in each st across, turn, fasten off.

NOTE: For **front post stitch (fp,** see page 159), yo, insert hook from front to back around post of corresponding st 3 rows below, yo, draw lp through, (yo, draw through 2 lps on hook. Skip next st on last row behind fp.

Row 4: Join black with sc in first st, sc in each of next 2 sts, (fp, sc in each of next 3 sts) across, turn.

Row 5: Ch 3, dc in each st across, turn, fasten off.

Rows 6-7: With mulberry, repeat rows 2 and 3.

Row 8: Join black with sc in first st, fp, (sc in each of next 3 sts, fp) across to last st, sc in last st, turn.

Row 9: Repeat row 5.

Continued on page 29

Cozy Toesies

Design by
Jo Ann Maxwell

Finished Sizes:

Instructions given fit 7½" sole; changes for 8½" and 9" sole are in [ ].

Materials:

★ Worsted-weight yarn:
2½ [3, 3½] oz. each variegated and matching solid color
★ I crochet hook or size needed to obtain gauge

Gauge:

With **2 strands held together,** 3 sc = 1"; 3 sc rnds = 1".

Skill Level:

Easy

Slipper (make 2)

NOTES: Use one strand each variegated and solid color held together throughout.

Do not join rnds unless otherwise stated. Mark first st of each rnd.

Rnd 1: Starting at **toe,** ch 3 [4, 4], sl st in first ch to form ring, ch 1, 8 [10, 11] sc in ring (8 sc) [10 sc, 11 sc].

Rnd 2: 2 sc in each st around (16) [20, 22].

Rnd 3 [3-5, 3-7]: Sc in each st around.

Rnds 4-11 [6-13, 8-15]: 2 sc in first st, sc in each st around, ending with 24 [28, 30] sc in last rnd. At end of last rnd, join with sl st in first sc.

Rnd 12 [14, 16]: Working this rnd in **back lps** only, ch 1, sc in each st around, **do not** join.

Row 13 [15, 17]: For **cuff,** working in rows, ch 14 [16, 18], sc in 2nd ch from hook, sc in next 11 [13, 15] chs, sc last ch and back lp of first st on last rnd tog; working in **back lps** only, sc in next 22 [26, 28] sts, sc last st and next ch on opposite side of beginning ch tog, sc in last 12 [14, 16] chs, turn (48) [56, 62].

Row 14 [16, 18]: Working this row in **front lps** only, ch 1, sc in each st across, turn.

Row 15 [17, 19]: Working this row in **back lps** only, ch 1, sc in each st across, turn.

Rows 16-18 [18-20, 20-22]: Repeat rows 14 and 15 [16 and 17, 18 and 19] alternately, ending with row 14 [16, 18].

Row 19 [21, 23]: Working this row in **back lps** only, ch 1, sc in first 17 [21, 24] sts, (sc next 2 sts tog) 7 times, sc in last 17 [21, 24] sts, turn (41) [49, 55].

Row 20 [22, 24]: Repeat row 14 [16, 18].

Row 21 [23, 25]: Working this row in **back lps** only, ch 1, sc in first 11 [15, 18] sts, (sc next 2 sts tog) 9 times, sc in last 12 [16, 19] sts, turn (32) [40, 46].

Row 22 [24, 26]: Repeat row 14 [16, 18].

Fold last rnd in half, ch 1, sl st in each st across through **back lps** only, fasten off.✿

Girl's Night Out

Continued from page 27

Rows 10-39: Repeat rows 2-9 consecutively, ending with row 7.

Row 40: For **flap,** join black with sl st in first st, ch 1, sc same st and next 2 sts tog, sc in each of next 2 sts, fp, (sc in each of next 3 sts, fp) across to last 5 sts, sc in each of next 2 sts, sc last 3 sts tog, turn (27).

NOTE: (Ch 2, dc next 2 sts tog) counts as dc first 3 sts tog.

Row 41: Ch 2, dc next 2 sts tog, dc in each st across to last 3 sts, dc last 3 sts tog, turn, fasten off (23).

Row 42: Join teal with sl st in first st, ch 1, sc same st and next 2 sts tog, sc in each st across to last 3 sts, sc last 3 sts tog, turn (19).

Row 43: Ch 1, sc first 3 sts tog, sc in each st across to last 3 sts, sc last 3 sts tog, turn, fasten off (15).

Rows 44-45: Repeat rows 40 and 41, ending with 7 sts in last row.

For **edging,** working around outer edge, with G hook, join black with sc in 4th st on last row, sc in each st and in end of each row around with 2 sc in each bottom corner; for **button loop,** ch 12; join with sl st in first sc, fasten off.

Fold row 1 to row 39 with wrong sides together, matching sts, working through both thicknesses, using Backstitch (see page 159), sew posts of sts on each side together.

Sew button to center front of row 10.

Sew one end of chain to each end of row 40.✿

Youth seems eternal for those who understand the
magic of Dolls & Delights. Share with them
your secrets, your dreams, your tears. Never has
there been a friend so true.

Chapter Two

Dolls and Delights

Pageant Queen

Design by
Sandra Miller Maxfield

Finished Size:

Fits 11½" fashion doll.

Note:

Dress is made to be used with either the crocheted Skirt Form given in this book, or the "No-Sew Skirt Form" available through *The Needlecraft Shop* catalog. Call 1-800-259-4000 or write to: 23 Old Pecan Rd., Big Sandy, TX, 75755 for a catalog.

Materials For Skirt Form:

★ 500 yds. ecru size-10 bedspread cotton
★ 10½" circle of mat board
★ Cardboard tube from paper towel roll
★ Masking tape
★ Polyester fiberfill
★ Craft glue or hot glue gun
★ Ecru sewing thread
★ Sewing and tapestry needles
★ No. 0 steel crochet hook or size needed to obtain gauge

Materials For Dress:

★ 600 yds. ecru with metallic gold twist size-10 bedspread cotton
★ Small amount of metallic gold embroidery floss
★ 3 yds. metallic gold ⅞" pleated trim
★ 1 yd. metallic gold ⅜" wire-edged ribbon
★ Ecru sewing thread
★ Craft glue or hot glue gun
★ Sewing and tapestry needles
★ No. 0 steel crochet hook or size needed to obtain gauge

Gauges:

With **No. 0 hook and 2 strands held together**, 5 dc = 1"; 2 dc rows = 1". With **No. 7 steel hook and one strand**, 8 sts = 1"; 7 dc rows = 2"; 10 sc rows = 1".

Skill Level:

Average

Skirt Form

Row 1: Starting at **waist**, with No. 0 hook and 2 strands held tog, ch 22, dc in 4th ch from hook, 2 dc in each ch across, turn (38 dc).

Row 2: Ch 3, dc in each st across, turn.

Row 3: Ch 3, 2 dc in next st, (dc in next st, 2 dc in next st) across, turn (57).

Row 4: Repeat row 2.

Row 5: Ch 3, dc in next st, 2 dc in next st, (dc in each of next 2 sts, 2 dc in next st) across, turn (76).

Row 6: Repeat row 2.

Rnd 7: Working in rnds, ch 3, dc in same st, dc in each of next 3 sts, (2 dc in next st, dc in each of next 2 sts) around, dc in same st as first st, join with

sl st in top of ch-3 (102).

Rnds 8-10: Ch 3, dc in each st around, join.

Rnd 11: Ch 3, dc in next st, 2 dc in next st, (dc in each of next 2 sts, 2 dc in next st) around, join (136).

Rnds 12-14: Repeat rnd 8.

Rnd 15: Ch 3, (dc in next 4 sts, 2 dc in next st) around, join (163).

Rnds 16-18: Repeat rnd 8.

Rnd 19: Working this rnd in **back lps** only, ch 1, sc in each st around, join with sl st in first sc, fasten off.

Row 20: For **tie**, ch 32; working in starting ch on opposite side of row 1, join with sc in first ch, sc in each ch across; for **tie**, ch 32, fasten off.

Finishing

1: For **Skirt Form base**, cut 7½" long piece of cardboard tube.

2: Mark center of mat board. Glue end of tube centered over mark.

3: Cover opposite edge of tube with masking tape for added stability.

4: Sew ends of rows 3-6 together on Skirt Form. Slip Form over top of base, positioning waist opening over top of tube and seam at center back. Glue last rnd on Skirt Form to bottom of mat board. Stuff Form and shape. Stuff bottom of tube with small amount of fiberfill.

5: Place legs of doll in tube, adjusting to proper height (so ties of Form are even with waist); tie Form around waist.

Dress

Bodice

Row 1: Starting at **waist**, ch 27, sc in 2nd ch from hook, sc in each ch across, turn (26 sc).

Row 2: Ch 1, sc in each st across, turn.

Rows 3-5: Ch 1, sc in each st across with 2 sc in last st, turn, ending with 29 sc in last row.

Row 6: Ch 1, sc in first 8 sts, 2 sc in next st, sc in next 11 sts, 2 sc in next st, sc in last 8 sts, turn (31).

Rows 7-8: Repeat row 2.

Row 9: Ch 1, sc in first 10 sts, 2 sc in next st, sc in next 9 sts, 2 sc in next st, sc in last 10 sts, turn (33).

Row 10: Repeat row 2.

Row 11: Ch 1, sc in first 13 sts, skip next st, 10 hdc in next st, skip next st, sc in next st, skip next st, 10 hdc in next st, skip next st, sc in last 13 sts, turn (47 sts).

Row 12: Ch 1, sc in first 12 sts, skip next st, hdc in next 10 sts, sc in next st, hdc in next 10 sts, skip next st, sc in last 12 sts, turn (45).

Row 13: Ch 1, sc in first 12 sts, skip next st, sc in

Continued on page 37

Mr. Bumble

Design by
Michele Wilcox

Finished Size:

16" tall.

Materials:

★ Worsted-weight yarn:
3½ oz. black
2 oz. white
1 oz. yellow
small amount each beige and red
★ ⅜" red pom-pom
★ Polyester fiberfill
★ Craft glue or hot glue gun
★ Tapestry needle
★ G crochet hook or size needed to obtain gauge

Gauge:

4 sc = 1"; 9 sc rows = 2".

Skill Level:

Average

Head & Body

NOTE: Do not join rnds unless otherwise stated. Mark first st of each rnd.

Rnd 1: Starting at **top of Head,** with black, ch 2, 6 sc in 2nd ch from hook (6 sc).

Rnd 2: 2 sc in each st around (12).

Rnd 3: (Sc in next st, 2 sc in next st) around (18).

Rnd 4: (Sc in each of next 2 sts, 2 sc in next st) around (24).

Rnd 5: (Sc in each of next 3 sts, 2 sc in next st) around (30).

Rnd 6: (Sc in next 4 sts, 2 sc in next st) around (36).

Rnds 7-15: Sc in each st around.

Rnd 16: (Sc in next 4 sts, sc next 2 sts tog) around (30).

Rnd 17: (Sc in each of next 3 sts, sc next 2 sts tog) around (24).

Rnd 18: (Sc in each of next 2 sts, sc next 2 sts tog) around (18).

Rnd 19: (Sc in next st, sc next 2 sts tog) around (12).

Rnd 20: Sc in each st around. Stuff. Continue stuffing as you work.

Rnd 21: For **Body,** repeat rnd 2 (24).

Rnds 22-23: Repeat rnds 5 and 6 (30, 36). At end of last rnd, join with sl st in first sc, fasten off.

Rnd 24: Join yellow with sc in first st, sc in each st around.

Rnd 25: (Sc in next 5 sts, 2 sc in next st) around (42).

Rnd 26: Sc in each st around, join with sl st in first sc, fasten off.

Rnd 27: Join black with sc in first st, sc in each st around.

Rnds 28-29: Sc in each st around. At end of last rnd, join with sl st in first sc, fasten off.

Rnd 30: Join yellow with sc in first st, sc in each st around.

Rnds 31-32: Sc in each st around. At end of last rnd, join with sl st in first sc, fasten off.

Rnds 33-39: Repeat rnds 27-32 consecutively, ending with rnd 27.

Rnd 40: (Sc in next 5 sts, sc next 2 sts tog) around (36).

Rnd 41: Sc in each st around, join with sl st in first sc, fasten off.

Rnd 42: Repeat rnd 30.

Rnd 43: Repeat rnd 16 (30).

Rnd 44: Sc in each st around, join with sl st in first sc, fasten off.

Rnd 45: Repeat rnd 27.

Rnds 46-48: Repeat rnds 17-19, ending with 12 sc in last rnd.

Rnd 49: Sc in each st around.

Rnd 50: (Sc next 2 sts tog) around (6).

Rnd 51: Sc in each st around, join with sl st in first sc, leaving 8" end for weaving, fasten off.

Weave end through sts of last rnd, pull tight to gather, secure.

Face

Rnds 1-4: With beige, repeat same rnds of Head.

Row 5: 2 sc in first st, hdc in next st, 2 dc in each of next 2 sts, (hdc, sc) in next st, sl st in next st, (sc, hdc) in next st, 2 dc in each of next 2 sts, hdc in next st, 2 sc in next st, sl st in next st leaving remaining sts unworked, fasten off.

With row 5 at top, sew Face to front of Head over rnds 9-17.

Hand & Arm (make 2)

Rnds 1-3: For **Hand,** with white, repeat same rnds of Head.

Rnds 4-5: Sc in each st around.

Rnd 6: (Sc next 2 sts tog) around (9).

Continued on next page

Mr. Bumble
Continued from page 35

Rnd 7: Sc in each st around, join with sl st in first sc, fasten off. Stuff Hand only.

Rnd 8: For **Arm,** join black with sc in first st, sc in each st around.

Rnds 9-22: Sc in each st around. At end of last rnd, join with sl st in first sc, fasten off.

Thumb

Rnd 1: With white, ch 2, 6 sc in 2nd ch from hook (6 sc).

Rnds 2-3: Sc in each st around. At end of last rnd, join with sl st in first sc, fasten off.

Sew last rnd of each Thumb to rnds 6 and 7 on Hand.

For **cuff,** with white, ch 12, sl st in first ch to form ring, ch 1, sc in each ch around, join with sl st in first sc, fasten off.

Easing to fit, sew right side of each cuff to rnd 7 on each Hand.

Flatten last rnd of each Arm; with Thumbs pointing forward, sew one arm to each side of Body over rnd 23.

Foot & Leg (make 2)

Rnd 1: Starting at **Foot,** with white, ch 6, sc in 2nd ch from hook, sc in each of next 3 chs, 3 sc in last ch; working on opposite side of ch, sc in each of next 3 chs, 2 sc in last ch (12 sc).

Rnd 2: 2 sc in first st, sc in each of next 3 sts, 2 sc in each of next 3 sts, sc in each of next 3 sts, 2 sc in each of last 2 sts (18).

Rnd 3: (Sc in each of next 2 sts, 2 sc in next st) around (24).

Rnds 4-6: Sc in each st around.

Rnd 7: Sc in first 5 sts, (sc next 2 sts tog) 6 times, sc in last 7 sts (18).

Rnd 8: Sc in each of first 2 sts, (sc next 2 sts tog) 6 times, sc in last 4 sts (12). Stuff Foot only.

Rnd 9: Sc in each st around, join with sl st in first sc, fasten off.

Rnd 10: For **Leg,** join black with sc in first st, sc in each st around.

Rnds 11-28: Sc in each st around. At end of last rnd, join with sl st in first sc, fasten off.

For **cuff,** with white, ch 15, sl st in first ch to form ring, ch 1, sc in each ch around, join with sl st in

first sc, fasten off.

Easing to fit, sew right side of each cuff to rnd 9 on Foot.

Flatten last rnd of each Leg; with Feet pointing forward, sew one arm to each side of Body over rnd 41.

Antennae (make 2)

With black, ch 9, 4 sc in 2nd ch from hook, sl st in each ch across, fasten off.

Sew Antennae to top of Head as shown in photo.

Wing Section (make 4)

Row 1: With white, ch 2, 3 sc in 2nd ch from hook, turn (3 sc).

Row 2: Ch 1, sc in first st, 2 sc in next st, sc in last st, turn (4).

Row 3: Ch 1, sc in first st, 2 sc in each of next 2 sts, sc in last st, turn (6).

Row 4: Ch 1, sc in first st, 2 sc in next st, sc in each of next 2 sts, 2 sc in next st, sc in last st, turn (8).

Rows 5-12: Ch 1, sc in each st across, turn.

Row 13: Ch 1, sc in first st, sc next 2 sts tog, sc in each of next 2 sts, sc next 2 sts tog, sc in last st, turn (6).

Rnd 14: Working in rnds, ch 1, sc first 2 sts tog, sc in each of next 2 sts, sc last 2 sts tog, sc in end of each row around with 3 sc in point, join with sl st in first sc, fasten off.

For **each wing,** matching points on row 1, overlap 2 Wing Sections ¾" on sides. Sew together. Repeat with remaining 2 Wing Sections.

Sew bottom of Wings over rnds 25-29 on back of Body 1" apart.

Finishing

1: With black, using French Knot (see page 159) embroider 2 eyes to top of rnd 4 on Face 1" apart.

2: For **nose,** glue pom-pom to center of rnd 1.

3: With black, using Backstitch (see page 159), embroider **mouth** between rnds 2 and 3 of Face centered below nose.

4: With red, using Straight Stitch (see page 159), starting at center front of rnd 8, embroider 2 **shoelaces** down to rnd 3 on each side of Foot as shown. ☆

Pageant Queen

Continued from page 33

next 8 sts, skip next st, sc in next st, skip next st, sc in next 8 sts, skip next st, sc in last 12 sts, turn (41 sc).

Row 14: Ch 1, sc in first 20 sts, skip next st, sc in last 20 sts, turn (40).

Row 15: Repeat row 2.

Row 16: Ch 1, sc in first 8 sts; *for **armhole**, ch 12; for **shoulder loop,** sl st in 6th ch from hook, ch 6, skip next 5 sts*; sc in next 6 sts, sc next 2 sts tog, sc in next 6 sts; repeat between **, sc in last 8 sts, turn (29).

Row 17: Skipping each shoulder loop, ch 1, sc in each st and in each ch across, fasten off.

Skirt

Row 1: Working in starting ch on opposite side of row 1 on Bodice, with right side facing you, join with sc in first ch, sc in each ch across, turn (26 sc).

Row 2: Ch 3, dc in same st, 3 dc in next st, (2 dc in next st, 3 dc in next st) across, turn (65 dc).

Row 3: Ch 3, dc in next st, (2 dc in next st, dc in each of next 2 sts) across, turn (86).

Row 4: Ch 3, dc in each st across, turn.

Rows 5-6: Repeat rows 3 and 4 (114).

Row 7: Ch 3, dc in next st, 2 dc in next st, (dc in each of next 2 sts, 2 dc in next st) across, turn (152).

Row 8: Repeat row 4.

Row 9: Repeat row 3 (202).

Row 10: Working this row in **back lps** only, ch 1, sc in first st, (ch 4, skip next 2 sts, sc in next st) across, turn (68 sc, 67 ch-4 sps).

Row 11: Working in row before last behind ch lps, ch 3, (dc in **both lps** of each of next 2 skipped sts, dc in remaining **front lp** of next st) across, turn (202 dc).

Row 12: Ch 3, (dc in each of next 2 sts, dc in next st and in next ch-4 sp on row before last at same time) across, turn.

Row 13: Working this row in **front lps** only, ch 1, sc in first st, (ch 4, skip next 2 sts, sc in next st) across, turn.

Row 14: Working in row before last in front of ch lps, ch 3, (dc in **both lps** of each of next 2 skipped sts, dc in remaining **back lp** of next st) across, turn.

Row 15: Repeat row 12.

Rows 16-51: Repeat rows 10-15 consecutively. At end of last row, fasten off.

Finishing

1: Cut 12½" piece of pleated trim. Glue bound edge across center back of Skirt Form ¾" from bottom edge. Cut next piece approximately ⅞" smaller than last piece. Glue bound edge of this piece centered above last piece ¾" above bound edge. Repeat in same manner all the way up Skirt Form forming a triangle.

2: Cut 4 pieces embroidery floss each 4" long. Holding 2 pieces together, tie into overhand knot (see illustration) around each shoulder loop. Separate strands.

3: Fold each back bottom corner of Skirt up to

OVERHAND KNOT

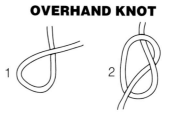

row 39, glue in place. Cut 2 pieces ribbon each 9" long. Tie each piece into a bow. Cut "V" in each end on each bow. Glue bow over each turned up corner.

4: Place Dress on doll. Overlapping back opening on Bodice ¼", sew back opening closed leaving Skirt open.

5: Tie remaining piece of ribbon into a bow around waist. Cut "V" in each end. ☆

Peach's Playdress

Design by Beverly Mewhorter

Finished Size:
Fits 10" doll.

Materials For One:
★ Worsted-weight yarn:
  2 oz. lt. coral
  small amount white
★ 2 peach 1¼" satin carnations with leaves
★ Craft glue or hot glue gun
★ Tapestry needle
★ H crochet hook or size needed to obtain gauge

Gauge:
13 sc = 4"; 7 sc rows = 2".

Skill Level:
Average

Dress

Bodice
Row 1: With lt. coral, ch 21, sc in 2nd ch from hook, sc in each ch across, turn (20 sc).

Row 2: Ch 1, sc in each st across, turn.

Row 3: Ch 1, sc in each of first 3 sts; for **armhole,** ch 6, skip next 3 sts; sc in next 8 sts; for **armhole,** ch 6, skip next 3 sts; sc in each of last 3 sts, turn (14 sc, 2 ch-6 sps).

Row 4: Ch 1, sc in each st and in each ch across, **do not** turn, fasten off (26 sc).

Row 5: For **trim,** join white with sl st in first st, sl st in each st across, fasten off.

Sleeves
Rnd 1: Working around one armhole, join lt. coral with sc in 2nd skipped st at underarm, sc in next st, sc in next 6 chs, sc in last st, join with sl st in first sc (9 sc).

Rnds 2-5: Ch 1, sc in each st around, join. At end of last rnd, fasten off.

Rnd 6: For **trim,** join white with sl st in first st, sl st in each st around, join with sl st in first sl st, fasten off.

Repeat on other armhole.

Skirt
Row 1: Working in starting ch on opposite side of row 1 on Bodice, with right side of work facing you, join lt. coral with sc in first ch, sc in each ch across, turn (20 sc).

Row 2: Ch 1, 3 sc in each st across, turn (60).

Rows 3-9: Ch 1, sc in each st across, turn. At end of last row, **do not** turn, fasten off.

Row 10: Join white with sl st in first st, sl st in each st across, fasten off.

For **ties,** join white with sl st in end of row 4 on Bodice, ch 20, fasten off. Repeat on opposite end of

row. Repeat on each end of row 1.

Sew ends of rows 2-10 on Skirt together.

Glue one carnation to center front of Bodice.

Panties

Row 1: For **front,** with white, ch 3, sc in 2nd ch from hook, sc in last ch, turn (2 sc).

Row 2: Ch 1, sc in each st across, turn.

Row 3: Ch 1, 2 sc in each st across, turn (4).

Row 4: Ch 1, sc in each st across, turn.

Rows 5-6: Ch 1, 2 sc in first st, sc in each st across with 2 sc in last st, turn (6, 8).

Row 7: Ch 1, sc in each st across, **do not** turn, fasten off.

Row 8: For **back,** working in starting ch on opposite side of row 1, join white with sc in first ch, sc in last ch, turn.

Rows 9-14: Repeat rows 2-7. At end of last row, **do not** fasten off.

Rnd 15: Working in rnds, ch 1, sc in end of each row and in each st around, join with sl st in first sc, fasten off.

Sew top corners of back and front together on each side.

Tie 6" piece of lt. coral into a bow around center front st on row 7 of front.

Headband

With lt. coral, ch 30, sl st in first ch to form ring, ch 1, sc in each ch around, join with sl st in first sc, fasten off.

Glue remaining carnation to one side of Headband. ☆

Miss Daisy

Design by
Carol Smith

Finished Size:

Fits 17½" doll.

Materials:

- ★ 6 oz. green pompadour baby sport yarn
- ★ 2 yds. white 2" gathered eyelet ruffle
- ★ 2½ yds. yellow ⅜" satin ribbon
- ★ 3 yds. green ⅜" satin ribbon
- ★ 2 yds. white and yellow 1" daisy trim
- ★ White sewing thread
- ★ Sewing needle
- ★ I crochet hook or size needed to obtain gauge

Gauge:

3 dc = 1"; 3 dc rows = 2".

Skill Level:

Average

Dress

Row 1: Starting at **neckline,** ch 27, 2 dc in 4th ch from hook, dc in next ch, (2 dc in next ch, dc in next ch) across, turn (37 dc).

Row 2: Ch 3, dc in each st across, turn.

Row 3: Ch 3, (2 dc in next st, dc in next st) across to last 2 sts, dc in each of last 2 sts, turn (54).

Row 4: Ch 3, dc in each st across, turn.

Rnd 5: Working in rnds, ch 3, dc in next 6 sts; for **armhole,** ch 4, skip next 13 sts; dc in next 14 sts; for **armhole,** ch 4, skip next 13 sts; dc in last 7 sts, join with sl st in top of ch-3, **turn** (28 dc, 2 ch-4 sps).

Rnd 6: For **skirt,** ch 4, skip next st, (dc in next st or ch, ch 1, skip next st or ch) around, join with sl st in 3rd ch of ch-4, **turn** (18 dc, 18 ch-1 sps).

NOTES: For **shell,** (2 dc, ch 1, 2 dc) in next st or ch sp.

For **front post stitch (fp,** see page 159), yo, insert hook from front to back around post of next st, yo, draw lp through, (yo, draw through 2 lps on hook) 2 times.

For **back post stitch (bp),** yo, insert hook from back to front around post of next st, yo, draw lp through, (yo, draw through 2 lps on hook) 2 times.

Rnd 7: Ch 3, shell in next ch, (bp around next st, shell in next ch) around, join, **turn** (18 sts, 18 shells).

Rnd 8: Ch 3, shell in ch sp of next shell, (fp around next post st, shell in ch sp of next shell) around, join, **turn.**

Rnd 9: Ch 3, shell in next shell, (bp around next post st, shell in next shell) around, join, **turn.**

Rnds 10-12: Repeat rnds 8 and 9 alternately, ending with rnd 8.

Rnd 13: Sl st in sp between last ch-3 and next shell, ch 4, dc in next shell, ch 1, dc in sp between last shell and next post st, ch 1, (dc in sp between last post st and next shell, ch 1, dc in next shell, ch 1, dc in sp between last shell and next post st, ch 1) around, join with sl st in 3rd ch of ch-4, **turn** (54 dc, 54 ch-1 sps).

Rnd 14: Ch 3, shell in next ch, (fp around next st, shell in next ch) around, join with sl st in top of ch-3, **turn** (54 shells, 54 sts).

Rnd 15: Repeat rnd 9, fasten off.

Armhole Trims

Working in skipped sts on row 4 of one armhole, with right side of work facing you, join with sl st around post of st before first skipped st, ch 3, shell in next st, (fp around next st, shell in next st) 6 times, fp around next st, fasten off.

Repeat on other armhole.

Bonnet

Row 1: Ch 4, sl st in first ch to form ring, ch 3, 2 dc in ring, (ch 1, 2 dc in ring) 5 times, ch 1, 3 dc in ring, turn (16 dc, 6 ch-1 sps).

Row 2: Ch 3, shell in next 6 ch-1 sps, dc in last st, turn (6 shells, 2 dc).

Row 3: Ch 3, shell in next shell, (dc in sp between last shell and next shell, shell in next shell) across to last st, dc in last st, turn (7 dc, 6 shells).

Row 4: Ch 3, shell in next shell, (fp around next dc between shells, shell in next shell) across to last st, dc in last st, turn (6 shells, 5 fp, 2 dc).

Row 5: Ch 3, shell in next shell, (bp around next post st, shell in next shell) across to last st, dc in last st, turn.

Row 6: Ch 3, shell in next shell, (fp around next post st, shell in next shell) across to last st, dc in last st, turn.

Row 7: Ch 4, dc in next shell, ch 1, (dc in sp between last shell and next post st, ch 1, dc in sp between last post st and next shell, ch 1, dc in next shell, ch 1) across to last st, dc in last st, turn (18 dc, 17 ch-1 sps).

Row 8: Ch 3, shell in next ch, (bp around next post st, shell in next ch) across to last st, dc in last st, turn (17 shells, 16 bp, 2 dc).

Rnd 9: Working around outer edge, ch 3, shell in

Continued on page 45

Diamond Bride

Design by
Judith Swingle

Finished Size:

10½" tall.

Materials:

- ★ Worsted-weight yarn:
  - 8 oz. white
  - 7 oz. white with iridescent glitter twist (glitter white)
- ★ White ⅞" flat button
- ★ White 2½" satin ribbon rose
- ★ 5½ yds. white/gold metallic 1¼" gathered lace
- ★ 18" white ½" trim
- ★ 3 crystal 10-mm x 12-mm oval gemstones
- ★ 8" pillow doll with white hair
- ★ Polyester fiberfill or 9" round pillow
- ★ White sewing thread
- ★ Craft glue or hot glue gun
- ★ Sewing and tapestry needles
- ★ G crochet hook or size needed to obtain gauge

Gauge:

4 sts = 1"; 2 dc rows = 1".

Skill Level:

Average

Dress

Bodice & Skirt

Row 1: Starting at **neckline,** with white, ch 24, sc in 2nd ch from hook, sc in each ch across, turn (23 sc).

Row 2: Ch 3, dc in same st, (skip next st, 3 dc in next st) across, turn (35 dc).

NOTE: For **3-double crochet cluster (3-dc cl),** yo, insert hook in next st, yo, draw lp through, yo, draw through 2 lps on hook, (yo, insert hook in same st, yo, draw lp through, yo, draw through 2 lps on hook) 2 times, yo, draw through all 4 lps on hook.

Row 3: Ch 3, (skip next st, 2 dc in next st) 3 times; for **armhole,** ch 7, skip next 5 sts; (2 dc in next st, skip next st) 2 times, 3-dc cl in each of next 3 sts, (skip next st, 2 dc in next st) 2 times; for **armhole,** ch 7, skip next 5 sts; (2 dc in next st, skip next st) 3 times, dc in last st, turn (25 sts, 2 ch-7 sps).

Row 4: Ch 3, skip next st, (2 dc in next st, skip next st) 2 times, 3 dc in next st, skip next ch, (dc next 2 chs tog) 3 times, (2 dc in next st, skip next st) 5 times, 2 dc in next st, (dc next 2 chs tog) 3 times, skip next ch, 3 dc in next st, (skip next st, 2 dc in next st) 2 times, skip next st, dc in last st, turn (34 dc).

NOTE: For **4-double crochet cluster (4-dc cl),** yo, insert hook in next st, yo, draw lp through, yo, draw through 2 lps on hook, (yo, insert hook in same st, yo, draw lp through, yo, draw through 2 lps on hook) 3 times, yo, draw through all 5 lps on hook.

Row 5: Ch 3, skip next st, (3 dc in next st, skip next st) 2 times, (dc next 2 sts tog) 3 times, skip next st, 2 dc in each of next 2 sts, 4-dc cl in each of next 4 sts, 2 dc in each of next 2 sts, skip next st, (dc next 2 sts tog) 3 times, skip next st, (3 dc in next st, skip next st) 2 times, dc in last st, turn (32 sts).

Rows 6-8: Ch 1, 2 sc in first st, sc in each st across, turn, ending with 35 sc in last row.

Row 9: For **skirt,** ch 3, 2 dc in same st, skip next st, (3 dc in next st, skip next st) across to last st, dc in last st, turn (52 dc).

Rnd 10: Working in rnds, ch 3, dc in same st, ch 2, (3 dc in sp between next 2 3-dc groups, ch 2) 16 times, dc in last st, join with sl st in top of ch-3 (17 3-dc groups, 17 ch-2 sps).

Rnd 11: Ch 3, dc in each st and in each ch around, join (85 dc).

Rnd 12: Ch 3, dc in each st around, join.

Rnd 13: Ch 3, dc in same st, dc in next 7 sts, 2 dc in next st, (dc in next 9 sts, 2 dc in next st) around to last 6 sts, dc in last 6 sts, join (94).

Rnd 14: Ch 3, dc in next 7 sts, 3 dc in next st, (dc in next 10 sts, 3 dc in next st) around to last 8 sts, dc in last 8 sts, join (110).

Rnd 15: Ch 3, dc in next 9 sts, 2 dc in next st, (dc in next 5 sts, 2 dc in next st) around to last 9 sts, dc in last 9 sts, join (126).

Rnd 16: Ch 3, dc in same st, dc in next 8 sts, 2 dc in each of next 3 sts, (dc in next 12 sts, 2 dc in each of next 3 sts) around to last 9 sts, dc in last 9 sts, join (151).

Rnd 17: Ch 3, dc in same st, dc in next 9 sts, 2 dc in each of next 3 sts, (dc in next 13 sts, 2 dc in each of next 3 sts) around to last 10 sts, dc in last 10 sts, join (179).

Rnd 18: Ch 3, dc in next 12 sts, 2 dc in next st, (dc in next 18 sts, 2 dc in next st) around to last 13 sts, dc in last 13 sts, join (188).

Rnd 19: Ch 3, dc in next 15 sts, skip next st, (dc in next 30 sts, skip next st) around to last 16 sts, dc in last 16 sts, join (182).

Rnd 20: Ch 3, dc in same st, dc in next 7 sts, (*skip next st, dc in next st, skip next st, 3 dc in next st, skip next st, dc in next st, skip next st*, dc in next 13 sts) 8 times; repeat between **, dc in last 7 sts, join (165).

Rnd 21: Ch 3, dc in next 9 sts, 2 dc in each of next 2 sts, (dc in next 16 sts, 2 dc in each of next 2 sts) around to last 9 sts, dc in last 9 sts, join (183).

Rnd 22: Ch 3, dc in next 9 sts, 2 dc in each of next 3 sts, (dc in next 17 sts, 2 dc in each of next 3 sts) around to last 10 sts, dc in last 10 sts, join (210).

Rnd 23: Ch 3, dc in next 10 sts, 2 dc in next st, dc in each of next 2 sts, 2 dc in next st, (dc in next 19 sts, 2 dc in next st, dc in each of next 2 sts, 2 dc in next st) around to last 11 sts, dc in last 11 sts, join, fasten off (228).

Continued on next page

Diamond Bride
Continued from page 43

First Ruffle

Rnd 1: Join glitter white with sc in first st on rnd 23, ch 3, skip next 2 sts, (sc in next st, ch 3, skip next 2 sts) around, join with sl st in first sc (76 ch sps).

Rnd 2: Working in skipped sts on rnd before last, behind ch sps on last rnd, sc in first skipped st on rnd before last, ch 3, skip next skipped st and next sc on last rnd, (sc in next skipped st on rnd before last, ch 3, skip next skipped st and next sc on last rnd) around, join.

Rnd 3: (Ch 3, sc) 4 times in first ch sp on rnd before last, (ch 3, sc) 4 times in first ch sp on last rnd, *(ch 3, sc) 4 times in next ch sp on rnd before last, (ch 3, sc) 4 times in next ch sp on last rnd; repeat from * around, join with sl st in first ch of first ch-3, fasten off.

Second Ruffle

Working around post of sts on rnd 21, work same as First Ruffle.

Third Ruffle

Rnd 1: Working around post of sts on rnd 18, join glitter white with sc in first st, ch 3, skip next st, (sc in next st, ch 3, skip next 2 sts) around, join with sl st in first sc (63 ch sps).

Rnd 2: Working in skipped sts on rnd before last, behind ch sps on last rnd, sc in first skipped st on rnd before last, ch 3, skip next sc on last rnd, (sc in next skipped st on rnd before last, ch 3, skip next skipped st and next sc on last rnd) around, join.

Rnd 3: Repeat same rnd of First Ruffle.

Fourth Ruffle

Working around post of sts on rnd 15, work same as First Ruffle.

Fifth Ruffle

Rnd 1: Working around post of sts on rnd 12, join glitter white with sc in first st, ch 3, skip next 3 sts, (sc in next st, ch 3, skip next 2 sts) around, join with sl st in first sc (28 ch sps).

Rnd 2: Working in skipped sts on rnd before last, behind ch sps on last rnd, sc in first skipped st on rnd before last, ch 3, skip next 2 skipped sts and next sc on last rnd, (sc in next skipped st on rnd before last, ch 3, skip next skipped st and next sc on last rnd) around, join.

Rnd 3: Repeat same rnd of First Ruffle.

Neck Trim

Working in starting ch on opposite side of row 1 on Bodice, join glitter white with sc in first ch, (ch 3, skip next ch, sc in next ch) across, **turn**; working in skipped chs, ch 3 (sc in next skipped ch, ch 3) across, join with sl st in first sc, fasten off.

Sleeves

Rnd 1: Working around one armhole, join white with sc in 4th skipped ch at underarm, sc in each of next 3 chs, 2 sc in end of next row, sc in next 5 sts, 2 sc in end of next row, sc in each of last 3 chs, join with sl st in first sc (16 sc).

Rnd 2: Ch 3, dc in next 6 sts, 2 dc in each of next 3 sts, dc in last 6 sts, join with sl st in top of ch-3 (19).

Rnds 3-4: Ch 3, dc in next 6 sts, tr in next 6 sts, dc in last 6 sts, join.

Rnd 5: Ch 1, sc in first 6 sts, hdc in next st, dc in next st, tr in each of next 3 sts, dc in next st, hdc in next st, sc in last 6 sts, join with sl st in first sc.

Rnd 6: Ch 1, sc in first 5 sts, (sc next 2 sts tog) 5 times, sc in last 4 sts, join (14 sc).

Rnd 7: Ch 1, sc in each st around, join.

Rnd 8: Ch 1, sc in first st, ch 3, (sc in next st, ch 3) around, join, fasten off.

Repeat on other armhole.

Base

NOTE: Do not join rnds unless otherwise stated. Mark first st of each rnd.

Rnd 1: With white, ch 2, 8 sc in 2nd ch from hook (8 sc).

Rnd 2: 2 sc in each st around (16).

Rnd 3: (Sc in next st, 2 sc in next st) around (24).

Rnd 4: (Sc in each of next 2 sts, 2 sc in next st) around (32).

Rnd 5: (Sc in each of next 3 sts, 2 sc in next st) around (40).

Rnd 6: (Sc in next 4 sts, 2 sc in next st) around (48).

Rnd 7: (Sc in next 5 sts, 2 sc in next st) around (56).

Rnd 8: (Sc in next 6 sts, 2 sc in next st) around (64).

Rnd 9: (Sc in next 7 sts, 2 sc in next st) around (72).

Rnd 10: (Sc in next 8 sts, 2 sc in next st) around (80).

Rnd 11: (Sc in next 9 sts, 2 sc in next st) around (88).

Rnd 12: (Sc in next 10 sts, 2 sc in next st) around (96).

Rnd 13: (Sc in next 11 sts, 2 sc in next st) around, join with sl st in first sc (104).

Rnd 14: Ch 3, dc in next 24 sts, 2 dc in next st, (dc in next 25 sts, 2 dc in next st) around, join with sl st in top of ch-3 (108 dc).

Rnds 15-16: Ch 3, dc in each st around, join, fasten off.

Finishing

1: Place Dress on doll. Sew back opening on Bodice closed. Sew last rnd of Base to rnd 14 on Skirt, inserting pillow or stuffing before closing.

2: Starting at center back, weave trim through ch sps of rnd 10 on Skirt, sew ends together.

3: Starting at center back, glue bound edge of 10" piece of lace around row 7 on Skirt, overlapping ends ½". With 23" piece, repeat on rnd 12. With 33½" piece, repeat on rnd 15. With 49" piece, repeat on rnd 18. With 48" piece, repeat on rnd 21. With 10" piece, repeat on row 2 of Bodice.

4: Tie a large loose knot in center of remaining piece of lace. Secure knot with small amounts of glue. Wrap around head and glue ends together.

5: Glue gemstones evenly spaced across top of head.

6: Glue rose to center back of waist.

7: Sew button to center of rnd 1 on Base. ☆

Miss Daisy
Continued from page 41

Continued from page 41

next shell, (fp around next post st, shell in next shell) across to last st, dc in last st; working in ends of rows, ch 1, (dc in next row, ch 1) 7 times, dc each end of row 1 together, ch 1, (dc in next row, ch 1) 7 times, join with sl st in top of ch-3, fasten off.

Finishing

1: Weave 15½" piece of green ribbon under one st and over 2 sts across row 1 of Bodice; fold ends to wrong side and tack in place. With 21" piece of ribbon, repeat across row 3.

2: Weave 3½" piece of green ribbon under one st and over 2 sts on row 5 of left back bodice; fold ends to wrong side and tack in place. Repeat on right back bodice. With 6½" piece of ribbon, repeat across front bodice.

3: Starting at center back, weave 39" piece of green ribbon through ch sps of rnd 13 on skirt. Sew ends together.

4: Weave 13½" piece of green ribbon through ch sps of row 7 on Bonnet; fold ends to wrong side and tack in place.

5: Sew 12½" piece of daisy trim to row 2 of bodice. Sew 18" piece across row 4 of bodice. Cut 27 daisies from trim. Sew one daisy to every other shell over rnd 15 of Skirt. Cut 9 daisies from trim. Sew one daisy to first shell over row 9 of Bonnet and to every other remaining shell.

6: Cut 8" piece of ruffle. Sew bound edge to wrong side of one Armhole Trim over row 4 of Bodice. Fold outer corners of ruffle down to wrong side and sew in place. Repeat on other Armhole Trim.

7: Cut 37" piece of ruffle. Starting at center back, sew bound edge to wrong side of rnd 13 on skirt. Sew ends together.

8: Cut 14½" piece of ruffle. Sew bound edge to wrong side of rnd 8 on Bonnet. Fold outer corners of ruffle down to wrong side and sew in place.

9: Starting at center front, weave 22" piece of yellow ribbon through rnd 6 of Skirt; place Dress on doll, tie ends into a bow.

10: For **back bodice ties,** cut 3 pieces of yellow ribbon each 12" long. Tie ends of row 1 on bodice together with one piece. Repeat on rows 3 and 5.

11: For **Bonnet ties,** weave remaining piece of yellow ribbon through ch sps across bottom neck opening on rnd 9 of Bonnet, pull ends even. ☆

Cuddle Babies

Design by
Beverly Mewhorter

Finished Size:

Fits 6½" baby doll.

Materials For One:

★ 1½ oz. desired color pompadour baby yarn
★ 1½ yds. white ⅛" satin ribbon
★ Optional — 1" white satin ribbon rose with ruffle
★ Optional — craft glue or hot glue gun
★ Tapestry needle
★ F crochet hook or size needed to obtain gauge

Gauge:

9 sts = 2"; 9 sc rows = 2"; 9 dc rows = 4".

Skill Level:

Average

Bonnet

Rnd 1: Ch 4, 11 dc in 4th ch from hook, join with sl st in top of ch-3 (12 dc).

Rnd 2: Ch 3, dc in same st, 2 dc in each st around, join (24).

Rnd 3: Ch 3, dc in same st, dc in next st, (2 dc in next st, dc in next st) around, join (36).

Rnd 4: Ch 1, sc in first st, ch 3, skip next st, (sc in next st, ch 3, skip next st) around, join with sl st in first sc (18 ch-3 sps).

Rnd 5: For **brim front**, sl st in first ch sp, ch 1, (sc, 3 dc, sc) in same sp and in each of next 8 ch sps; for **brim back**, 2 sc in each of last 9 ch sps, join, fasten off.

Starting at center front, weave 16" piece of ribbon through rnd 4, place Bonnet on doll's head; pull ends to gather and tie into a bow.

Nightgown

Bodice

Row 1: Ch 31, sc in 2nd ch from hook, sc in each ch across, turn (30 sc).

Row 2: Ch 1, sc in first 5 sts; for **armhole**, ch 8, skip next 3 sts; sc in next 14 sts; for **armhole**, ch 8, skip next 3 sts; sc in last 5 sts, turn (24 sc, 2 ch-8 sps).

Row 3: Ch 1, sc in each st and in each ch across, turn (40 sc).

Row 4: Ch 1, sc in first st, ch 3, sc in next st, (ch 3, skip next st, sc in next st) across, turn.

Row 5: Sl st in first st, (sc, 3 dc, sc) in each ch sp across, sl st in last st, fasten off.

Skirt

Row 1: Working in starting ch on opposite side of row 1 on Bodice, with right side facing you, join with sc in first ch, sc in each ch across, turn (30 sc).

Row 2: Ch 3, dc in same st, 2 dc in each st across, turn (60 dc).

Rows 3-9: Ch 3, dc in each st across, turn.

Rows 10-11: Repeat rows 4 and 5 of Bodice.

Sleeves

Rnd 1: Working around one armhole, join with sc in 2nd skipped st at underarm, sc in next st, sc in next 8 chs, sc in last st, join with sl st in first sc (11 sc).

Rnds 2-6: Ch 1, sc in each st around, join. At end of last rnd, fasten off.

Repeat on other armhole.

Finishing

1: Sew ends of rows on Skirt together leaving Bodice open.

2: Starting at back, weave 16" piece of ribbon through row 4 of Bodice, place Nightgown on doll, pull ends to gather and tie into a bow.

3: Starting at center front, weave remaining ribbon through row 10 of Skirt; pull ends to gather and tie into a bow.

4: Optional — glue rose to center front of Bodice. ☆

Petunia Pigihoof

Design by
Michele Wilcox

Finished Size:
9½" tall.

Materials:
- ★ 100% cotton worsted-weight yarn:
  6 oz. pink
  1½ oz. white
- ★ 2 blue ⁹⁄₁₆" flat buttons
- ★ 3 blue ⅜" satin ribbon roses with leaves
- ★ 1 yd. floral print 2⅝" cotton ribbon
- ★ White sewing thread
- ★ Craft glue or hot glue gun
- ★ Polyester fiberfill
- ★ Sewing and tapestry needles
- ★ G crochet hook or size needed to obtain gauge

Gauge:
4 sc = 1"; 9 sc rows = 2".

Skill Level:
Average

Head & Body

NOTE: **Do not** join rnds unless otherwise stated. Mark first st of each rnd.

Rnd 1: Starting at **top of Head,** with pink, ch 2, 6 sc in 2nd ch from hook (6 sc).

Rnd 2: 2 sc in each st around (12).

Rnd 3: (Sc in next st, 2 sc in next st) around (18).

Rnd 4: (Sc in each of next 2 sts, 2 sc in next st) around (24).

Rnd 5: (Sc in each of next 3 sts, 2 sc in next st) around (30).

Rnd 6: (Sc in next 4 sts, 2 sc in next st) around (36).

Rnd 7: Sc in each st around.

Rnd 8: (Sc in next 5 sts, 2 sc in next st) around (42).

Rnds 9-16: Sc in each st around.

Rnd 17: (Sc in next 5 sts, sc next 2 sts tog) around (36).

Rnd 18: (Sc in next 4 sts, sc next 2 sts tog) around (30).

Rnd 19: (Sc in each of next 3 sts, sc next 2 sts tog) around (24).

Rnd 20: (Sc in each of next 2 sts, sc next 2 sts tog) around (18).

Rnd 21: Sc in each st around. Stuff.

Rnds 22-24: For **Body,** repeat rnds 4-6, ending with 36 sc in last rnd.

Rnd 25: (Sc in next 5 sts, 2 sc in next st) around (42).

Rnd 26: (Sc in next 6 sts, 2 sc in next st) around (48).

Rnds 27-41: Sc in each st around.

Rnd 42: (Sc in next 6 sts, sc next 2 sts tog) around (42).

Rnd 43: (Sc in next 5 sts, sc next 2 sts tog)

around (36). Stuff.

Rnd 44: (Sc next 2 sts tog) around (18).

Rnd 45: (Sc in next st, sc next 2 sts tog) around (12).

Rnd 46: (Sc next 2 sts tog) around, join with sl st in first sc, leaving 8" end for weaving, fasten off.

Weave end through sts of last rnd, pull tight to gather; secure end.

Leg (make 2)

Rnds 1-5: Repeat same rnds of Head & Body. At end of last rnd, join with sl st in first sc.

Rnd 6: Working this rnd in **back lps** only, ch 1, sc in each st around.

Rnds 7-18: Sc in each st around.

Rnd 19: (Sc in each of next 3 sts, sc next 2 sts tog) around, join with sl st in first sc, fasten off. Stuff.

For **trim,** working in **front lps** of rnd 5, join pink with sl st in any st, sl st in each st around, join with sl st in first sl st, fasten off.

Flatten last rnd of each Leg and sew at an angle over rnds 34-42 on each side of Body as shown in photo.

Arm (make 2)

Rnds 1-4: Repeat same rnds of Head & Body. At end of last rnd, join with sl st in first sc.

Rnd 5: Working this rnd in **back lps** only, ch 1, sc in each st around.

Rnds 6-17: Sc in each st around.

Rnd 18: (Sc in next st, sc next 2 sts tog) around, join with sl st in first sc, fasten off. Stuff.

For **trim,** working in **front lps** of rnd 4, join pink with sl st in any st, sl st in each st around, join with sl st in first sl st, fasten off.

Flatten last rnd of each Arm and sew over rnds 25-32 on each side of Body as shown. Tack inside of rnd 15 on each Arm to Body.

Snout

Rnds 1-3: Repeat same rnds of Head & Body.

Rnd 4: Working this rnd in **back lps** only, ch 1, sc in each st around.

Rnds 5-7: Sc in each st around. At end of last rnd, join with sl st in first sc, fasten off. Stuff.

For **trim,** working in **front lps** of rnd 3, join pink with sl st in any st, sl st in each st around, join with sl st in first sl st, fasten off.

Sew rnd 7 of Snout to center front of Head over rnds 8-14.

Mouth

Rnds 1-2: Repeat same rnds of Head & Body on

Continued on page 55

Sir Snowfellow

Design by
Tammy Hildebrand

Finished Size:
10½" tall.

Materials:
- ★ Worsted-weight yarn:
  2 oz. white
  1 oz. black
  ½ oz. each green and red
  small amount orange
- ★ Two 20-mm wiggle eyes
- ★ 2 red 1" pom-poms
- ★ 4½" red feather
- ★ Polyester fiberfill
- ★ Craft glue or hot glue gun
- ★ Tapestry needle
- ★ G crochet hook or size needed to obtain gauge

Gauge:
4 sc = 1"; 4 sc rows = 1".

Skill Level:
Average

Head & Body

Rnd 1: Starting at **bottom,** with white, ch 3, sl st in first ch to form ring, ch 1, 12 sc in ring, join with sl st in first sc (12 sc).

Rnd 2: Ch 1, sc in first st, 2 sc in next st, (sc in next st, 2 sc in next st) around, join (18).

Rnd 3: Ch 1, sc in first st, sc in next st, 2 sc in next st, (sc in each of next 2 sts, 2 sc in next st) around, join (24).

Rnd 4: Ch 1, sc in first st, sc in each of next 2 sts, 2 sc in next st, (sc in each of next 3 sts, 2 sc in next st) around, join (30).

Rnd 5: Ch 1, sc in first st, sc in each of next 3 sts, 2 sc in next st, (sc in next 4 sts, 2 sc in next st) around, join (36).

Rnd 6: Ch 1, sc in first st, sc in next 4 sts, 2 sc in next st, (sc in next 5 sts, 2 sc in next st) around, join (42).

Rnd 7: Ch 1, sc in first st, sc in next 5 sts, 2 sc in next st, (sc in next 6 sts, 2 sc in next st) around, join (48).

Rnd 8: Ch 1, sc in first st, sc in next 6 sts, 2 sc in next st, (sc in next 7 sts, 2 sc in next st) around, join (54).

Rnd 9: Ch 1, sc in first st, sc in next 7 sts, 2 sc in next st, (sc in next 8 sts, 2 sc in next st) around, join (60).

Rnd 10: Ch 1, sc in first st, sc in next 8 sts, 2 sc in next st, (sc in next 9 sts, 2 sc in next st) around, join (66).

Rnd 11: Ch 1, sc in first st, sc in next 9 sts, 2 sc in next st, (sc in next 10 sts, 2 sc in next st) around, join (72).

Rnd 12: Working this rnd in **back lps** only, ch 1, sc in each st around, join.

Rnds 13-28: Ch 1, sc in each st around, join.

Rnds 29-30: Ch 1, sc in first 4 sts, sc next 2 sts tog, (sc in next 4 sts, sc next 2 sts tog) around, join (60, 50).

Rnd 31: Ch 1, sc in each of first 3 sts, sc next 2 sts tog, (sc in each of next 3 sts, sc next 2 sts tog) around, join (40).

Rnd 32: Ch 1, sc in first 8 sts, sc next 2 sts tog, (sc in next 8 sts, sc next 2 sts tog) around, join (36).

Rnds 33-35: Ch 1, sc in each st around, join.

Rnd 36: Ch 1, sc in first st, 2 sc in next st, (sc in next st, 2 sc in next st) around, join (54).

Rnds 37-39: Ch 1, sc in each st around, join.

Rnd 40: Repeat rnd 36 (81).

Rnds 41-43: Ch 1, sc in each st around, join.

Rnds 44-45: Ch 1, sc in first st, sc next 2 sts tog, (sc in next st, sc next 2 sts tog) around, join (54, 36).

Rnds 46-48: Ch 1, sc in each st around, join.

Rnd 49: Ch 1, sc in first st, sc next 2 sts tog, (sc in next st, sc next 2 sts tog) around, join (24). Stuff.

Rnd 50: Ch 1, sc first 2 sts tog, (sc next 2 sts tog) around, join. Leaving 8" end for sewing, fasten off (12). Sew opening closed.

Arm (make 2)

Rnd 1: With white, ch 16, sl st in first ch to form ring, ch 1, sc in each ch around, join with sl st in first sc (16 sc).

Rnds 2-6: Ch 1, sc in each st around, join. At end of last rnd, fasten off.

Rnd 7: For **mitten;** working in starting ch on opposite side of rnd 1, join red with sc in first ch, sc in each ch around, join.

Rnds 8-10: Ch 1, sc in each st around, join.

Rnd 11: For **thumb,** ch 1, sc in first 6 sts, skip last 10 sts, join (6 sc).

Rnd 12: Ch 1, sc in each st around, join. Leaving 6" end for sewing, fasten off. Sew opening closed.

Rnd 11: For **fingers,** join red with sc in first skipped st on rnd 10, sc in each st around, join (10).

Rnds 12-13: Ch 1, sc in each st around, join.

Rnd 14: Ch 1, sc first 2 sts tog, (sc next 2 sts tog) around, join. Leaving 6" end for sewing, fasten off. Sew opening closed.

Sew opening at base of thumb closed. Stuff Arms and fingers. With thumbs pointing up, sew Arms to each side of Body over rnds 24-28.

Scarf

Row 1: With green, ch 5, sc in 2nd ch from hook, sc in each ch across, turn (4 sc).

Rows 2-89: Working these rows in **back lps** only, ch 1, sc in each st across, turn. At end of last row, fasten off.

Tie around neck.

Continued on page 55

1800s Day Outfit

Design by
Beverly Mewhorter

Finished Size:

Fits 11½" fashion doll.

Materials:

★ Size-10 bedspread cotton:
  500 yds. violet
  75 yds. white
  small amount black
★ 6" x 52" piece of violet tulle
★ 2¼ yds. black ⅛" satin ribbon
★ One yd. black 4-mm strung beads
★ 10 black 4" boa feathers
★ 3 small rubber bands
★ One straight pin
★ Black sewing thread
★ Small amount polyester fiberfill
★ Craft glue or hot glue gun
★ Sewing and tapestry needles
★ No. 7 steel crochet hook or size needed to obtain gauge

Gauge:

15 sts = 2"; 8 sc rows = 1"; 15 dc rows = 4".

Skill Level:

Average

Blouse

Bodice

Row 1: Starting at **waist,** with violet, ch 23, sc in 2nd ch from hook, sc in each ch across, turn (22 sc).

Rows 2-3: Ch 1, sc in each st across, turn.

Row 4: Ch 1, sc in first 4 sts, 2 sc in next st, sc in next 12 sts, 2 sc in next st, sc in last 4 sts, turn (24).

Row 5: Repeat row 2.

Row 6: Ch 1, sc in first 5 sts, 2 sc in next st, sc in next 12 sts, 2 sc in next st, sc in last 5 sts, turn (26).

Rows 7-8: Repeat row 2.

Row 9: Ch 1, sc in first 4 sts, 2 sc in next st, sc in next 16 sts, 2 sc in next st, sc in last 4 sts, turn (28).

Row 10: Repeat row 2.

Row 11: Ch 1, sc in each of first 3 sts, (2 sc in next st, sc in each of next 2 sts) across to last st, sc in last st, turn (36).

Row 12: Repeat row 2.

Row 13: Ch 1, sc in first 7 sts; for **armhole,** ch 10, skip next 4 sts; sc in next 14 sts; for **armhole,** ch 10, skip next 4 sts; sc in last 7 sts, turn (28 sc, 2 ch-10 sps).

Row 14: Ch 1, sc in each st and in each ch across, turn (48 sc).

Rnd 15: Working around outer edge, ch 1, sc in each st across, sc in end of each row across; for **peplum,** working in starting ch on opposite side of row 1, 2 sc in first ch, sc in next ch, hdc in each of next 3 chs, dc in each of next 3 chs, 2 tr in each of next 6 chs, dc in each of next 3 chs, hdc in each of next 3 chs, sc in next ch, 2 sc in last ch; sc in end of each row across, join with sl st in first sc, fasten off.

Bodice Ruffle

Row 1: Working in **front lps** of rnd 15 on Bodice, with right side facing you, and waist opening towards you, join white with sc in first st, 2 sc in same st, 3 sc in each of next 47 sts leaving remaining sts unworked, turn.

Row 2: Ch 1, sc in each st across, fasten off.

Neck Trim

Row 1: Working in **remaining lps** of rnd 15 on Bodice, with right side facing you, join violet with sc in first st, sc in next 47 sts leaving remaining sts unworked, turn (48 sc).

Row 2: Ch 1, sc in each of first 2 sts, sc next 2 sts tog, (sc in each of next 2 sts, sc next 2 sts tog) across, fasten off.

Sleeves

Rnd 1: Working around one armhole, join violet with sc in 3rd skipped st at underarm, sc in next st, sc in next 10 chs, sc in each of last 2 sts, join with sl st in first sc (14 sc).

Rnd 2: Ch 1, sc in first 4 sts, 3 sc in each of next 6 sts, sc in last 4 sts, join (26).

Rnds 3-12: Ch 1, sc in each st around, join.

Rnd 13: Ch 1, sc in first 4 sts, (sc next 3 sts tog) 6 times, sc in last 4 sts, join (14).

Rnd 14: Ch 1, sc first 2 sts tog, (sc next 2 sts tog) around, join, fasten off (7).

Rnd 15: Join white with sc in first st, 2 sc in same st, 3 sc in each st around, join.

Rnd 16: Ch 1, sc in each st around, join, fasten off. Repeat on other armhole. Place Bodice on doll. Sew back opening closed.

Skirt

Row 1: With violet, ch 23, sc in 2nd ch from hook,

Continued on next page

1800's Day Outfit

Continued from page 53

sc in each ch across, turn (22 sc).

Row 2: Ch 1, sc in each of first 3 sts, 2 sc in next st, (sc in each of next 2 sts, 2 sc in next st) across, turn (29).

Row 3: Ch 1, sc in first 4 sts, 2 sc in next st, (sc in each of next 3 sts, 2 sc in next st) across, turn (36).

Row 4: Ch 1, sc in first st, 2 sc in next st, (sc in next st, 2 sc in next st) across, turn (54).

Row 5: Ch 1, 3 sc in first st, 4 sc in next st, (3 sc in next st, 4 sc in next st) across, turn (189).

Rows 6-32: Ch 3, dc in each st across, turn. At end of last row, fasten off.

Row 33: Join white with sc in first st, 2 sc in same st, 3 sc in each st across, fasten off.

Run gathering thread across long edge of tulle, pull tight to fit across row 1 of Skirt. Sew gathered edge to wrong side of row 1 on Skirt.

Starting at bottom of Skirt, sew ends of rows together across to row 10, place Skirt on doll, sew remaining ends of rows together.

Hat

Rnd 1: With violet, ch 4, 13 dc in 4th ch from hook, join with sl st in top of ch-3 (14 dc).

Rnd 2: Ch 3, dc in same st, 2 dc in each st around, join (28).

Rnd 3: Ch 3, dc in same st, dc in next st, (2 dc in next st, dc in next st) around, join (42).

Rnd 4: Working this rnd in **back lps** only, ch 3, dc in each st around, join.

Rnd 5: Repeat rnd 3 (63).

Rnd 6: Ch 3, dc in same st, dc in each of next 2 sts, (2 dc in next st, dc in each of next 2 sts) around, join (84).

Rnd 7: Ch 1, sc in each st around, join with sl st in first sc, fasten off.

Purse

Rnd 1: With black, ch 4, 11 dc in 4th ch from hook, join with sl st in top of ch-3 (12 dc).

Rnd 2: Ch 3, dc in same st, 2 dc in each st around, join (24).

Rnds 3-5: Ch 3, dc in each st around, join.

Rnds 6-7: Ch 1, sc first 2 sts tog, (sc next 2 sts tog) around, join with sl st in first sc (12 sc, 6 sc).

Rnd 8: Ch 3, 2 dc in same st, 3 dc in each st around, join with sl st in top of ch-3; for **handles**, ch 20, skip next 8 sts, sl st in next st, ch 20, skip next 8 sts, join with sl st in joining sl st, fasten off.

For **tassel,** cut 11 strands black each 2½" long. Tie separate strand tightly around middle of all strands; fold strands in half. Wrap another strand around folded strands ³⁄₁₆" from top of fold, covering ⅛"; secure and hide ends inside Tassel. Trim all ends evenly. Tie Tassel to center of rnd 1 on Purse.

Finishing

1: Glue 7" piece of strung beads around row 1 of Neck Trim.

2: Cut 6 pieces of ribbon each 6" long. Tie each piece into a bow. Glue one bow to outside of each Sleeve over rnd 14. Glue one bow to center back of row 1 on Skirt. Glue remaining bows down center front of Bodice as shown in photo.

3: Cut 3 pieces of strung beads each 8" long. Glue one end of each piece ½" apart across center front of row 1 on Skirt. Glue other end of beads 3¼" apart across row 29 as shown. Cut 3 pieces of ribbon each 6" long. Tie each piece into a bow. Glue one bow to bottom end of each strand of beads. Glue peplum over top end of beads on Skirt.

4: Stuff Purse with small amount of fiberfill. Tie 12" piece of ribbon tightly into a bow around rnd 7. Trim.

5: Insert one end of 12" piece of ribbon from bottom to top through one side of rnd 3 on Hat, insert same end from top to bottom through opposite side of rnd 3, pull ends even.

6: Glue 5 feathers to back half of Hat on underside and remaining feathers to same half on top side.

7: Tie 12" piece of ribbon into a bow. Glue to back edge of Hat slightly off-center as shown.

Hair Arrangement

Divide hair on top of head into one section and secure with rubber band. Divide hair in back into 2 separate sections. Braid each back section of hair separately leaving approximately 2" ends. Secure each braid with rubber bands. Bring ends of both braids up to top section of hair. Remove rubber band from top section and smooth over cords of braid.

Pin Hat to top of head; tie ribbon ends into a bow under chin. ✩

Petunia Pigihoof

Continued from page 49

page 49.

Rnds 3-4: Sc in each st around. At end of last rnd, join with sl st in first sc, fasten off.

Flatten last rnd and sew directly below Snout as shown.

Ear (make 2)

Rnd 1: With pink, ch 2, 6 sc in 2nd ch from hook (6 sc).

Rnd 2: Sc in each st around.

Rnd 3: 2 sc in each st around (12).

Rnd 4: Sc in each st around.

Rnd 5: (Sc in next st, 2 sc in next st) around (18).

Rnds 6-8: Sc in each st around. At end of last rnd, join with sl st in first sc, fasten off.

Flatten last rnd of each Ear. Cup each Ear and sew one to each side of Head over rnds 6-10.

Tail

With pink, ch 14, 3 sc in 2nd ch from hook, 3 sc in each ch across to last ch, sl st in last ch, fasten off.

Sew one end of tail to center back of rnd 41 on Body. Sew 9th st from end to center back of rnd 39.

Apron

Row 1: With white, ch 43, 2 dc in 4th ch from hook, 2 dc in each ch across, turn (81 dc).

Row 2: Ch 3, (2 dc in next st, dc in next st) across, turn (121).

Row 3: Ch 1, sc in first st, (skip next 2 sts, 5 dc in next st, skip next 2 sts, sc in next st) across, fasten off.

For **tie**, with white, ch 30; working in starting ch on opposite side of row 1, sc in each ch across; for **tie**, ch 30, fasten off.

Tie Apron around waist of Pig.

Finishing

1: For **eyes**, sew buttons to rnds 9 and 10 of Head on each side of Snout.

2: Tie ribbon into a bow around neck of Pig.

3: Glue ribbon roses evenly spaced across first row of Apron. ✪

Sir Snowfellow

Continued from page 51

Hat

Rnd 1: With black, ch 3, sl st in first ch to form ring, ch 3, 19 dc in ring, join with sl st in top of ch-3 (20 dc).

Rnd 2: Ch 3, 2 dc in next st, (dc in next st, 2 dc in next st) around, join (30).

Rnd 3: Ch 3, dc in next st, 2 dc in next st, (dc in each of next 2 sts, 2 dc in next st) around, join (40).

Rnd 4: Working this rnd in **back lps** only, ch 1, sc in each st around, join with sl st in first sc.

Rnds 5-10: Ch 1, sc in each st around, join.

Rnd 11: Working this rnd in **back lps** only, ch 3, dc in each st around, join with sl st in top of ch-3.

Rnd 12: Repeat rnd 2, fasten off (60). Stuff lightly; sew rnd 10 to top of Head.

Nose

Rnd 1: With orange, ch 4, sl st in first ch to form ring, ch 1, sc in each ch around, join with sl st in first sc (4 sc).

Rnd 2: Ch 1, 2 sc in each st around, join (8).

Rnds 3-4: Ch 1, sc in each st around, join. At end of last rnd, leaving 6" end for sewing, fasten off.

Stuff. Sew to center front of Head over rnds 40 and 41.

Coal (make 5)

With black, ch 2, 5 sc in 2nd ch from hook, join with sl st in first sc. Leaving 6" end for sewing, fasten off.

Sew Coal pieces over rnds 37-39 centered below Nose as shown in photo.

Finishing

1: Glue wiggle eyes 1" apart over rnds 42-44 centered above Nose.

2: Sew red pom-poms to center front of body as shown.

3: Insert feather through one side of Hat and through Head, glue in place. ✪

Happy Scrappy

Design by Joyce Keklock

Finished Size:

19" tall.

Materials:

★ Worsted-weight yarn:
 2½ oz. each teal and blue
 2 oz. each lt. yellow, lt. brown and off-white
 ½ oz. each dk. brown and black
 small amount each orange, red and white
★ Powder blush
★ Polyester fiberfill
★ Tapestry needle
★ G crochet hook or size needed to obtain gauge

Gauge:

4 sc = 1"; 4 sc rows = 1".

Skill Level:

Average

Note:

Do not join rnds unless otherwise stated. Mark first st of each rnd.

Scarecrow

Head

Rnd 1: Starting at **top of Head,** with off-white, ch 2, 6 sc in 2nd ch from hook (6 sc).

Rnd 2: 2 sc in each st around (12).

Rnd 3: (Sc in next st, 2 sc in next st) around (18).

Rnd 4: (Sc in each of next 2 sts, 2 sc in next st) around (24).

Rnd 5: (Sc in each of next 3 sts, 2 sc in next st) around (30).

Rnd 6: (Sc in next 4 sts, 2 sc in next st) around (36).

Rnds 7-12: Sc in each st around.

Rnd 13: (Sc in next 4 sts, sc next 2 sts tog) around (30).

Rnd 14: (Sc in each of next 3 sts, sc next 2 sts tog) around (24).

Rnd 15: Sc in each st around.

Rnd 16: (Sc in next 4 sts, sc next 2 sts tog) around, join with sl st in first sc (20).

Rnd 17: For **neck ruffle,** working this rnd in **front lps** only, ch 3, 2 dc in same st, 3 dc in each st around, join with sl st in top of ch-3, fasten off. Stuff Head.

Body

Rnd 1: Working in **back lps** of rnd 16 on Head, join teal with sc in first st, sc in each st around (20 sc).

Rnd 2: (Sc in next st, 2 sc in next st) around (30).

Rnd 3: (Sc in next 4 sts, 2 sc in next st) around (36).

Rnd 4: (Sc in next 5 sts, 2 sc in next st) around (42).

Rnds 5-16: Sc in each st around. At end of last rnd, join with sl st in first sc, fasten off.

Rnd 17: Join blue with sc in first st, sc in each st around.

Rnds 18-26: Sc in each st around.

Rnd 27: (Sc in next 5 sts, sc next 2 sts tog) around (36).

Rnd 28: (Sc in next 4 sts, sc next 2 sts tog) around (30).

Rnd 29: (Sc in next st, sc next 2 sts tog) around (20). Stuff.

Rnd 30: (Sc next 2 sts tog) around, join with sl st in first sc. Leaving 8" for sewing, fasten off (10). Sew opening closed.

Arm (make 2)

Rnd 1: With teal, ch 15, sl st in first ch to form ring, ch 3, dc in each ch around, join with sl st in top of ch-3 (15 dc).

Rnds 2-10: Ch 3, dc in each st around, join.

Rnd 11: Working this rnd in **front lps** only, ch 2, hdc in each st around, join with sl st in top of ch-2, fasten off. Stuff lightly.

For **each fringe,** cut 2 pieces of lt. yellow each 3" long. Holding both pieces tog, insert hook in **back lp** of any st on rnd 10, draw fold through, draw all loose ends through fold, tighten. Fringe in each st on rnd 10. Trim ends.

Hand (make 2)

Rnd 1: With off-white, ch 2, 6 sc in 2nd ch from hook (6 sc).

Rnd 2: 2 sc in each st around (12).

Rnds 3-6: Sc in each st around. Stuff, continue stuffing as you work.

Rnds 7-8: (Sc next 2 sts tog) around. At end of last rnd, join with sl st in first sc, fasten off.

Insert rnds 7 and 8 of one Hand inside each Arm. With teal, sew rnd 11 of each Arm to rnd 6 of each Hand.

Continued on next page

Happy Scrappy
Continued from page 57

Leg (make 2)
Rnd 1: With blue, ch 20, sl st in first ch to form ring, ch 3, dc in each ch around, join with sl st in top of ch-3 (20 dc).

Rnds 2-15: Ch 3, dc in each st around, join.

Rnd 16: Working this rnd in **front lps** only, ch 2, hdc in each st around, join with sl st in top of ch-2, fasten off. Stuff lightly.

For **each fringe,** cut 2 pieces of lt. yellow each 3" long. Holding both pieces tog, insert hook in **back lp** of any st on rnd 15, draw fold through, draw all loose ends through fold, tighten. Fringe in each st on rnd 15. Trim.

Shoe (make 2)
Rnd 1: Starting at **toe,** with dk. brown, ch 2, 6 sc in 2nd ch from hook (6 sc).

Rnd 2: 2 sc in each st around (12).

Rnd 3: (Sc in each of next 3 sts, 2 sc in next st) around (15).

Rnds 4-6: Sc in each st around.

Row 7: Working in rows, ch 1, sc in first 9 sts leaving remaining sts unworked, turn (9).

Rows 8-10: Ch 1, sc in each st across, turn.

Row 11: Ch 1, sc in first st, (sc next 2 sts tog) across, turn (5).

Rnd 12: Working in rnds, ch 1, sc in first st, (sc next 2 sts tog) 2 times, join with sl st in first sc, **turn** (3).

Rnd 13: Working in sts and in ends of rows around opening, ch 1, evenly space 18 sc around opening, join (18).

Rnd 14: Sc in each st around.

Rnd 15: (Sc next 2 sts tog) around, join with sl st in first sc, fasten off. Stuff. Sew opening closed.

Insert top back of each Shoe inside of each Leg; working around outside of Leg, with blue, sew rnd 14 of each Leg to each Shoe as shown.

Hair
For **each fringe around back of Head,** cut 2 pieces of lt. yellow each 5" long. Holding both pieces tog, insert hook in st, draw fold through st, draw all loose ends through fold, tighten. Fringe in each st on rnd 9 across back of Head. Using 3" pieces of lt. yellow, fringe in 10 sts across center front of rnd 6. Using 5" pieces of lt. yellow, fringe at an angle across rnds 7-8 on each side of Head between fringe on back and front. Trim fringe on back and sides to 2" and front to 1".

Nose
Row 1: With red, ch 3, sc in 2nd ch from hook, sc in last ch, turn.

Row 2: Sl st next 2 sts tog, fasten off.

Sew over rnds 9-11 on center front Head as shown.

Eye (make 2)
With black, ch 2, sc in 2nd ch from hook changing to white (see page 158), ch 1, 2 sc in same ch, fasten off.

With white sts on top, sew Eyes over rnds 8 and 9 centered above Nose ⅜" apart.

Hat
Rnd 1: With lt. brown, ch 2, 8 sc in 2nd ch from hook (8 sc).

Rnd 2: 2 sc in each st around (16).

Rnd 3: (Sc in next st, 2 sc in next st) around (24).

Rnd 4: (Sc in each of next 2 sts, 2 sc in next st) around (32).

Rnds 5-7: Sc in each st around.

Rnd 8: (Sc in each of next 3 sts, 2 sc in next st) around (40).

Rnds 9-10: Sc in each st around. At end of last rnd, join with sl st in first sc, **turn.**

Rnd 11: Working this rnd in **back lps** only, ch 3, dc in same st, dc in next st, (2 dc in next st, dc in next st) around, join with sl st in top of ch-3 (60 dc).

Rnd 12: Ch 3, dc in next st, 2 dc in next st, (dc in each of next 2 sts, 2 dc in next st) around, join, fasten off.

Sew rnd 10 to top of Head, covering knots on Hair fringes.

Neck Tie
With lt. brown, ch 50, fasten off. Starting at center front, weave through rnd 16 of Head, tie ends into a bow.

Waist Tie
With lt. brown, ch 75, fasten off. Starting at center front, weave through rnd 17 of Body, tie ends into a bow.

Knee Patch (make 2)
Row 1: With orange, ch 6, sc in 2nd ch from hook, sc in each ch across, turn (5 sc).

Rows 2-4: Ch 1, sc in each st across, turn. At end of last row, fasten off.

For **fringes behind patches,** cut one piece of lt. yellow 4" long. Insert hook in st, draw fold through, draw both loose ends through fold, tighten. Trim.

Working in center front of rnds 8 and 9 on each Leg, work 5 fringes at random over a 1" square area. Sew one Patch over same area, covering knots as shown.

Shirt and Hip Patch (make 2)
Row 1: With orange, ch 4, sc in 2nd ch from

hook, sc in each ch across, turn (3 sc).

Rows 2-3: Ch 1, sc in each st across, turn. At end of last row, fasten off.

For **fringes behind patches,** work same as fringes behind patches on Knees.

Working on right front of rnds 6-10 on Body and rnds 19-23 on back of Body, work 5 fringes at random over a ¾" square area. Sew one Patch over same areas, covering knots as shown

Finishing

With one 2-ply strand red, using Backstitch (see page 159), embroider **mouth** over rnds 12 and 13 of Head centered below Nose as shown.

Apply blush to cheeks.

Crow

Body & Head

Rnd 1: With black, ch 2, 6 sc in 2nd ch from hook (6 sc).

Rnd 2: 2 sc in each st around (12).

Rnds 3-5: Sc in each st around.

Rnd 6: (Sc next 2 sts tog) around (6). Stuff. Continue stuffing as you work.

Rnd 7: For **head,** (sc in next st, 2 sc in next st) around (9).

Rnds 8-10: Sc in each st around.

Rnd 11: Sc first 3 sts tog, (sc next 2 sts tog) around, join with sl st in first sc, fasten off. For **feather,** trim end to ½"; separate strands.

Wing (make 2)

Row 1: With black, ch 3, sc in 2nd ch from hook, sc in last ch, turn (2 sc).

Row 2: Ch 1, 2 sc in each st across, fasten off.

Sew row 1 of each Wing to each side of Body over rnd 6.

Beak

With lt. yellow, ch 2, sc in 2nd ch from hook, fasten off. Sew wide end to center front of Head over rnd 9.

Feet

With lt. yellow, ch 4, (sl st, ch 4, sl st) in 4th ch from hook, fasten off. Sew straight end to front of rnd 1 on Body.

Finishing

1: With one 2-ply strand orange, using French Knot (see page 159), embroider eyes between rnds 10 and 11 centered above Beak ¼" apart.

2: Cut 6" piece of orange; tie into a bow around center front st on rnd 6 of Body.

3: Sew back of rnd 2 on Body to top of Scarecrow's left Arm between rnds 1 and 2. ✿

Imagine a cozy fireside chat, snuggly storytime in the
children's room, a relaxing afternoon nap in the
front porch swing. Imagine how grand your life could be
with a little Afghan Fancy.

Chapter Three

Afghan Fancy

Rosebud Ripple

Design by Margret Willson

Finished Size:
54" x 73½".

Materials:
- ★ Brushed acrylic worsted-weight yarn:
  - 35 oz. off-white
  - 31 oz. mulberry
  - 28 oz. green
- ★ H crochet hook or size needed to obtain gauge.

Gauge:
4 dc and 3 ch-1 sps = 2"; rows 1-4 = 2½".

Skill Level:
Average

Afghan

NOTE: For **shell**, dc in next ch or ch sp, (ch 1, dc in same ch or ch sp) 3 times.

Row 1: With off-white, ch 222, dc in 4th ch from hook, ch 1, skip next ch, (dc in next ch, ch 1, skip next ch) 4 times, shell in next ch, *(ch 1, skip next ch, dc in next ch) 6 times, skip next 3 chs, (dc in next ch, ch 1, skip next ch) 6 times, shell in next ch; repeat from * 6 more times, (ch 1, skip next ch, dc in next ch) 5 times, skip next ch, dc in last ch, turn (96 dc, 94 ch-1 sps, 8 shells). Front of row 1 is right side of work.

Row 2: Ch 3, (dc in next ch sp, ch 1) 5 times, skip next ch sp, shell in next ch sp, *ch 1, skip next ch sp, dc in next ch sp, (ch 1, dc in next ch sp) 5 times, skip next 2 sts, (dc in next ch sp, ch 1) 6 times, skip next ch sp, shell in next ch sp; repeat from * 6 more times, ch 1, skip next ch sp, dc in next ch sp, (ch 1, dc in next ch sp) 4 times, dc in last st, turn, fasten off.

NOTES: For **cluster (cl)**, yo, insert hook in next st, yo, draw lp through, yo, draw through 2 lps on hook, yo, insert hook in same st, yo, draw lp through, yo, draw through 2 lps on hook, yo, draw through all 3 lps on hook.

For **cluster shell (cl-shell)**, (cl, ch 3, cl) in next st or ch sp.

Row 3: Join green with sl st in first st, ch 3, skip next dc, cl in next dc, skip next dc, (cl-shell in next dc, skip next dc) 2 times, cl-shell in next ch sp, *skip next dc, (cl-shell in next dc, skip next dc) 3 times, dc in each of next 2 ch sps, skip next dc, (cl-shell in next dc, skip next dc) 3 times, cl-shell in next ch sp; repeat from * 6 more times, skip next dc, (cl-shell in next dc, skip next dc) 2 times, cl in next dc, skip next dc, dc in last dc, turn, fasten off (54 cl-shells, 16 dc, 2 cls).

NOTE: For **popcorn (pc)**, 5 dc in next ch sp, drop lp from hook, insert hook in first st of 5-dc group, draw dropped lp through. Push to right side of work.

Row 4: Join mulberry with sl st in first st, ch 3, dc in sp between next 2 cls, ch 1, pc in next ch-3 sp, (ch 2, dc in sp between next 2 cls, ch 2, pc in next ch-3 sp) 5 times, *ch 1, pc in next ch-3 sp, (ch 2, dc in sp between next 2 cls, ch 2, pc in next ch-3 sp) 6 times; repeat from * 5 more times, ch 1, pc in next ch-3 sp, (ch 2, dc in sp between next 2 cls, ch 2, pc in next ch-3 sp) 5 times, ch 1, dc in sp between next 2 cls, dc in last st, turn, fasten off (92 ch-2 sps, 54 pcs, 50 dc, 9 ch-1 sps).

Row 5: Join off-white with sl st in first st, ch 3; working in ch-1 sps and ch-2 sps, (dc in next ch sp, ch 1) 5 times, shell in next pc, *(ch 1, dc in next ch sp) 6 times, skip next ch sp, dc in next ch sp, ch 1) 6 times, shell in next pc; repeat from * 6 more times, (ch 1, dc in next ch sp) 5 times, dc in last st, turn (96 dc, 94 ch-1 sps, 8 shells).

Rows 6-98: Repeat rows 2-5 consecutively, ending with row 2. At end of last row, **do not** fasten off.

Rnd 99: Working around outer edge, ch 1, sc in first 14 sts and ch sps, 3 sc in next ch sp, (sc in next 14 sts and ch sps, skip next 2 sts, sc in next 14 ch sps and sts, 3 sc in next ch sp) 7 times, sc in last 14 sts and ch sps, 3 sc in end of each row across; working in starting ch on opposite side of row 1, 3 sc in first ch sp, sc in next 10 chs and ch sps, skip next ch, (sc in next 12 ch sps and chs, 7 sc in next ch sp, sc in next 12 chs and ch sps, skip next ch) 7 times, sc in next 10 ch sps and chs, 3 sc in last ch sp, 3 sc in end of each row across, join with sl st in first sc, fasten off. ☆

Sunnyside Up

Design by
Katherine Eng

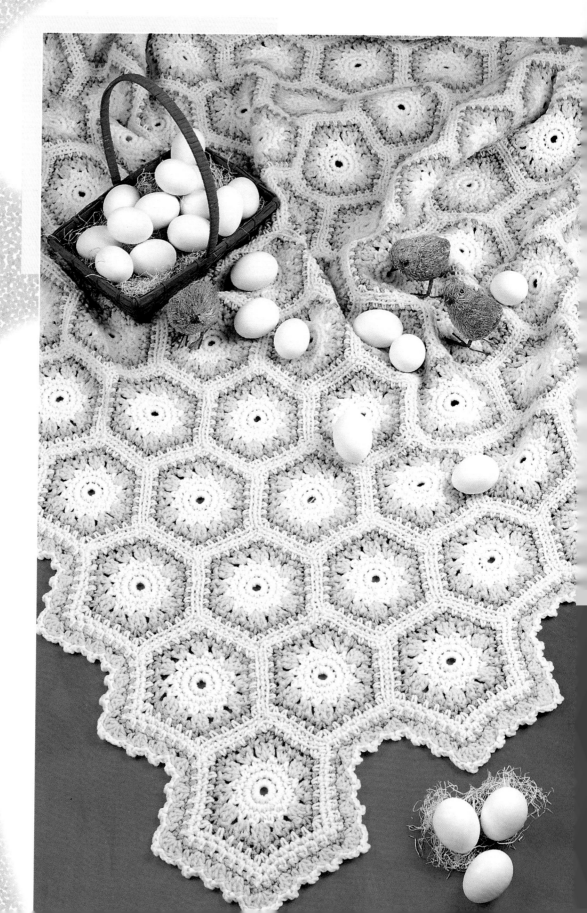

Finished Size:
45½" x 58".

Materials:
★ Worsted-weight yarn:
14 oz. bright yellow
13 oz. each pale yellow and white
10 oz. lilac
★ Tapestry needle
★ H crochet hook or size needed to obtain gauge

Gauge:
Rnds 1-3 of Motif = 3" across. Each Motif is 5" across.

Skill Level:
Average

Motif (make 95)

Rnd 1: With white, ch 5, sl st in first ch to form ring, ch 1, 12 sc in ring, join with sl st in first sc (12 sc).

Rnd 2: Ch 1, 2 sc in each st around, join (24).

Rnd 3: Ch 1, (sc, ch 2, sc) in first st, skip next st, *(sc, ch 2, sc) in next st, skip next st; repeat from * around, join, fasten off (12 ch-2 sps).

Rnd 4: Join bright yellow with sc in any ch sp, ch 2, sc in same sp, ch 1, 3 dc in next ch sp, ch 1, *(sc, ch 2, sc) in next ch sp, ch 1, 3 dc in next ch sp, ch 1; repeat from * around, join, fasten off (12 ch-1 sps, 6 3-dc groups, 6 ch-2 sps).

Rnd 5: Join lilac with sc in center dc of any 3-dc group, ch 2, sc in same st, ch 1, (sc in next ch-1 sp or ch-2 sp, ch 1) 3 times, *(sc, ch 2, sc) in center dc of next 3-dc group, ch 1, (sc in next ch-1 sp or ch-2 sp, ch 1) 3 times; repeat from * around, join, fasten off (24 ch-1 sps, 6 ch-2 sps).

Rnd 6: Join pale yellow with sc in any ch-2 sp, ch 2, sc in same sp, ch 1, (sc in next ch-1 sp, ch 1) 4 times, *(sc, ch 2, sc) in next ch-2 sp, ch 1, (sc in next ch-1 sp, ch 1) 4 times; repeat from * around, join, fasten off.

Start
Border
here.

**ASSEMBLY
DIAGRAM**

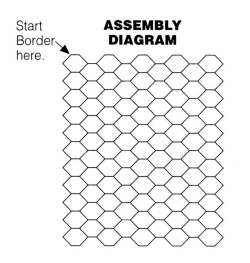

Holding Motifs wrong sides together, matching sts, with pale yellow, sew together through **back lps** according to Assembly Diagram.

Border

Rnd 1: Working around entire outer edge, join pale yellow with sc in corner ch-2 sp as indicated on diagram, ch 2, sc in same sp, ch 1, (sc in next ch-1 sp or ch-2 sp before and after each seam, ch 1) across to next corner ch-2 sp or ch-2 sp at next tip, *(sc, ch 2, sc) in next ch-2 sp, ch 1, (sc in next ch-1 sp or ch-2 sp before and after each seam, ch 1) across to next corner ch-2 sp or ch-2 sp at next tip; repeat from * around, join with sl st in first sc.

Rnd 2: Sl st in first ch-2 sp, ch 1, (sc, ch 2, sc) in same sp; skipping ch-1 sp at each indentation, ch 1, (sc in next ch-1 sp, ch 1) across to next ch-2 sp, *(sc, ch 2, sc) in next ch-2 sp; skipping ch-1 sp at each indentation, ch 1, (sc in next ch-1 sp, ch 1) across; repeat from * around, join, fasten off.

Rnd 3: Join lilac with sc in first ch-2 sp, ch 2, sc in same sp, ch 1, (sc in next ch-1 sp, ch 1) across to next ch-2 sp, *(sc, ch 2, sc) in next ch-2 sp, ch 1, (sc in next ch-1 sp, ch 1) across to next corner ch-2 sp; repeat from * around, join, fasten off.

Rnd 4: Join bright yellow with sl st in first ch-2 sp, ch 3, 4 dc in same sp, ◊skip next sc, sc in next sc, (3 dc in next sc, sc in next sc) 3 times, skip next sc, 5 dc in next ch-2 sp, *skip next sc, sc in next sc, (3 dc in next sc, sc in next sc) 2 times, skip next sc, 3 dc in next sc, skip next sc, sc in next sc, (3 dc in next sc, sc in next sc) 2 times, skip next sc, 5 dc in next ch-2 sp*; repeat between ** 9 more times, skip next sc, sc in next sc, (3 dc in next sc, sc in next sc) 3 times, skip next sc, 5 dc in next ch-2 sp, skip next sc, sc in next sc, (3 dc in next sc, sc in next sc) 3 times, skip next sc, [5 dc in next ch-2 sp, skip next sc, sc in next sc, (3 dc in next sc, sc in next sc) 2 times, skip next sc, 3 dc in next sc, skip next sc, sc in next sc, 3 dc in next sc, sc in next sc, skip next sc, 3 dc in next sc, skip next sc, sc in next sc, (3 dc in next sc, sc in next sc) 2 times, skip next sc, 5 dc in next ch-2 sp, skip next sc, sc in next sc, (3 dc in next sc, sc in next sc) 3 times, skip next sc]; repeat between [ ] 3 more times◊, 5 dc in next sc; repeat between ◊◊, join with sl st in top of ch-3, fasten off.

Rnd 5: Join white with sl st in center dc of first 5-dc group, ch 2, sl st in same st, ch 3, sl st in next sc, *ch 1, (sl st, ch 2, sl st) in center dc of next 3-dc group, ch 1, sl st in next sc; repeat from * across to next 5-dc group, ch 3, ◊(sl st, ch 2, sl st) in center dc of next 5-dc group, ch 3, sl st in next sc, [ch 1, (sl st, ch 2, sl st) in center dc of next 3-dc group, ch 1, sl st in next sc]; repeat between [ ] across to next 5-dc group, ch 3; repeat from ◊ around, join with sl st in first sl st, fasten off. ✪

Afghan Fancy
65

Milan Chenille Strips

Design by
Tammy Hildebrand

Finished Size:
40½" x 57".

Materials:
★ Worsted-weight chenille yarn:
30 oz. antique white
17 oz. variegated purple
★ G crochet hook or size needed to obtain gauge

Gauge:
2 sc and 2 ch-1 sps = 1"; 4 sc rows = 1". Each Strip is 2½" wide.

Skill Level:
Average

First Strip

Center
Row 1: With antique white, ch 8, sc in 2nd ch from hook, (ch 1, skip next ch, sc in next ch) across, turn (4 sc, 3 ch-1 sps).

Rows 2-224: Ch 1, sc in first st, (ch 1, skip next ch sp, sc in next st) across, turn. At end of last row, fasten off.

Border
Working around outer edge, join variegated with sc in first sc on last row, ch 1, sc in same sc, (sc, ch 1, sc) in each of last 3 sc; working in ends of rows, skip first row, (sc, ch 3, sc) in next row, *skip next row, (sc, ch 3, sc) in next row; repeat from * 110 more times; working in starting ch on opposite side of row 1, (sc, ch 1, sc) in first ch, [skip next ch, (sc, ch 1, sc) in next ch]; repeat between [ ] 2 more times; working in ends of rows, (sc, ch 3, sc) in first row, skip next row, ◊(sc, ch 3, sc) in next row, skip next row; repeat from ◊ across, join with sl st in first sc, fasten off.

Next Strip

Center
Work same as First Strip's Center.

Border
Working around outer edge, join variegated with sc in first sc on last row, ch 1, sc in same sc, (sc, ch 1, sc) in each of last 3 sc; working in ends of rows, skip first row, sc in next row; joining to last Strip, ch 1, sl st in first ch-3 sp on last Strip, ch 1, sc in same row on this Strip, *skip next row, sc in next row, ch 1, sl st in next ch-3 sp on last Strip, ch 1, sc in same row on this Strip; repeat from * 110 more times; working in starting ch on opposite side of row 1, (sc, ch 1, sc) in first ch, [skip next ch, (sc, ch 1, sc) in next ch]; repeat between [ ] 2 more times; working in ends of rows, (sc, ch 3, sc) in first row, skip next row, ◊(sc, ch 3, sc) in next row, skip next row; repeat from ◊ across, join, fasten off.

Repeat Next Strip 14 more times for a total of 16 Strips.

Edging
Working around entire outer edge, join variegated with sc in first ch-1 sp on one short end, (sc, ch 2, 2 sc) in same sp, [[(sc, ch 1, sc) in each of next 2 ch-1 sps, (2 sc, ch 2, 2 sc) in next ch-1 sp, *sc in next joining seam, (2 sc, ch 2, 2 sc) in next ch-1 sp, (sc, ch 1, sc) in each of next 2 ch-1 sps, (2 sc, ch 2, 2 sc) in next ch-1 sp; repeat from * 14 more times, 2 sc in each of next 112 ch-3 sps], (2 sc, ch 2, 2 sc) in next ch-1 sp; repeat between [ ], join with sl st in first sc, fasten off. ✰

Razz-Ma-Taz Afghan

Design by
Katherine Eng

Finished Size:
46" x 65".

Materials:
★ Worsted-weight yarn:
27 oz. black
16 oz. sage
14 oz. coral
8 oz. brown
★ Tapestry needle
★ G crochet hook or size needed to obtain gauge

Gauge:
Rnds 1 and 2 of Motif = 2½" across. Each Motif is 4¾" square.

Skill Level:
Average

Motif A (make 59)

Rnd 1: With black, ch 4, 15 dc in 4th ch from hook, join with sl st in top of ch-3, fasten off (16 dc).

Rnd 2: Join sage with sc in any st, ch 2, sc in same st, ch 1, skip next st, *(sc, ch 2, sc) in next st, ch 1, skip next st; repeat from * around, join with sl st in first sc, fasten off (8 ch-1 sps, 8 ch-2 sps).

Rnd 3: Join brown with sc in any ch-2 sp, ch 2, sc in same sp, ch 2, skip next ch-1 sp, *(sc, ch 2, sc) in next ch-2 sp, ch 2, skip next ch-1 sp; repeat from * around, join, fasten off (16 ch-2 sps).

Rnd 4: Join coral with sl st in first ch sp, ch 3, (dc, ch 2, 2 dc) in same sp, *[ch 1, dc around next ch sps of rnds 2 and 3 at same time, ch 1, sc in next ch sp on last rnd, ch 1, dc around next ch sps of rnds 2 and 3 at same time, ch 1], (2 dc, ch 2, 2 dc) in next ch sp on last rnd; repeat from * 2 more times; repeat between [ ], join, **turn** (28 sts, 16 ch-1 sps, 4 ch-2 sps).

Rnd 5: Ch 1, sc in first ch-1 sp, ch 1, skip next st, (sc in next ch-1 sp, ch 1, skip next st) 3 times, *[sc in next st, (sc, ch 2, sc) in next ch-2 sp, sc in next st, ch 1, skip next st], (sc in next ch-1 sp, ch 1, skip next st) 4 times; repeat from * 2 more times; repeat between [ ], join with sl st in first sc, **turn**, fasten off (32 sc, 20 ch-1 sps, 4 ch-2 sps).

NOTE: For **long single crochet (lsc)**; working over next ch-1 sp, insert hook in next dc on rnd before last, yo, draw up long lp, yo, draw through both lps on hook.

Rnd 6: Join black with sc in any corner ch-2 sp, ch 3, sc in same sp, *[sc in each of next 2 sts, lsc, (sc in next st, lsc) 4 times, sc in each of next 2 sts], (sc, ch 3, sc) in next corner ch-2 sp; repeat from * 2 more times; repeat between [ ], join, fasten off.

Motif B (make 58)

Rnd 1: Repeat same rnd of Motif A.
Rnd 2: With coral, repeat same rnd of Motif A.
Rnd 3: Repeat same rnd of Motif A.
Rnds 4-5: With sage, repeat same rnds of Motif A.
Rnd 6: Repeat same rnd of Motif A.

Holding Motifs wrong sides together, matching sts, starting with Motif A in any corner, alternating Motifs B and A, with black, sew together through **back lps** in 9 rows of 13 Motifs each.

Border

Rnd 1: Working around entire outer edge, join black with sc in any corner ch-3 sp, ch 3, sc in same sp, sc in each st, sc in each ch-2 sp on each side of seams and hdc in each seam around with (sc, ch 3, sc) in each corner ch-3 sp, join with sl st in first sc, **turn** (161 sc across each short end between corner ch-3 sps, 233 sc across each long edge between corner ch-3 sps).

Rnd 2: Sl st in next st, ch 1, sc in same st, *ch 1, skip next st, (sc in next st, ch 1, skip next st) across to next corner ch sp, (sc, ch 3, sc) in next corner ch sp; repeat from * 3 more times, ch 1, skip last st, join, **turn**.

Rnd 3: Sl st in first ch-1 sp, ch 4, *[(dc, ch 1, dc, ch 3, dc, ch 1, dc) in next corner ch-3 sp, ch 1, (dc in next ch-1 sp, ch 1) across] to next corner ch-3 sp; from * 2 more times; repeat between [ ], join with sl st in 3rd ch of ch-4, **turn**.

Rnd 4: Sl st in first ch-1 sp, ch 1, sc in same sp, *ch 1, (sc in next ch-1 sp, ch 1) across to next corner ch-3 sp, (sc, ch 3, sc) in next ch-3 sp; repeat from * 3 more times, ch 1, (sc in next ch-1 sp, ch 1) across, join with sl st in first sc, **turn**.

Rnd 5: Ch 1, sc in each st and in each ch-1 sp around with (sc, ch 3, sc) in each corner ch sp, join, **do not** turn, fasten off.

Rnd 6: Join sage with sc in any corner ch sp, (ch 2, sc, ch 3, sc, ch 2, sc) in same sp, [◊skip next st, *(sc, ch 2, sc) in next st, skip next st; repeat from * across◊ to next corner ch sp, (sc, ch 2, sc, ch 3, sc, ch 2, sc) in next corner ch sp]; repeat between [ ] 2 more times; repeat between ◊◊, join, fasten off. ★

Picnic

Summer Cherry Picnic

Design by
Eleanor Albano-Miles

Finished Size:
43½" x 54".

Materials:
- ★ Worsted-weight yarn:
  24½ oz. white
  14 oz. yellow
  7 oz. black
  3½ oz. each green and red
- ★ Tapestry needle
- ★ H crochet hook or size needed to obtain gauge

Gauge:
7 sts = 2"; 4 sc rows = 1". Each Block is 10½" square.

Skill Level:
Average

Cherry Block (make 10)

Row 1: With white, ch 26, sc in 2nd ch from hook, sc in each ch across, turn (25 sc).

Rows 2-29: Ch 1, sc in each st across, turn. At end of last row, **do not** turn, fasten off.

Rnd 30: Working around outer edge, join yellow with sc in first st, sc in same st, sc in each st across to last st, 3 sc in last st; *working in ends of rows, sc in first 4 rows, skip next row, (sc in each of next 3 rows, skip next row) across to last 4 rows, sc in last 4 rows*; working in starting ch on opposite side of row 1, 3 sc in first ch, sc in each ch across to last ch, 3 sc in last ch; repeat between **, sc in same st as first st, join with sl st in first sc, **turn** (104 sc).

Rnds 31-32: Ch 1, 2 sc in first st, sc in each st around with 3 sc in each center corner st, sc in same st as first st, join, **turn** (112, 120). At end of last rnd, **do not** turn, fasten off.

NOTE: When changing colors (see page 158), always drop color to wrong side of work, work over dropped color and pick up again when needed.

Rnd 33: Join white with sc in any center corner st, sc in same st, *[sc in next st changing to black, sc in each of next 3 sts changing to white in last st made, (sc in each of next 3 sts changing to black in last st made, sc in each of next 3 sts changing to white in last st made) 4 times, sc in next st], 3 sc in next center corner st; repeat from * 2 more times; repeat between [ ], sc in same st as first st changing to black, join, **turn** (128).

Rnd 34: Ch 1, sc in first st changing to white, *[sc in same st, sc in each of next 2 sts changing to black in last st made, sc in each of next 3 sts changing to white in last st made, (sc in each of next 3 sts changing to black in last st made, sc in each of next 3 sts changing to white in last st made) 4 times, sc in each of next 2 sts], sc in next center corner st changing to black, sc in same st changing to white; repeat from * 2 more times; repeat between [ ], sc in same st as first st changing to black, join, **turn** (136).

Rnd 35: Ch 1, 2 sc in first st changing to white, *[sc in each of next 3 sts changing to black in last st made, (sc in each of next 3 sts changing to white in last st made, sc in each of next 3 sts changing to black in last st made) 5 times], 3 sc in next center corner st changing to white; repeat from * 2 more times; repeat between [ ], sc in same st as first st, join, fasten off (144).

Leaf (make 2)

With green, ch 10, sc in 2nd ch from hook, *hdc in next ch, dc in next ch, tr in each of next 3 chs, dc in next ch, hdc in next ch*, 3 sc in last ch; working on opposite side of chs; repeat between **, sc in last ch, join with sl st in first sc, fasten off.

Cherry & Stem (make 3)

For **Cherry**, with red, ch 3, sl st in first ch to form ring, ch 1, 10 sc in ring, join with sl st in first sc, fasten off.

For **Stem**, join green with sl st in first st, ch 8, fasten off.

Sew Leaves, Cherries and Stems over center of Block as shown in photo.

Solid Block (make 10)

Rows/Rnds 1-32: Repeat same rows/rnds of Cherry Block.

Rnd 33: Join black with sc in any center corner st, sc in same st, *[sc in next st changing to white, sc in each of next 3 sts changing to black in last st made, (sc in each of next 3 sts changing to white in last st made, sc in each of next 3 sts changing to black in last st made) 4 times, sc in next st], 3 sc in next center corner st; repeat from * 2 more times; repeat between [ ], sc in same st as first st changing to white, join, **turn** (128).

Rnd 34: Ch 1, sc in first st changing to black, *[sc in same st, sc in each of next 2 sts changing to white in last st made, sc in each of next 3 sts changing to black in last st made, (sc in each of next 3 sts changing to white in last st made, sc in each of next 3 sts changing to black in last st made) 4 times, sc in each of next 2 sts], sc in next center corner st changing to white, sc in same st changing to black; repeat from * 2 more times; repeat between [ ], sc in same st as first st changing to white, join, **turn** (136).

Rnd 35: Ch 1, 2 sc in first st changing to black, *[sc in each of next 3 sts changing to white in last st made, (sc in each of next 3 sts changing to black in last st made, sc in each of next 3 sts changing to white in last st made) 5 times], 3 sc in next center corner st changing to black; repeat from * 2 more times; repeat between [ ], sc in same st as first st, join, fasten off (144).

Holding Blocks wrong sides together, matching sts, working through both thicknesses, with white, sew Blocks together through **back lps** according to Assembly Diagram.

Edging

Rnd 1: Working around entire outer edge, join yellow with sc in center st on any corner, ch 2, sc in same st, sc in each st and in each seam around with (sc, ch 2, sc) in each center corner st, join with sl st in first sc, **turn.**

Rnd 2: Ch 1, sc in each st around with (sc, ch 2, sc) in each corner ch sp, join, **turn.**

Rnd 3: Ch 1, sc in each st around with 3 sc in each corner ch sp, join, fasten off. ☆

ASSEMBLY DIAGRAM

Ocean Waves

Design by
Eleanor Albano-Miles

Finished Size:
41" x 59".

Materials:
★ Worsted-weight yarn:
17 oz. med. blue
12 oz. each lt. blue and lt. green
8 oz. each lt. lavender and lt. aqua
★ H crochet hook or size needed to obtain gauge

Gauge:
7 sts = 2"; 2 sc rows and 2 dc rows = 1½".

Skill Level:
Average

Afghan

Row 1: With med. blue, ch 204, sc in 2nd ch from hook, sc in each ch across, turn, fasten off (203 sc).

Row 2: Join lt. blue with sl st in first st, ch 3, dc in each st across, turn, fasten off.

Row 3: Join lt. lavender with sc in first st, sc in each st across, turn, fasten off.

Row 4: Join lt. aqua with sl st in first st, ch 4, skip next st, dc in next st, (ch 1, skip next st, dc in next st) across, turn, fasten off (102 dc, 101 ch-1 sps).

Row 5: Join lt. green with sc in first st, sc in each st and in each ch sp across, turn (203 sc).

Row 6: Ch 3, dc in each st across, turn.

Row 7: Ch 1, sc in each st across, turn, fasten off.

Row 8: Repeat row 4.

Row 9: Join lt. lavender with sc in first st, sc in each st and in each ch sp across, turn, fasten off.

Row 10: Repeat row 2.

Row 11: Join med. blue with sc in first st, sc in each st across, turn.

Row 12: Ch 3, skip next 3 sts; for **diamond,** dc in next st, ch 3, 3 dc around last dc made; (skip next 3 sts; for **next diamond,** dc in next st, ch 3, 3 dc around last dc made) across to last 2 sts, skip next st, dc in last st, turn (50 diamonds).

Row 13: Ch 5, sc in ch-3 on top of next diamond, (ch 3, sc in ch-3 on top of next diamond) 49 times, ch 2, dc in first ch of last ch-3, turn (50 sc, 49 ch-3 sps, 2 dc, 2 ch-2 sps).

Row 14: Ch 1, sc in first st, 2 sc in next ch-2 sp, sc in next st, (3 sc in next ch-3 sp, sc in next st) 49 times, 2 sc in next ch-2 sp, sc in 3rd ch of last ch-5, turn, fasten off (203 sc).

Rows 15-102: Repeat rows 2-14 consecutively, ending with row 11.

Edging

Row 1: Working in ends of rows across one short end, join med. blue with sc in first row, sc in each row across, turn.

Row 2: Ch 1, sc in each st across, turn, fasten off.
Repeat Edging on opposite short end. ☆

Earthtone Chevron

Design by
Eleanor Albano-Miles

Finished Size:
45" x 57½".

Materials:
- ★ Worsted-weight yarn:
  - 21 oz. each brown variegated and taupe
  - 17 oz. rust
  - 8 oz. natural
- ★ Tapestry needle
- ★ I crochet hook or size needed to obtain gauge

Gauge:
3 sc = 1"; 4 sc rows = 1". Each Strip is 5½" wide.

Skill Level:
Average

Strip (make 8)

Center
Row 1: With taupe, ch 12, sc in 2nd ch from hook, sc in each ch across, turn (11 sc).

Row 2: Ch 3, dc in next st, hdc in each of next 2 sts, sc in next st, sl st in next st, sc in next st, hdc in each of next 2 sts, dc in each of last 2 sts, turn.

Rows 3-5: Ch 1, 2 sc in first st, sc in each of next 3 sts; for **decrease (dec),** insert hook in next st, yo, draw lp through, skip next st, insert hook in next st, yo, draw lp through, yo, draw through all 3 lps on hook; sc in each of next 3 sts, 2 sc in last st, turn. At end of last row, fasten off.

Row 6: Join natural with sc in first st, sc in same st, sc in each of next 3 sts, dec, sc in each of next 3 sts, 2 sc in last st, turn.

Row 7: Ch 1, 2 sc in first st, sc in each of next 3 sts, dec, sc in each of next 3 sts, 2 sc in last st, turn, fasten off.

Row 8: With variegated, repeat row 6.

Rows 9-13: Repeat row 3. At end of last row, fasten off.

Rows 14-15: Repeat rows 6 and 7.

Row 16: With taupe, repeat row 6.

Rows 17-21: Repeat row 3. At end of last row, fasten off.

Rows 22-154: Repeat rows 6-21 consecutively, ending with row 10.

Row 155: Ch 1, sc in each of first 2 sts, hdc in each of next 2 sts, dc in next st, tr in next st, dc in next st, hdc in each of next 2 sts, sc in each of last 2 sts, turn.

Row 156: Ch 1, sc in each st across, **do not** turn, fasten off.

Border
Rnd 1: Join rust with sc in first st of last row, ch 2, sc in same st, (sc next 2 sts tog) 2 times, sc in next st, (sc next 2 sts tog) 2 times, (sc, ch 2, sc) in last st, skip end of first row, sc in end of each row across; working in starting ch on opposite side of row 1, (sc, ch 2, sc) in first ch, (sc next 2 chs tog) 2 times, sc in next ch, (sc next 2 chs tog) 2 times, (sc, ch 2, sc) in last ch, sc in end of each row across to last row, skip end of last row, join with sl st in first sc, **turn** (7 sc across each short end between corner ch-2 sps, 157 sc across each long edge between corner ch-2 sps).

Rnds 2-3: Ch 1, sc in each st around with (sc, ch 2, sc) in each corner ch sp, join, **turn.** At end of last row, **do not** turn, fasten off.

NOTE: For **long single crochet (lsc);** working over last rnd, insert hook in next st on rnd before last, yo, draw up long lp, yo, draw through both lps on hook.

Rnd 4: Join taupe with sc in any corner ch sp, sc in next st, (lsc, sc in next st on last rnd) across to next corner ch sp, *(sc, ch 2, sc) in next corner ch sp, sc in next st, (lsc, sc in next st on last rnd) across to next corner ch sp; repeat from * around, join, **turn.**

Rnd 5: Ch 1, sc in each st around with (sc, ch 2, sc) in each corner ch sp, join, **turn,** fasten off.

Rnds 6-7: With variegated, repeat rnds 4 and 5.

Holding Strips wrong sides together, with every other Strip held upside down, matching sts and ch sps, working through both thicknesses, with variegated, sew long edges together through **back lps.**

Edging

Working around entire outer edge, join variegated with sl st in any corner ch sp, ch 5, dc in same sp, dc in each st and in each ch sp on each side of seams around with (dc, ch 2, dc) in each corner ch sp, join with sl st in 3rd ch of ch-5, fasten off. ✰

Baby's Bric-A-Brac

Design by Diane Poellot

Finished Size:
32½" x 40".

Materials:
★ Sport yarn:
   28 oz. white
   5 oz. pink
★ G crochet hook or size needed to obtain gauge

Gauge:
4 sts = 1"; 5 sc rows and 4 dc rows = 3".

Skill Level:
Advanced

Afghan

Row 1: With white, ch 152, sc in 2nd ch from hook, sc in each of next 2 chs, (ch 1, skip next ch, sc in each of next 3 chs) across, turn (114 sc, 37 ch-1 sps).

Row 2: Ch 3, dc in each st and in each ch-1 sp across, turn (151 dc).

NOTE: For **treble split cluster (split-cl)**, working in front of last row, yo 2 times, insert hook in same skipped ch or st on row before last, yo, draw lp through, (yo, draw through 2 lps on hook) 2 times, yo 2 times, insert hook in next skipped ch or st on row before last, yo, draw lp through, (yo, draw through 2 lps on hook) 2 times, yo, draw through all 3 lps on hook, skip next st on last row behind cluster.

Row 3: Ch 1, sc in first st; working in front of last row, tr in next skipped ch or st on row before last, skip next st on last row, sc in next st, ch 1, skip next st, sc in next st, (split-cl, sc in next st, ch 1, skip next st, sc in next st) 36 times; working in front of last row, tr in same skipped ch or st on row before last, skip next st on last row, sc in last st, turn (76 sc, 37 ch-1 sps, 36 split-cls, 2 tr).

Row 4: Ch 3, dc in each st and in each ch-1 sp across, turn, fasten off (151 dc).

Row 5: Join pink with sc in first st; working in front of last row, tr in next skipped ch or st on row before last, skip next st on last row, sc in next st, ch 1, skip next st, sc in next st, (split-cl, sc in next st, ch 1, skip next st, sc in next st) 36 times; working in front of last row, tr in same skipped ch or st on row before last, skip next st on last row, sc in last st, turn, fasten off.

Row 6: Join white with sl st in first st, ch 3, dc in each st and in each ch-1 sp across, turn.

Rows 7-8: Repeat rows 3 and 2.

NOTE: For **treble front post cluster (fp-cl)**, working in front of last row, yo 2 times, insert hook from front to back around post of first half of last split-cl worked on row before last, yo, draw lp through, (yo, draw through 2 lps on hook) 2 times, yo 2 times, insert hook from front to back around post of 2nd half of next split-cl on row before last, yo, draw

lp through, (yo, draw through 2 lps on hook) 2 times, yo, draw through all 3 lps on hook, skip next st on last row.

Row 9: Ch 1, sc in first st, ch 1, skip next st, sc in next st; working in front of last row, yo 2 times, insert hook from front to back around post of next tr on row before last, yo, draw lp through, (yo, draw through 2 lps on hook) 2 times, yo 2 times, insert hook from front to back around post of 2nd half of next split-cl on row before last, yo, draw lp through, (yo, draw through 2 lps on hook) 2 times, yo, draw through all 3 lps on hook, skip next st on last row, sc in next st, ch 1, skip next st, sc in next st, (fp-cl, sc in next st, ch 1, skip next st, sc in next st) 35 times; working in front of last row, yo 2 times, insert hook from front to back around post of first half of last split-cl worked on row before last, yo, draw lp through, (yo, draw through 2 lps on hook) 2 times, yo 2 times, insert hook from front to back around post of next tr on row before last, yo, draw lp through, (yo, draw through 2 lps on hook) 2 times, yo, draw through all 3 lps on hook, skip next st on last row, sc in next st, ch 1, skip next st, sc in last st, turn (76 sc, 38 ch-1 sps, 37 fp-cls).

Row 10: Repeat row 4.

NOTE: For **beginning treble split cluster (beg split-cl)**, working in front of last row, yo 2 times, insert hook in first skipped st on row before last, yo, draw lp through, (yo, draw through 2 lps on hook) 2 times, yo 2 times, insert hook in next skipped st on row before last, yo, draw lp through, (yo, draw through 2 lps on hook) 2 times, yo, draw through all 3 lps on hook, skip next st on last row.

Row 11: Join pink with sc in first st, ch 1, skip next st, sc in next st, beg split-cl, sc in next st, ch 1, skip next st, sc in next st, (split-cl, sc in next st, ch 1, skip next st, sc in next st) 36 times, turn, fasten off.

Row 12: Repeat row 6.

Row 13: Ch 1, sc in each of first 3 sts, **beg split-cl**, (sc in next st, ch 1, skip next st, sc in next st, split-cl) 36 times, sc in each of last 3 sts, turn (78 sc, 37 split-cls, 36 ch-1 sps).

Row 14: Repeat row 2.

NOTE: For **treble crochet front post (fp)**, working in front of last row, yo 2 times, insert hook from front to back around post of designated st, yo, draw lp through, (yo, draw through 2 lps on hook) 3 times, skip st on last row.

Row 15: Ch 1, sc in first st, fp around 2nd half of first split-cl on row before last, sc in next st, ch 1, skip next st, sc in next st, (fp-cl, sc in next st, ch 1, skip next st, sc in next st) 36 times, fp around first half of last split-cl on row before last, sc in last st, turn (76 sc, 37 ch-1 sps, 36 fp-cls, 2 fp).

Rows 16-97: Repeat rows 4-15 consecutively, ending with row 13. At end of last row, **do not** turn or fasten off.

Continued on page 89

Holiday Lace Over

Design by
Eleanor
Albano-Miles

Finished Size:
41¾" x 58¼".

Materials:
★ Worsted-weight yarn:
48 oz. aran
29 oz. red/green/white variegated
★ Tapestry needle
★ H crochet hook or size needed to obtain gauge

Gauge:
13 sc = 4"; 13 sc rows = 4". Each Block is 8¼" square.

Skill Level:
Average

Block (make 35)

Back
Row 1: With aran, ch 18, sc in 2nd ch from hook, sc in each ch across, turn (17 sc).

Rows 2-17: Ch 1, sc in each st across, turn.

Rnd 18: Working around outer edge, ch 1, (sc, ch 2, sc) in first st, sc in next 15 sts, (sc, ch 2, sc) in last st; *working in ends of rows, skip first row, sc in next 15 rows, skip last row*; working in starting ch on opposite side of row 1, (sc, ch 2, sc) in first ch, sc in next 15 chs, (sc, ch 2, sc) in last ch; repeat between **, join with sl st in first sc (17 sc across each side between corner ch-2 sps).

Rnd 19: Ch 1, sc in each st around with (sc, ch 2, sc) in each corner ch sp, join, fasten off (19 sc across each side between corner ch-2 sps).

Front
Row 1: With variegated, ch 24, sc in 9th ch from hook, turn; for **diamond**, *[ch 1, sc in first sc, 3 sc in next ch sp, **turn**, (ch 1, sc in next 4 sc, **turn**) 2 times, ch 1, sc in next 4 sc, **do not** turn, skip next 2 chs on starting ch, dc in next ch], ch 3, skip next 2 chs, sc in next ch, **turn**; repeat from *; repeat between [ ], turn (4 dc, 3 diamonds).

Row 2: Ch 6, sc in tip of next diamond, ch 2, (tr in next dc, ch 2, sc in tip of next diamond, ch 2) across to last ch-8, tr in 6th ch of last ch-8, turn (6 ch-2 sps, 4 tr, 3 sc). Front of row 2 is right side of work.

Row 3: Ch 6, sc in next sc, **turn**; for **diamond**, *[ch 1, sc in first sc, 3 sc in next ch sp, **turn**, (ch 1, sc in next 4 sc, **turn**) 2 times, ch 1, sc in next 4 sc, **do not** turn, skip next ch-2 sp, dc in next st on last row], ch 3, skip next ch-2 sp, sc in next st, **turn**; repeat from *; repeat between [ ], turn (4 dc, 3 diamonds).

Row 4: Ch 6, sc in tip of next diamond, ch 2, (tr in next dc, ch 2, sc in tip of next diamond, ch 2) across to last ch-6, tr in 4th ch of ch-6, turn.

Rows 5-6: Repeat rows 3 and 4.

Rnd 7: Working around outer edge, ch 1, (sc, ch 2, sc) in first st, 2 sc in next ch sp, (sc in next st, 2 sc in next ch sp) across to last st, (sc, ch 2, sc) in last st, 2 sc in end of first row, 3 sc in end of each row across; working in starting ch on opposite side of row 1, (sc, ch 2, sc) in first ch, 2 sc in next ch sp, (sc in next ch, 2 sc in next ch sp) across to last ch, (sc, ch 2, sc) in last ch, 3 sc in end of each row across to last row, 2 sc in last row, join with sl st in first sc, **do not** fasten off (19 sc across each side between corner ch-2 sps).

Rnd 8: To **join Back to Front,** holding one Back and one Front wrong sides together, matching sts, working through both thicknesses, ch 1, sc in each st around with (sc, ch 2, sc) in each corner ch sp, join, **turn,** fasten off.

Rnd 9: Join aran with sl st in any corner ch sp, ch 5, dc in same sp, dc in each st around with (dc, ch 2, dc) in each corner ch sp, join with sl st in 3rd ch of ch-5, **turn.**

Rnd 10: Ch 1, sc in each st around with (sc, ch 2, sc) in each corner ch sp, join with sl st in first sc, fasten off.

Holding Blocks wrong sides together, matching sts, with aran, sew Blocks together through **back lps** in 5 rows of 7 Blocks each.

Edging
Working around entire outer edge, join aran with sc in any corner ch sp, 2 sc in same sp, sc in each st, sc in each ch sp on each side of seams and sc in each seam around with 3 sc in each corner ch sp, join with sl st in first sc, fasten off. ✫

Hearts & Flowers

Design by
Katherine Eng

Finished Size:
43" x 62½".

Materials:
- ★ Worsted-weight yarn:
  - 20 oz. raspberry
  - 14 oz. pink
  - 12 oz. med. green
  - 7 oz. lt. green
  - 3½ oz. lt. yellow
- ★ Tapestry needle
- ★ G crochet hook or size needed to obtain gauge

Gauge:
Rnds 1 and 2 of Motif = 2½" across. Each Motif is 6½" square.

Skill Level:
Average

Motif A (make 36)

Rnd 1: With lt. yellow, ch 5, sl st in first ch to form ring, ch 1, 12 sc in ring, join with sl st in first sc, fasten off (12 sc).

NOTE: For **popcorn (pc)**, 4 dc in next st, drop lp from hook, insert hook in first dc of 4-dc group, draw dropped lp through.

Rnd 2: Join pink with sc in first st, ch 1, pc in next st, ch 1, (sc in next st, ch 1, pc in next st, ch 1) around, join, fasten off (12 ch-1 sps, 6 sc, 6 pc).

Rnd 3: Join raspberry with sc in first sc, ch 3, (sc in next sc, ch 3) around, join (6 sc, 6 ch-3 sps).

Rnd 4: Ch 1, sc in first st, (sc, hdc, 3 dc) in next ch sp, 2 dc in next st, 3 hdc in next ch sp, sc in next st, 3 sc in next ch sp, (sc, ch 2, sc) in next st, 3 sc in next ch sp, sc in next st, 3 hdc in next ch sp, 2 dc in next st, (3 dc, hdc, sc) in last ch sp, join, **turn** (31 sts, 1 ch-2 sp).

Rnd 5: Ch 1, sc in each of next 2 sts, 2 sc in each of next 6 sts, sc in next 7 sts, (2 sc, ch 2, 2 sc) in next ch sp, sc in next 7 sts, 2 sc in each of next 6 sts, sc in each of last 2 sts, join with sl st in joining sl st on last rnd, **turn,** fasten off (46 sts, 1 ch-2 sp).

Rnd 6: Join med. green with sc in 4th st before joining sl st, ch 1, skip next st, hdc in next st, ch 1, skip next st, dc in next sl st, ch 1, skip next st, hdc in next st, ch 1, skip next st, sc in next st, ch 1, skip next st, (2 dc, ch 2, 2 dc) in next st, ch 1, skip next st, (hdc in next st, ch 1, skip next st) 2 times, sc in next st, ch 1, skip next st, hdc in next st, ch 1, skip next st, dc in next st, ch 1, skip next st, (2 tr, ch 2, 2 tr) in next st, ch 1, skip next st, dc in next st, ch 1, skip next st, hdc in next st, ch 1, skip next st, sl st in next ch sp, ch 1, skip next st, hdc in next st, ch 1, skip next st, dc in next st, ch 1, skip next st, (2 tr, ch 2, 2 tr) in next st, ch 1, skip next st, dc in next st, ch 1, skip next st,

hdc in next st, ch 1, skip next st, sc in next st, ch 1, skip next st, (hdc in next st, ch 1, skip next st) 2 times, (2 dc, ch 2, 2 dc) in next st, ch 1, skip last st, join, **turn** (36 sts, 24 ch-1 sps, 4 ch-2 sps).

Rnd 7: Ch 1, sc in first ch sp, ch 1, skip next st, sc in next st, (sc, ch 2, sc) in next ch-2 sp, *sc in next st, (ch 1, skip next st, sc in next ch-1 sp) 6 times, ch 1, skip next st, sc in next st, (sc, ch 2, sc) in next ch-2 sp; repeat from * 2 more times, sc in next st, ch 1, skip next st, (sc in next ch-1 sp, ch 1, skip next st) 5 times, join, **turn** (40 sc, 28 ch-1 sps, 4 ch-2 sps).

Rnd 8: Ch 1, sc in each st and in each ch-1 sp around with (sc, ch 2, sc) in each corner ch-2 sp, join, **turn,** fasten off (76 sc, 4 ch-2 sps).

Rnd 9: Join pink with sc in any corner ch-2 sp, ch 2, sc in same sp, *[ch 1, skip next st, (sc in next st, ch 1, skip next st) across] to next corner ch-2 sp, (sc, ch 2, sc) in next ch-2 sp; repeat from * 2 more times; repeat between [ ], join, **turn,** fasten off (44 sc, 40 ch-1 sps, 4 ch-2 sps).

Rnd 10: Join raspberry with sc in any corner ch-2 sp, ch 2, sc in same sp, ch 1, (sc in next ch-1 sp, ch 1) across to next corner ch-2 sp, *(sc, ch 2, sc) in next corner ch-2 sp, ch 1, (sc in next ch-1 sp, ch 1) across; repeat from * around, join, fasten off (48 sc, 44 ch-1 sps, 4 ch-2 sps).

Motif B (make 18)

Rnds 1-5: Repeat same rnds of Motif A.

Rnds 6-8: With lt. green, repeat same rnds of Motif A.

Rnds 9-10: Repeat same rnds of Motif A.

Holding Motifs wrong sides together, matching sts, with raspberry, sew together through **back lps** in 6 rows of 9 Motifs each according to Assembly Diagram.

ASSEMBLY DIAGRAM

A	A	A	A	A	A
A	B	B	B	B	A
A	B	A	A	B	A
A	B	A	A	B	A
A	B	A	A	B	A
A	B	A	A	B	A
A	B	A	A	B	A
A	B	B	B	B	A
A	A	A	A	A	A

A = Motif A
B = Motif B

Continued on page 90

Crazy Patch

Crazy Patch

Design by
Sandra Jean Smith

Finished Size:
53" x 73½".

Materials:
- ★ Worsted-weight yarn:
  - 32 oz. black
  - 8 oz. each purple, burgundy, rose, yellow, med. green and lt. green
- ★ Tapestry needle
- ★ G crochet hook or size needed to obtain gauge

Gauge:
3 sc = 1"; 3 sc rows = 1". Each Block is 20½" square.

Skill Level:
Average

Block A

Row 1: With black, ch 61, sc in 2nd ch from hook, sc in each ch across, turn (60 sc).

Rows 2-5: Ch 1, sc in each st across, turn.

NOTES: When changing colors (see page 158), always drop yarn to wrong side of work. Use a separate skein of yarn for each color section. **Do not** carry yarn across from one section to another. Fasten off at end of each color section.

Work odd-numbered rows on graph from left to right and even-numbered rows from right to left.

Each square on graph equals one sc.

Row 6: For **row 6 of Block A graph** (see page 88), ch 1, sc in first 5 sts changing to med. green in last st made, sc in next 15 sts changing to purple in last st made, sc in next 15 sts changing to yellow in last st made, sc in next 5 sts changing to lt. green in last st made, sc in next 15 sts changing to black in last st made, sc in last 5 sts, turn.

Rows 7-60: Ch 1, sc in each st across changing colors according to Block A graph, turn.

Rnd 61: Working around outer edge, ch 1, (sc, ch 2, sc) in first st, sc in next 58 sts, (sc, ch 2, sc) in last st; working in ends of rows, skip first row, sc in next 59 rows; working in starting ch on opposite side of row 1, (sc, ch 2, sc) in first ch, sc in next 58 chs, (sc, ch 2, sc) in last ch; working in ends of rows, sc in first 59 rows, skip last row, join with sl st in first sc, fasten off (60 sc across each short end between corner ch sps, 61 sc across each long edge between corner ch sps).

Block B

Rows 1-5: Repeat same rows of Block A.

Row 6: For **row 6 of Block B graph** (see page 89), ch 1, sc in first 5 sts changing to med. green in last st made, sc in next 11 sts changing to burgundy in last st made, sc in next 14 sts changing to purple in last st made, sc in next 10 sts changing to rose in last st made, sc in next 10 sts changing to yellow in last st made, sc in next 5 sts changing to black in last st made, sc in last 5 sts, turn.

Rows 7-60: Ch 1, sc in each st across changing colors according to Block B graph, turn.

Rnd 61: Repeat same rnd of Block A.

Block C

Rows 1-5: Repeat same rows of Block A.

Row 6: For **row 6 of Block C graph** (see page 90), ch 1, sc in first 5 sts changing to yellow in last st made, sc in next 15 sts changing to rose in last st made, sc in next 15 sts changing to burgundy in last st made, sc in next 14 sts changing to yellow in last st made, sc in next 6 sts changing to black in last st made, sc in last 5 sts, turn.

Rows 7-60: Ch 1, sc in each st across changing colors according to Block C graph, turn.

Rnd 61: Repeat same rnd of Block A.

Block D

Rows 1-5: Repeat same rows of Block A.

Row 6: For **row 6 of Block D graph** (see page 91), ch 1, sc in first 5 sts changing to lt. green in last st made, sc in next 15 sts changing to purple in last st made, sc in next 15 sts changing to yellow in last st made, sc in next 5 sts changing to lt. green in last st made, sc in next 15 sts changing to black in last st made, sc in last 5 sts, turn.

Rows 7-60: Ch 1, sc in each st across changing colors according to Block D graph, turn.

Rnd 61: Repeat same rnd of Block A.

Block E

Rows 1-5: Repeat same rows of Block A.

Row 6: For **row 6 of Block E graph** (see page 92), ch 1, sc in first 5 sts changing to lt. green in last st made, sc in next 15 sts changing to yellow in last st made, sc in next 5 sts changing to purple in last st made, sc in next 15 sts changing to lt. green in last st made, sc in next 15 sts changing to black in last st made, sc in last 5 sts, turn.

Rows 7-60: Ch 1, sc in each st across changing colors according to Block E graph, turn.

Rnd 61: Repeat same rnd of Block A.

Block F

Rows 1-5: Repeat same rows of Block A.

Row 6: For row 6 of Block F graph (see page 93), ch 1, sc in first 5 sts changing to purple in last st made, sc in next 11 sts changing to med. green in last st made, sc in next 14 sts changing to rose in last st made, sc in next 10 sts changing to burgundy in last st made, sc in next 10 sts changing to purple in last st made, sc in next 5 sts changing to black in last st made, sc in last 5 sts, turn.

Rows 7-60: Ch 1, sc in each st across changing colors according to Block F graph, turn.

Rnd 61: Repeat same rnd of Block A.

With black, using Feather Stitch (see illustration), outline each color section other than black on each Block.

Holding Blocks wrong sides together, matching sts, with black, sew Blocks together through **back lps** according to Assembly Diagram.

FEATHER STITCH

Border

Rnd 1: Working around outer edge, in **back lps** only, join black with sc in corner ch sp before one short end, ch 2, sc in same sp, *evenly space 123 more sc across to next corner ch sp, (sc, ch 2 sc) in next corner ch sp, evenly space 187 sc across long edge to next corner ch sp*, (sc, ch 2, sc) in next corner ch sp; repeat between **, join with sl st in first sc (125 sc across each short end between corner ch sps, 189 sc across each long edge between corner ch sps).

Rnd 2: Sl st in first ch sp, ch 1, (sc, ch 2, sc) in same sp, *[ch 1, skip next st, (sc in next st, ch 1, skip next st) across] to next corner ch sp, (sc, ch 2, sc) in next corner ch sp; repeat from * 2 more times; repeat between [ ], join, fasten off.

Rnd 3: Join yellow with sl st in first ch-2 sp, ch 5, dc in same sp, dc in each st and in each ch-1 sp around with (dc, ch 2, dc) in each corner ch-2 sp, join with sl st in 3rd ch of ch-5, fasten off.

NOTE: Skip st on last rnd behind tr.

Rnd 4: Join black with sc in first corner ch sp, ch 2, sc in same sp, *[sc in each of next 2 sts; working

in front of last 2 rnds, tr in next skipped st 3 rnds below, (sc in next st on last rnd, ch 1, skip next st, sc in next st, working in front of last 2 rnds, tr in next skipped st 3 rnds below) across to 2 sts before next corner ch-2 sp, sc in each of next 2 sts on last rnd], (sc, ch 2, sc) in next corner ch-2 sp; repeat from * 2 more times; repeat between [ ], join, fasten off.

Rnd 5: Working this rnd in **back lps** only, join burgundy with sl st in first ch of any corner ch-2 sp, ch 5, dc in next ch, dc in each st and in each ch-1 sp across to next corner ch-2 sp, *dc in next ch, ch 2, dc in next ch, dc in each st and in each ch-1 sp across to next corner ch-2 sp; repeat from * around, join with sl st in 3rd ch of ch-5, fasten off.

Rnd 6: Join black with sc in any corner ch-2 sp, ch 2, sc in same sp, *[ch 1, skip next st, sc in next st; working in front of last 2 rnds, tr in corner ch sp 3 rnds below, sc in next st on last rnd, ch 1, skip next st, sc in next st; (working in front of last 2 rnds, tr in next skipped st 3 rnds below, sc in next st on last rnd, ch 1, skip next st, sc in next st) across to 3 sts before next corner ch-2 sp, working in front of last 2 rnds, tr in next corner ch sp 3 rnds below, sc in next st on last rnd, ch 1, skip next st], (sc, ch 2, sc) in next corner ch-2 sp; repeat from * 2 more times; repeat between [ ], join with sl st in first sc, fasten off.

Rnd 7: With lt. green, repeat rnd 5.

Rnd 8: Join black with sc in any corner ch-2 sp, ch 2, sc in same sp, *[ch 1, skip next st, sc in next st; working in front of last 2 rnds, tr in next skipped st 3 rnds below, (sc in next st on last rnd, ch 1, skip next st, sc in next st; working in front of last 2 rnds, tr in next skipped st 3 rnds below) across to 2 sts before next corner ch sp, sc in next st on last rnd, ch 1, skip next st], (sc, ch 2, sc) in next corner ch-2 sp; repeat from * 2 more times; repeat between [ ], join with sc in first sc, fasten off.

Rnd 9: With rose, repeat rnd 5.

Rnd 10: Repeat rnd 8.

Rnd 11: With lt. green, repeat rnd 5.

Rnd 12: Repeat rnd 8.

Rnd 13: With purple, repeat rnd 5.

Rnd 14: Join black with sc in any corner ch-2 sp, ch 2, sc in same sp, *[sc in each of next 2 sts; working in front of last 2 rnds, tr in next skipped st 3 rnds below, (sc in each of next 3 sts; working in front of last 2 rnds, tr in next skipped st 3 rnds below) across to last 2 sts, sc in each of last 2 sts], (sc, ch 2, sc) in next corner ch sp; repeat from * 2 more times; repeat between [ ], join with sl st in first sc, fasten off. ✰

ASSEMBLY DIAGRAM

A	B
C	D
E	F

Graphs continued on page 88

BLOCK A

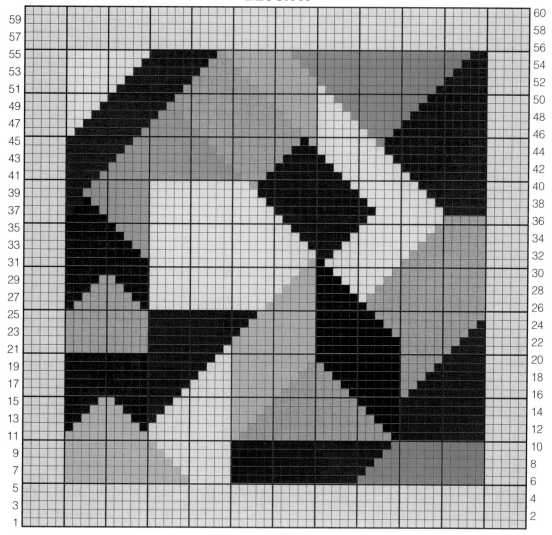

COLOR KEY

■ = Burgundy
■ = Purple
■ = Rose
□ = Yellow
■ = Med. Green
■ = Lt. Green
□ = Black

BLOCK B

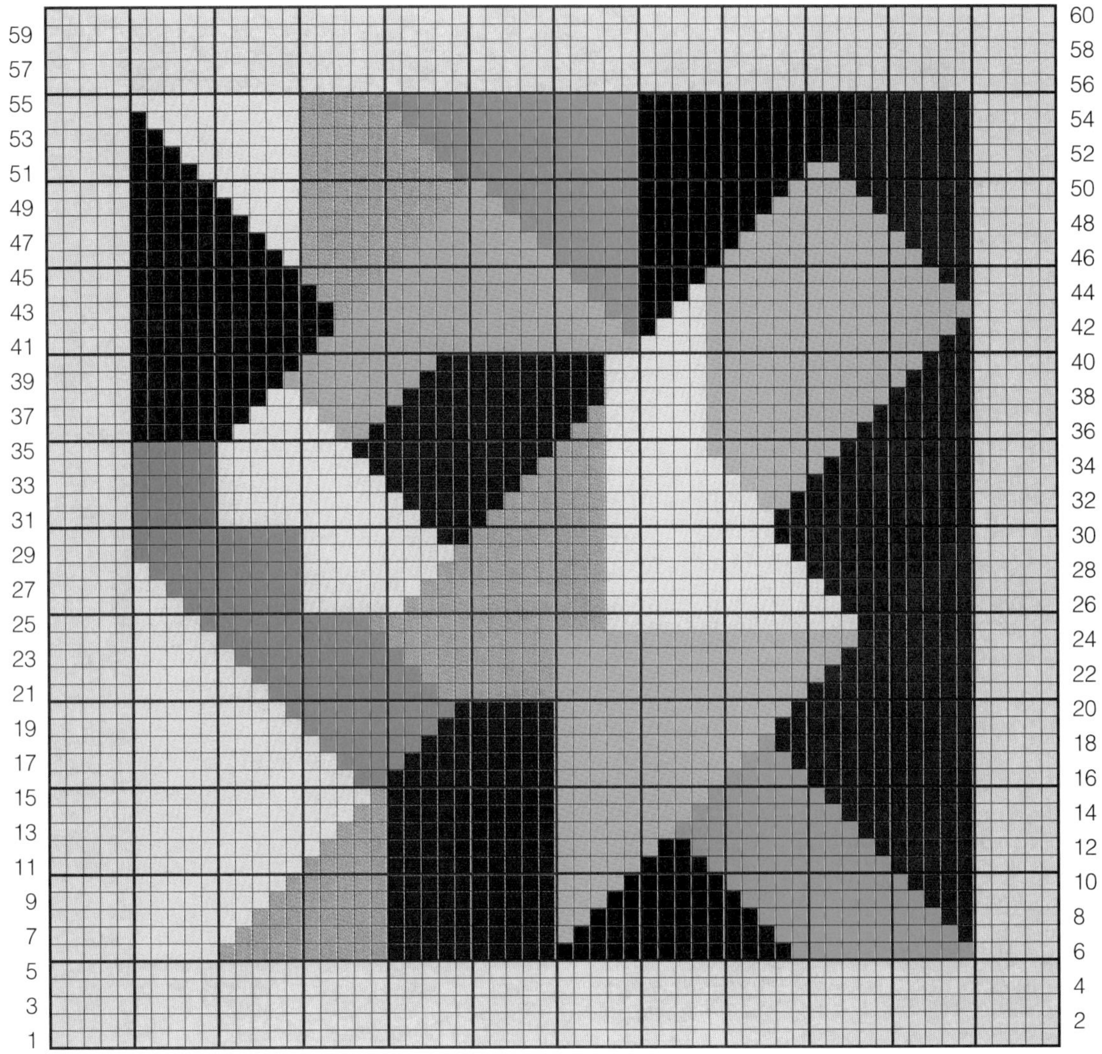

(chart grid with row numbers 1–59 on left side and 2–60 on right side)

Baby's Bric-A-Brac

Continued from page 79

Edging

Row 1: For **first side**, working in ends of rows, ch 3, 2 dc in next dc row, 3 dc in each dc row across to last dc row, 2 dc in last dc row, dc in last sc row, **do not** turn, fasten off (144 dc).

NOTES: Second half of last split-cl, fp-cl and last fp on Afghan will be referred to as tr.

Skip next st on last row behind each tr or fp .

Row 2: Join white with sc in first st, *[(tr in same st as next tr on Afghan, sc in each of next 2 sts on last row) 2 times, skip next tr on Afghan, fp around next tr on Afghan, sc in each of next 2 sts on last row

of Edging, (fp around next tr on Afghan, sc in each of next 2 sts on last row of Edging) 2 times, skip next dc row, fp around sc between 3-dc groups on next sc row], sc in each of next 2 sts on last row of Edging; repeat from * 6 more times; repeat between [ ], sc in last st on this row, fasten off.

Row 1: For **2nd side**, working in ends of rows on opposite end, join white with sl st in row 1, ch 3, 2 dc in next dc row, 3 dc in each dc row across to last dc row, 2 dc in last dc row, dc in last sc row, **do not** turn, fasten off (144 dc).

Row 2: Repeat same row of Edging on First Side.

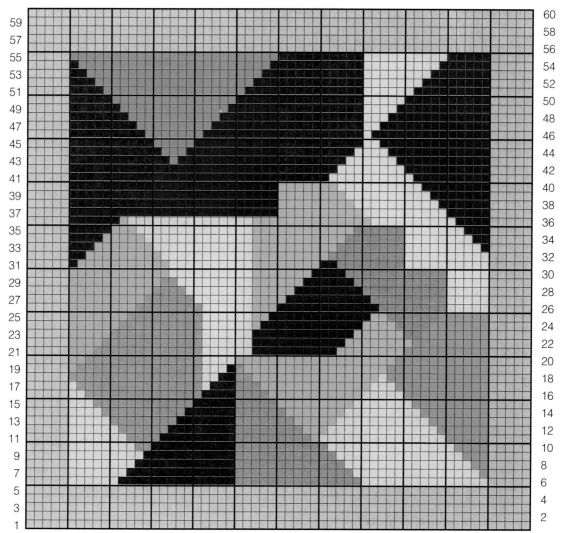

Hearts & Flowers

Continued from page 83

Border

Rnd 1: Working around entire outer edge, join raspberry with sc in any corner ch-2 sp, ch 3, sc in same sp, [◊(sc, ch 2, sc) in each of next 11 ch-1 sps, *sc in next ch-2 sp, ch 2, skip next seam, sc in next ch-2 sp, (sc, ch 2, sc) in each of next 11 ch-1 sps; repeat from * across◊ to next corner ch-2 sp, (sc, ch 3, sc) in next ch-2 sp]; repeat between [ ] 2 more times; repeat between ◊◊, join with sl st in first sc, fasten off.

Rnd 2: Join pink with sl st in any corner ch-3 sp, ch 3, 4 dc in same sp, *[sc in next ch-2 sp, (3 dc in next ch-2 sp, sc in next ch-2 sp) across] to next corner ch-3 sp, 5 dc in next ch-3 sp; repeat from * 2 more times; repeat between [ ], join with sl st in top of ch-3, **turn,** fasten off.

Rnd 3: Join lt. yellow with sc in center dc of any corner 5-dc group, ch 3, sc in same st, *[ch 1, sc in next st, ch 3, (sc in center dc of next 3-dc group, ch 3) across to next corner 5-dc group, skip next st, sc in next st, ch 1], (sc, ch 3, sc) in next st; repeat from * 2 more times; repeat between [ ], join with sl st in first sc, **turn,** fasten off.

Rnd 4: Join pink with sl st in any corner ch-3 sp, ch 3, 4 dc in same sp, *[sc in next ch-1 sp, 3 dc in next

BLOCK D

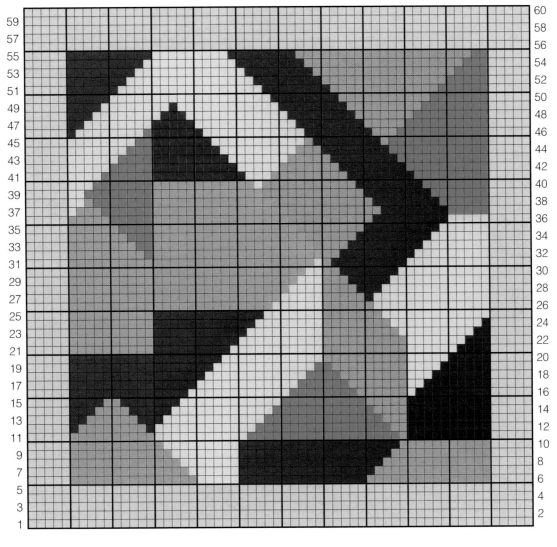

COLOR KEY

- ■ = Burgundy
- ■ = Purple
- ■ = Rose
- □ = Yellow
- ■ = Med. Green
- ■ = Lt. Green
- □ = Black

sc, (sc in next ch-3 sp, 3 dc in next sc) across to ch-1 sp before next corner ch-3 sp, sc in next ch-1 sp], 5 dc in next ch-3 sp; repeat from * 2 more times; repeat between [ ], join with sl st in top of ch-3.

Rnd 5: Sl st in next dc, ch 1, sc in same st, ch 1, (sc, ch 2, sc) in next dc, [◊ch 1, sc in next dc, ch 1, skip next st, sc in next sc, ch 1, *(sc, ch 2, sc) in center dc of next 3-dc group, ch 1, sc in next sc, ch 1; repeat from * across to next corner 5-dc group, skip next dc, sc in next dc, ch 10, (sc, ch 2, sc) in next st]; repeat between [ ] 2 more times; repeat between ◊◊, join with sl st in first sc, fasten off. ✰

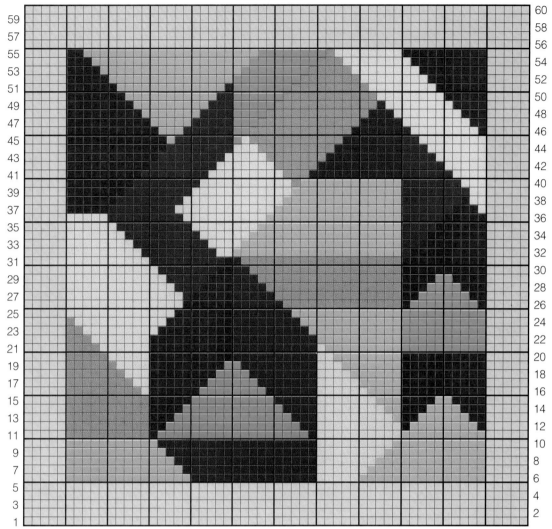

COLOR KEY

- ■ = Burgundy
- ■ = Purple
- ■ = Rose
- ☐ = Yellow
- ■ = Med. Green
- ■ = Lt. Green
- ☐ = Black

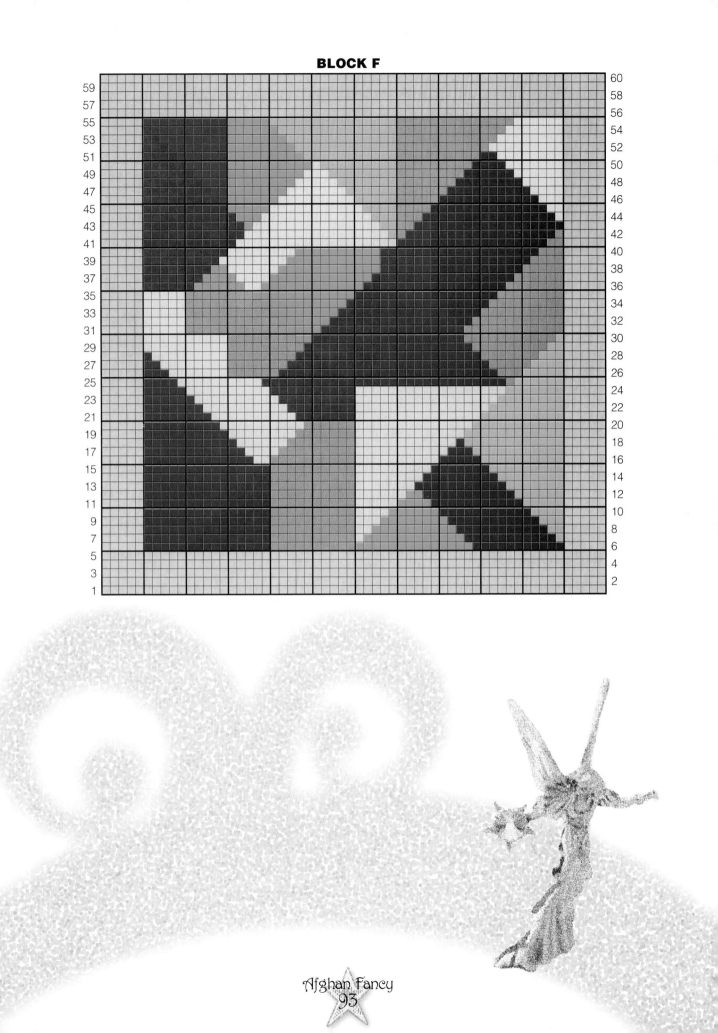

It's the little things in life that make the most unforgettable
moments. Capture them in crochet and create
memories galore, all with an individual style you get only
from Enchantments and Accents.

Chapter Four

Enchantments and Accents

Basket of Sunflowers Coasters

Design by
Patricia Hall

Finished Sizes:

Basket is 2" deep x 6" in diameter. Each Coaster is 5" across.

Materials:

- ★ 1½ oz. each green, orange and brown worsted-weight yarn
- ★ 6" metal ring
- ★ F and G crochet hooks or size needed to obtain gauge

Gauge:

With **G hook**, rnds 1 and 2 of Basket is 2½" across. Rnds 1 and 2 of Coaster is 2¾" across.

Skill Level:

Average

Basket

Rnd 1: With G hook and green, ch 5, sl st in first ch to form ring, ch 3, 17 dc in ring, join with sl st in top of ch-3 (18 dc).

Rnd 2: Ch 3, dc in same st, 2 dc in each st around, join (36).

Rnd 3: Ch 3, dc in same st, dc in each of next 3 sts, (2 dc in next st, dc in each of next 3 sts) around, join (45).

Rnd 4: Ch 3, dc in same st, dc in each of next 2 sts, (2 dc in next st, dc in each of next 2 sts) around, join (60).

Rnd 5: Repeat rnd 3 (75).

Rnd 6: Ch 3, skip next 2 sts, (sl st in next st, ch 3, skip next 2 sts) around, join with sl st in joining sl st of last rnd (25 ch-3 sps).

Rnd 7: Sl st in each of next 2 chs, ch 3, dc in same ch, ch 2, (2 dc in 2nd ch of next ch-3, ch 2) around, join with sl st in top of ch-3 (50 dc, 25 ch-2 sps).

Rnd 8: Sl st in next st, sl st in next ch sp, ch 3, dc in same sp, ch 2, (2 dc in next ch sp, ch 2) around, join.

Rnd 9: Ch 1, sc in each st and in each ch sp around, join with sl st in first sc (75 sc).

Rnd 10: Working around ring (see page 159), ch 1, sc in each st around, join, fasten off.

Coaster (make 4)

Rnd 1: With G hook and brown, ch 4, sl st in first ch to form ring, ch 4, 16 tr in ring, join with sl st in top of ch-4 (17 tr).

Rnd 2: Ch 3, dc in same st, 2 dc in each st around to last st, dc in last st, join with sl st in top of ch-3, fasten off (33 dc).

Rnd 3: With F hook and orange, join with sc in any st, sl st in next st, ch 4, tr same st and next st tog, ch 4, sl st in same st, (sc in next st, sl st in next st, ch 4, tr same st and next st tog, ch 4, sl st in same st) around, join with sl st in first sc (11 petals).

Rnd 4: Ch 1, 4 sc around next ch-4, (sc, ch 3, sc) in next tr, 4 sc around next ch-4, *sl st in next sc, 4 sc around next ch-4, (sc, ch 3, sc) in next tr, 4 sc around next ch-4; repeat from * around, join with sl st in joining sl st on last rnd, fasten off. ✿

Poinsettia Pillow

Design by
Sandra
Miller Maxfield

Finished Size:
17" square.

Materials:
★ Worsted-weight yarn:
  7 oz. white
  1 oz. each red and green
  small amount yellow
★ 16" square pillow form
★ G crochet hook or size needed to obtain gauge

Gauge:
4 sts = 1"; one 3-dc group and one ch-1 sp = 1". Rnds 1-3 of Front = 5" across; 2 3-dc group rnds worked in pattern = 1".

Skill Level:
Average

Pillow

Front
Rnd 1: With yellow, ch 4, sl st in first ch to form ring, ch 1, 8 sc in ring, join with sl st in first sc, fasten off (8 sc).

Rnd 2: Join red with sc in any st, (*ch 8, sl st in 2nd ch from hook, hdc in next ch, dc in next 4 chs, hdc in next ch, sc in same st on last rnd*, sc in next st) 7 times; repeat between **, join (8 petals).

Rnd 3: Working behind petals, ch 2, skip first st, sc in **back bar** (see page 159) of next st, (*ch 8, sl st in 2nd ch from hook, hdc in next ch, dc in next 4 chs, hdc in next ch, skip next st on last rnd*, sc in back bar of next st) 7 times; repeat between **, join with sl st in first ch of first ch-2, fasten off.

Rnd 4: Join white with sl st in tip of any petal on rnd 3, ch 3, (2 dc, ch 3, 3 dc) in same petal, *[ch 1, 3 dc in tip of next petal on rnd 2, ch 1, 3 dc in tip of next petal on rnd 3, ch 1, 3 dc in tip of next petal on rnd 2, ch 1], (3 dc, ch 3, 3 dc) in tip of next petal on rnd 3; repeat from * 2 more times; repeat between [ ], join with sl st in top of ch-3, fasten off (20 3-dc groups, 16 ch-1 sps, 4 ch-3 sps).

Rnd 5: Join green with sl st in any corner ch-3 sp, ch 3, (2 dc, ch 3, 3 dc) in same sp, *[ch 1, (3 dc in next ch-1 sp, ch 1) across] to next corner ch-3 sp, (3 dc, ch 3, 3 dc) in next ch-3 sp; repeat from * 2 more times; repeat between [ ], join, fasten off (20 ch-1 sps, 4 ch-3 sps).

Rnd 6: With white, repeat rnd 5, **do not** fasten off (24 ch-1 sps, 4 ch-3 sps).

Rnds 7-9: Sl st in each of next 2 sts, sl st in next ch-3 sp, ch 3, (2 dc, ch 3, 3 dc) in same sp, *[ch 1, (3 dc in next ch-1 sp, ch 1) across] to next corner ch-3 sp, (3 dc, ch 3, 3 dc) in next ch-3 sp; repeat from * 2 more times; repeat between [ ], join, ending with 36 ch-1 sps and 4 ch-3 sps in last rnd. At end of last rnd, fasten off.

Rnds 10-12: Working in color sequence of red, white and green, repeat rnd 5, ending with 48 ch-1 sps and 4 ch-3 sps in last rnd.

Rnds 13-14: Repeat rnds 6 and 7, ending with 56 ch-1 sps and 4 ch-3 sps in last rnd. At end of last rnd, fasten off.

Back
Rnd 1: With white, ch 4, sl st in first ch to form ring, ch 3, 2 dc in ring, ch 3, (3 dc in ring, ch 3) 3 times, join with sl st in top of ch-3 (4 3-dc groups, 4 ch-3 sps).

Rnd 2: Sl st in each of next 2 sts, sl st in next ch sp, ch 3, (2 dc, ch 3, 3 dc) in same sp, ch 1, *(3 dc, ch 3, 3 dc) in next ch sp, ch 1; repeat from * around, join (4 ch-3 sps, 4 ch-1 sps).

Rnd 3: Sl st in each of next 2 sts, sl st in next ch-3 sp, ch 3, (2 dc, ch 3, 3 dc) in same sp, ch 1, 3 dc in next ch-1 sp, ch 1, *(3 dc, ch 3, 3 dc) in next ch-3 sp, ch 1, 3 dc in next ch-1 sp, ch 1; repeat from * around, join (8 ch-1 sps, 4 ch-3 sps).

Rnds 4-15: Sl st in each of next 2 sts, sl st in next ch-3 sp, ch 3, (2 dc, ch 3, 3 dc) in same sp, *[ch 1, (3 dc in next ch-1 sp, ch 1) across] to next corner ch-3 sp, (3 dc, ch 3, 3 dc) in next ch-3 sp; repeat from * 2 more times; repeat between [ ], join, ending with 56 ch-1 sps and 4 ch-3 sps in last rnd. At end of last rnd, fasten off.

Edging
Holding Front and Back wrong sides together, matching sts, with Front facing you, working through both thicknesses, join white with sc in any corner ch-3 sp, (sc, ch 1, 2 sc) in same sp, sc in each st and in each ch-1 sp around with (2 sc, ch 1, 2 sc) in each corner ch-3 sp, inserting pillow form before closing, join with sl st in first sc, fasten off. ☆

Bathtime Elegance

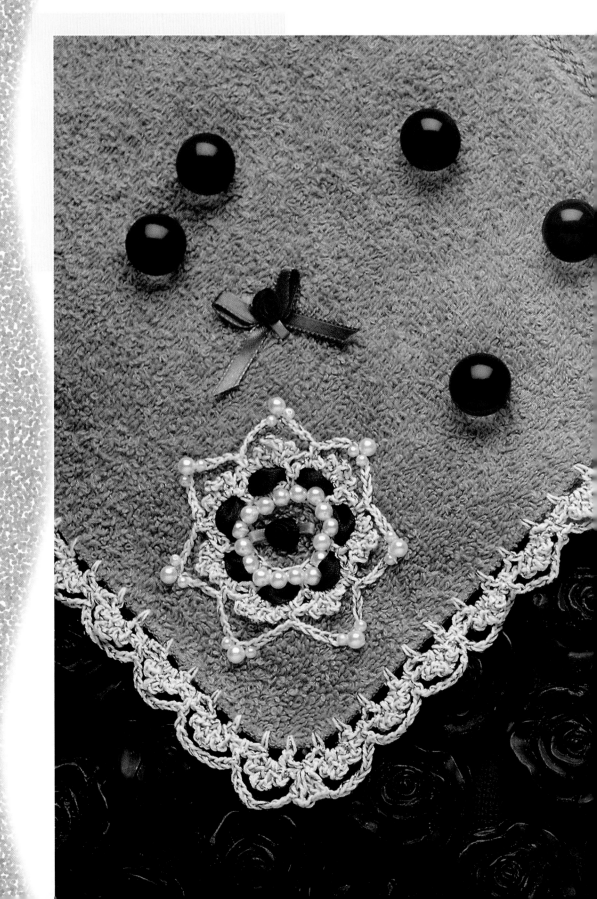

Bathtime Elegance

Design by
Jo Ann Maxwell

Green Washcloth

Finished Size:

Edging is ⅞" wide. Motif is 3¼" across.

Materials:

- ★ Size-10 bedspread cotton:
  - 60 yds. ecru
  - 30 yds. green
- ★ Green washcloth
- ★ 16" pink ⅜" satin ribbon
- ★ 20 gold 3-mm beads
- ★ 2 pink ⅝" satin ribbon roses with leaves
- ★ Off-white sewing thread
- ★ Straight pins
- ★ Sewing needle
- ★ No. 2 steel crochet hook or size needed to obtain gauge

Gauge:

Rnds 1 and 2 of Motif = 1¾" across.

Skill Level:

Average

Motif

Rnd 1: With ecru, ch 4, sl st in first ch to form ring, ch 3, 19 dc in ring, join with sl st in top of ch-3 (20 dc).

Rnd 2: Ch 5, (dc in next st, ch 2) around, join with sl st in 3rd ch of ch-5 (20 dc, 20 ch-2 sps).

Rnd 3: Ch 2, hdc in same st, hdc in each ch and 2 hdc in each st around, join with sl st in top of ch-2 (60 hdc).

NOTES: For **beginning cluster (beg cl)**, ch 3, (yo, insert hook in same st, yo, draw lp through, yo, draw through 2 lps on hook) 3 times, yo, draw through all 4 lps on hook.

For **cluster (cl)**, yo, insert hook in next st, yo, draw lp through, yo, draw through 2 lps on hook, (yo, insert hook in same st, yo, draw lp through, yo, draw through 2 lps on hook) 3 times, yo, draw through all 5 lps on hook.

Rnd 4: Beg cl, ch 4, skip next 2 sts, (cl in next st, ch 4, skip next 2 sts) around, join with sl st in top of beg cl, fasten off.

Edging

Rnd 1: Working around outer edge of washcloth, with ecru, place slip knot on hook, push hook through washcloth ⅛" from edge, yo, complete as sc, ch 4; spacing sts approximately ⅜" apart, (sc, ch 4) evenly spaced around, join with sl st in first sc.

Rnd 2: Sl st in first ch sp, beg cl, ch 4, (cl in next ch sp, ch 4) around, join with sl st in top of beg cl, fasten off.

NOTE: For **picot,** ch 3, sl st in top of last sc made.

Rnd 3: Join green with sc in ch sp after any corner ch sp, picot, ch 3, *(sc in next ch sp, picot, ch 3) across to next corner ch sp, (2 dc, ch 2, 2 dc) in next ch sp, ch 3; repeat from * around, join with sl st in first sc, fasten off.

Finishing

1: Cut ribbon in half. Weave one piece through rnd 2 of Motif; sew ends together.

2: Pin Motif to one corner of washcloth. Sew one bead to center of each ch sp on last rnd of Motif and to washcloth at same time. Sew one ribbon rose to center of Motif and to washcloth at same time.

3: Tie remaining ribbon into a bow. Position center of bow 1⅜" above Motif as shown in photo. Sew remaining ribbon rose to center of bow and to washcloth at same time.

Mauve Washcloth

Finished Size:

Edging is ⅞" wide. Motif is 3¼" across.

Materials:

- ★ 75 yds. cream size-10 bedspread cotton
- ★ 75 yds. copper filament
- ★ Mauve washcloth
- ★ 8" each mauve and burgundy ¼" satin ribbon
- ★ 14 off-white 4-mm pearl beads
- ★ 23 off-white 6-mm pearl beads
- ★ 2 burgundy ½" satin ribbon roses with leaves
- ★ Off-white sewing thread
- ★ Straight pins
- ★ Sewing needle
- ★ No. 2 steel crochet hook or size needed to obtain gauge

Gauge:

With **bedspread cotton and filament held together,** rnds 1 and 2 of Motif = 2" across.

Skill Level:

Average

Motif

Rnd 1: With ecru and filament held together, ch 21, sl st in first ch to form ring, ch 1, 2 sc in each ch around, join with sl st in first sc (42 sc).

Rnd 2: Ch 1, sc in first st, ch 4, skip next 2 sts, (sc in next st, ch 4, skip next 2 sts) around, join (14 ch-4 sps).

NOTES: For **small picot (sm picot)**, ch 3, sl st in top of last sc made.

For **large picot (lg picot)**, ch 5, sl st in top of last sc made.

Rnd 3: Sl st in first ch sp, ch 1, sc in same sp, *[ch 2, (sc, sm picot, sc, lg picot, sc, sm picot, sc) in next ch sp, ch 2], sc in next ch sp; repeat from * 5 more times; repeat between [ ], join.

Rnd 4: Ch 1, sc in first sc, ch 11, skip next ch-2 sp, next 3 picots and next ch-2 sp, (sc in next sc, ch 11, skip next ch-2 sp, next 3 picots and next ch-2 sp) around, join, fasten off.

Edging

Rnd 1: Working around outer edge of washcloth, with ecru and filament held together, place slip knot on hook, push hook through washcloth 1/8" from edge, yo, complete as sc, ch 4; spacing sts approximately 3/8" apart, (sc, ch 4) evenly spaced around ending with an even-number of sts and ch sps, join with sl st in first sc.

Rnd 2: Repeat rnd 3 of Motif.

Rnd 3: Ch 1, sc in first sc, ch 9, skip next ch-2 sp, next 3 picots and next ch-2 sp, (sc in next sc, ch 9, skip next ch-2 sp, next 3 picots and next ch-2 sp) around, join, fasten off.

Finishing

1: Weave burgundy ribbon through rnd 2 of Motif; sew ends together.

2: Pin Motif to one corner of washcloth. Sew one 4-mm bead, one 6-mm bead and one more 4-mm bead to center of each ch sp on last rnd of Motif and to washcloth at same time. Sew remaining 6-mm beads around rnd 1 of Motif and to washcloth at same time.

3: Sew one ribbon rose to washcloth in center of Motif.

4: Tie mauve ribbon into a bow. Position center of bow 1 1/4" above Motif as shown in photo. Sew remaining ribbon rose to center of bow and to washcloth at same time.

Ecru Washcloth

Finished Size:

Edging is 5/8" wide. Motif is 2 1/4" across.

Materials:

★ 60 yds. ecru size-10 bedspread cotton
★ 60 yds. gold filament
★ Ecru washcloth
★ 16" pink 1/4" satin ribbon
★ 33 white 4-mm pearl beads
★ One pink 1/2" satin ribbon rose with leaves
★ White sewing thread
★ Straight pins
★ Sewing needle
★ No. 2 steel crochet hook or size needed to obtain gauge

Gauge:

With **bedspread cotton and filament held together**, rnds 1 and 2 of Motif = 1 1/2" across.

Skill Level:

Average

Motif

Rnd 1: With ecru and filament held together, ch 4, sl st in first ch to form ring, ch 3, 19 dc in ring, join with sl st in top of ch-3 (20 dc).

Rnd 2: Ch 4, (hdc in next st, ch 2) around, join with sl st in 2nd ch of ch-4 (20 hdc, 20 ch-2 sps).

NOTE: For **shell**, (2 dc, ch 2, 2 dc) in next st.

Rnd 3: Ch 1, sc in first st, ch 2, skip next ch sp, shell in next st, ch 2, skip next ch sp, (sc in next st, ch 2, skip next ch sp, shell in next st, ch 2, skip next ch sp) around, join with sl st in first sc, fasten off.

Edging

Rnd 1: Working around outer edge of washcloth, with ecru and filament held together, place slip knot on hook, push hook through washcloth 1/8" from edge, yo, complete as sc, ch 4; spacing sts approximately 3/8" apart, (sc, ch 4) evenly spaced around ending with an even-number of sts and ch sps, join with sl st in first sc.

Rnd 2: Sl st in first ch sp, ch 1, sc in same sp, ch 2, shell in next ch sp, ch 2, (sc in next ch sp, ch 2, shell in next ch sp, ch 2) around, join, fasten off.

Finishing

1: Cut ribbon in half. Weave one piece through rnd 2 of Motif; sew ends together.

2: Pin Motif to one corner of washcloth. Sew one bead to dc before ch sp, one to ch sp and one to dc after ch sp of each shell on last rnd of Motif and to washcloth at same time. Sew ribbon rose to center of rnd 1 on Motif and to washcloth at same time.

3: Tie remaining ribbon into a bow. Position center of bow 1" above Motif as shown in photo. Sew remaining beads to center of bow and to washcloth at same time. ☆

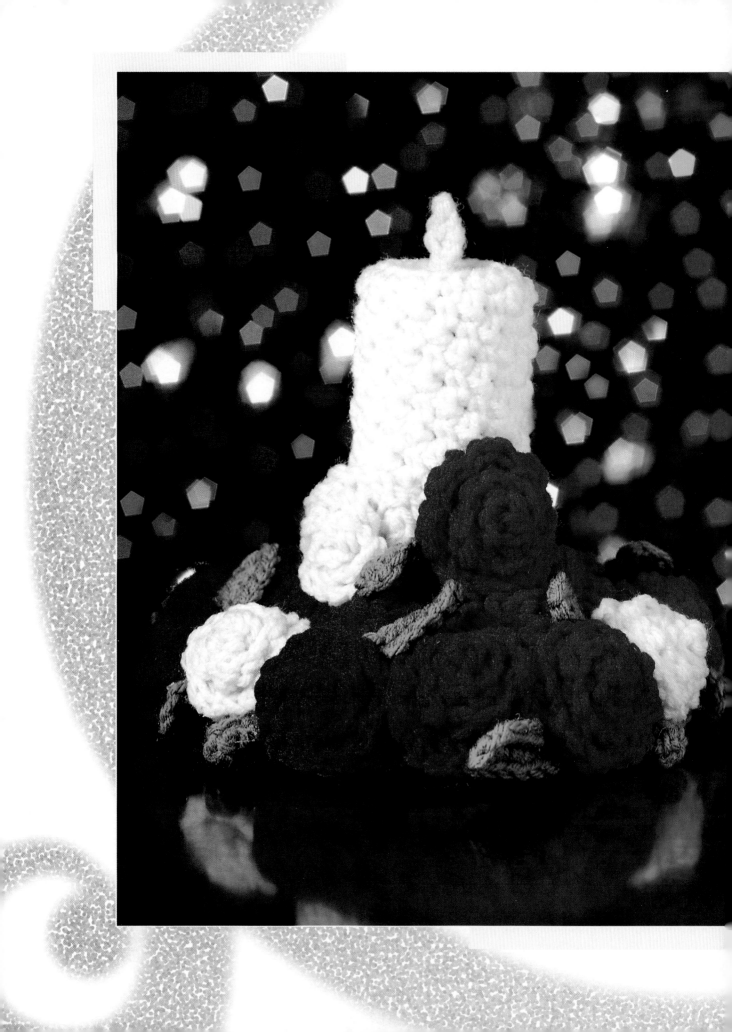

Candle & Roses Centerpiece

Design by
Beverly Mewhorter

Finished Size:
6½" tall x 7½" across base.

Materials:
★ Worsted-weight yarn:
  6 oz. red
  2 oz. each white, pink and green
  small amount yellow
★ Cardboard center from toilet tissue roll
★ 1" deep x 6" round Styrofoam® circle
★ Craft glue or hot glue gun
★ I crochet hook or size needed to obtain gauge

Gauge:
3 sts = 1"; 3 dc rows and 3 sc rows = 2". Rose is 2" across. Leaf is 2" long.

Skill Level:
Average

Candle

Rnd 1: With white, ch 3, sl st in first ch to form ring, ch 1, 6 sc in ring, join with sl st in first sc (6 sc).

Rnd 2: Ch 1, 2 sc in each st around, join (12).

Rnd 3: Ch 1, sc in first st, 2 sc in next st, (sc in next st, 2 sc in next st) around, join (18).

Rnd 4: Working this rnd in **back lps** only, ch 1, sc in each st around, join.

Rnd 5: Ch 1, sc in first st, dc in next st, (sc in next st, dc in next st) around, join.

Rnd 6: Ch 3, sc in next st, (dc in next st, sc in next st) around, join with sl st in top of ch-3.

Rnds 7-18: Repeat rnds 5 and 6 alternately. At end of last rnd, fasten off.

For **flame,** with yellow, ch 5, sl st in 2nd ch from hook, dc in next ch, sc in next ch, sl st in last ch, fasten off.

Sew one end to center of rnd 1 on Candle. Slip Candle over cardboard center from toilet tissue roll.

Rose (make 17 red and 4 pink)

Ch 29, sc in 2nd ch from hook, 2 dc in next ch, (sc in next ch, 2 dc in next ch) across to last ch, sl st in last ch, fasten off. Roll into shape of a rose and tack to secure.

Leaf (make 18)

With green, ch 7, sc in 2nd ch from hook, sc in each ch across; working on opposite side of ch, sc in each ch across, join with sl st in first sc, fasten off.

Finishing

1: Glue bottom end of Candle to center of Styrofoam®.

2: Arrange and glue Roses over Styrofoam® and over bottom of Candle as desired covering completely.

3: Glue Leaves among Roses as desired. ☆

Christmas Kitchen

Set

Christmas Kitchen Set

Design by
Carol Smith

Poinsettias

Finished Size:
Each Poinsettia is 7½" across.

Materials:
- ★ Worsted-weight yarn with metallic gold wrap:
  - 3½ oz. red
  - 2½ oz. green
  - 1 oz. variegated
- ★ 18 glitter gold plastic 6-mm x 9-mm pony beads
- ★ Gold ⅝" jingle bell
- ★ Dish towel
- ★ Off-white sewing thread
- ★ Sewing and tapestry needles
- ★ I crochet hook or size needed to obtain gauge

Gauge:
3 dc = 1"; 3 dc rows = 2".

Skill Level:
Average

Poinsettia (make 3)
Row 1: With red, ch 6, sl st in first ch to form ring; for **first petal**, ch 3, 2 dc in ring, turn (3 dc).

Row 2: Ch 3, dc in same st, dc in next st, 2 dc in last st, turn (5).

Row 3: Ch 3, dc in each of next 3 sts, 2 dc in last st, turn (6).

NOTE: (Ch 2, dc in next st) counts as dc first 2 sts tog.

Row 4: Ch 2, dc in next st, dc in each of next 2 sts, dc last 2 sts tog, turn (4).

Row 5: Ch 2, dc in next st, dc last 2 sts tog, **do not** turn; working across side of petal, work 2 sl sts in end of each row across, sl st in ring on row 1.

Row 1: For **second petal**, ch 3, 2 dc in ring, turn (3 dc).

Rows 2-5: Repeat same rows of first petal.

Repeat second petal 5 more times for a total of 7 petals. At end of last row on last petal, fasten off.

For **flower center,** with green, join with sl st in ring on row 1 between 2 petals, ch 3, sl st around post of center st on row 1 of next petal, ch 3, (sl st in ring between last petal and next petal, ch 3, skip next petal, sl st around post of center st on row 1 of next petal, ch 3, sl st in ring between last petal and next petal, ch 3, sl st around post of center st on row 1 of next petal, ch 3) 2 times, join with sl st in first sl st, fasten off.

With green, sew one bead to center of flower center and one bead to sl st worked on each Poinsettia petal.

Leaves (make 2)
With green, work same as Poinsettia, working 5 petals instead of 7.

Towel Topper
Rnd 1: With variegated, ch 48, sl st in first ch to form ring, ch 3, dc in each ch around, join with sl st in top of ch-3 (48 dc).

Rnds 2-5: Ch 3, dc in each st around, join. Flatten last rnd.

Row 6: Working in rows and through both thicknesses, ch 3, dc in each st across, turn (24).

Row 7: Ch 2, dc in next st, (dc next 2 sts tog) across, turn (12).

Row 8: Ch 3, dc in each st across, turn.

Row 9: Repeat row 7 (6).

Rows 10-17: Ch 3, dc in each st across, turn.

Row 18: Ch 2, (yo, insert hook in next st, yo, draw lp through, yo, draw through 2 lps on hook) 5 times, yo, draw through all 6 lps on hook, fasten off.

Finishing
1: Cut hem and/or fringe off one end of towel. With sewing needle and thread, gather across cut end. Insert into rnds 1 and 2 of Towel Topper; sew opening closed.

2: With right sides facing you, place one set of Leaves behind one Poinsettia with Leaves between petals. Sew over rnds/rows 1-9 on front of Towel Topper.

3: For **button,** sew jingle bell to center of row 11 on front of Towel Topper using sp between center 2 sts on row 17 for buttonhole.

Pot Holder
Holding remaining 2 Poinsettias wrong sides together with remaining Leaves between, matching petals on Poinsettias and placing Leaves between petals as desired, with red, sew end of rows on petals together. With green, sew piece together through center.

Stockings

Finished Size:
Each Stocking is 8" x 8½" not including hanging loop.

Materials:
- ★ Worsted-weight yarn with metallic gold wrap:
  - 4 oz. red
  - 1 oz. each green and variegated
- ★ 2 gold 1" jingle bells
- ★ Dish towel
- ★ Red sewing thread
- ★ Sewing and tapestry needles
- ★ J crochet hook or size needed to obtain gauge

Gauge:
5 hdc = 2"; 2 hdc rows = 1".

Skill Level:
Average

Stocking Side (make 4)
NOTE: Ch-2 at beginning of each row counts as first st.

Row 1: With red, ch 21, hdc in 3rd ch from hook, hdc in each ch across, turn (20 hdc).

Rows 2-6: Ch 2, hdc in each st across, turn.

Row 7: Ch 2, hdc in next 9 sts leaving remaining sts unworked, turn (10).

Rows 8-10: Ch 2, hdc in each st across, turn. At end of last row, fasten off.

NOTE: For **triple treble crochet (ttr),** yo 4 times, insert hook in next st, yo, draw lp through, (yo, draw through 2 lps on hook) 5 times.

Row 11: For **toe,** join variegated with sl st in first st, skip next 3 sts, 10 ttr in next st, skip next 4 sts, sl st in last st, fasten off.

Pot Holder
For **trim,** holding 2 Stocking Sides wrong sides together, matching sts and ends of rows, working through both thicknesses in starting ch on opposite side of row 1, join green with sc in first ch, sc in same ch, sc in next 18 chs, 3 sc in last ch; working in ends of rows, evenly space 16 sc across bottom; working across toe, (2 sc in first ttr, sc in next ttr) 5 times, 2 sc in end of each of next 4 rows, sc in each skipped st across row 6 with 3 sc in last st, evenly space 10 sc across end of last 6 rows across top, sc in same st as first st, join with sl st in first sc; for **hanging loop,** ch 12, sl st in same st, fasten off.

Cuff
NOTES: For **front post (fp,** see page 159), yo, insert hook from front to back around post of next st, yo, draw lp through, (yo, draw through 2 lps on hook) 2 times.

For **back post (bp,)** yo, insert hook from back to front around post of next st, yo, draw lp through, (yo, draw through 2 lps on hook) 2 times.

Rnd 1: Working around top of Stocking, in sts below trim, join variegated with sl st around post of any st, ch 3, fp around same st, 2 fp around post of each st around with 2 dc in st on trim at each seam, join with sl st in top of ch-3.

Rnd 2: Ch 3, bp around next st, (fp around next st, bp around next st) around, join, fasten off.

Fold Cuff down. Sew one jingle bell to top corner below hanging loop.

Towel Topper
For **trim,** holding remaining 2 Stockings wrong sides together with toe pointing left, matching sts and ends of rows, working through both thicknesses in skipped sts across row 6, join green with sc in first st, sc in each st across, 2 sc in end of each of next 4 rows, (2 sc in first ttr, sc in next ttr) 5 times; evenly space 16 sc in ends of rows across bottom; working in starting ch on opposite side of row 1, 3 sc in first ch, sc in each ch across; working through one thickness on front only, evenly space 10 sc across ends of rows, **turn;** working through one thickness on back only, evenly space 10 sc across ends of rows, join with sl st in next st; for **hanging loop,** ch 12, sl st in same st, fasten off.

Working in ends of rows across bottom of Stocking on back, join green with sc in first row, evenly space 15 sc across, sl st in next st on toe, fasten off.

Cut hem and/or fringe off one end of towel. With sewing needle and thread, gather across cut end. Insert into opening on bottom of Stocking; sew opening closed.

Cuff
Work same as Pot Holder's Cuff.

Sew remaining jingle bell to top corner below hanging loop.

Wreaths

Finished Size:
Each Wreath is 8" across not including hanging loop.

Materials:
- ★ Worsted-weight yarn with metallic gold wrap:
  - 5 oz. green
  - 1 oz. variegated
- ★ 2 yds. red ¼" satin ribbon
- ★ Gold ⅝" jingle bell
- ★ Dish towel
- ★ 63 glitter plastic 6-mm x 9-mm pony beads in assorted colors
- ★ Green sewing thread
- ★ Sewing and tapestry needles
- ★ I crochet hook or size needed to obtain gauge

Gauge:
Rnds 1 and 2 of Wreath Side = 3½" across.

Continued on page 115

Harvest Tweed Rug

Design by Aline Suplinskas

Finished Size:

24½" x 31" not including fringe.

Materials:

- ★ 2-ply chunky yarn:
  9 oz. each gold and rust
  1½ oz. each aqua, taupe, variegated, lt. gray and off-white
- ★ Tapestry needle
- ★ G crochet hook or size needed to obtain gauge

Gauge:

2 hdc and 2 ch-1 sps = 1"; 11 hdc rows = 6".

Skill Level:

Easy

Rug

NOTES: Leave 3½" ends at beginning and end of each row for fringe.

Ch-3 at beginning of each row counts as first hdc and ch-1 sp.

Row 1: With gold, ch 127, hdc in 5th ch from hook, (ch 1, skip next ch, hdc in next ch) across, turn, fasten off (63 hdc, 62 ch-1 sps).

Row 2: Join rust with sl st in first st, ch 3, (hdc in next hdc, ch 1) across to last ch-4, hdc in 3rd ch of last ch-4, turn, fasten off.

Row 3: Join gold with sl st in first st, ch 3, (hdc in next hdc, ch 1) across to last ch-3, hdc in 2nd ch of last ch-3, turn, fasten off.

Rows 4-45: Alternating rust and gold, repeat row 3.

Stripes

For **each Stripe,** cut one strand of any 2 colors plus one strand each of gold and rust each 46" long. Holding all 4 pieces together, weave through ch sps of first row leaving 3½" ends for fringe. Cut off any excess. Repeat on each row.

Trim

Working in ends of rows on one end of Rug, holding fringe on first row to front, join rust with sc in first row, (ch 1, working around last fringe and holding fringe on next row to front, sc in end of next row) across. Trim ends.

Repeat on opposite end.☆

Chef's Choice

Design by
Ellen Anderson
Eaves

Striped Ric-Rac Pot Holder

Finished Size:
9" x 10½" not including hanging loop.

Materials:
★ Size-3 crochet cotton:
 125 yds. orange
 115 yds. peach
 95 yds. green
★ E crochet hook or size needed to obtain gauge

Gauge:
3 3-dc groups = 2"; 3 dc rows worked in pattern = 1".

Skill Level:
Average

Pot Holder

Side (make 2)
Row 1: With peach, ch 46, 2 dc in 4th ch from hook, (skip next 2 chs, 3 dc in next ch) across, turn, fasten off (15 3-dc groups).

Row 2: Join orange with sl st in sp between first 2 dc, ch 3, 2 dc in same sp, (3 dc in sp between first and 2nd dc of next 3-dc group) across, turn, fasten off.

Rows 3-25: Working in color sequence of green, peach and orange, repeat row 2, ending with peach.

Edging
Rnd 1: Holding Sides wrong sides together, matching sts, working through both thicknesses, join orange with sc in last st on last row; for **hanging loop,** ch 10, sc in same st; *working in ends of rows, ch 3, skip first row, (sc in next row, ch 3, skip next row) across*; working in starting ch on opposite side of row 1, (sc, ch 3, sc) in first ch, ch 3, (sc in next ch-2 sp, ch 3) across to last ch, (sc, ch 3, sc) in last ch; repeat between **, (sc, ch 3, sc) in first st on last row, ch 3, sc in sp between last 3-dc group and next 3-dc group, ch 3, (sc in sp between next 2 3-dc groups, ch 3) across, join with sl st in first sc.

Rnd 2: Sl st in first ch-10 lp, ch 1, 20 sc in same lp, 5 sc in each ch-3 sp around, join, fasten off.

Star Pot Holder

Finished Size:
8½" across not including hanging loop.

Materials:
★ 40 yds. each orange, yellow and ecru size-3 crochet cotton
★ E crochet hook or size needed to obtain gauge

Gauge:
5 dc = 1"; 5 dc rows = 2".

Skill Level:
Average

Pot Holder

Side (make 2)
Rnd 1: With ecru, ch 4, 11 dc in 4th ch from hook, join with sl st in top of ch-3, fasten off (12 dc).

Rnd 2: Join yellow with sc in first st, (hdc, dc) in same st, (hdc, sc) in next st, *(sc, hdc, dc) in next st, (hdc, sc) in next st; repeat from * around, join with sl st in first sc, fasten off (30 sts).

Rnd 3: Join orange with sl st in 2nd st, ch 3, 5 dc in next st, dc in next st, skip next 2 sts, (dc in next st, 5 dc in next st, dc in next st, skip next 2 sts) around, join with sl st in top of ch-3, fasten off (42 dc).

Rnd 4: Join ecru with sl st in 2nd st, ch 3, dc in next st, 5 dc in next st, dc in each of next 2 sts, skip next 2 sts, (dc in each of next 2 sts, 5 dc in next st, dc in each of next 2 sts, skip next 2 sts) around, join, fasten off (54).

Rnd 5: Join yellow with sl st in 2nd st, ch 3, dc in each of next 2 sts, 5 dc in next st, dc in each of next 3 sts, skip next 2 sts, (dc in each of next 3 sts, 5 dc in next st, dc in each of next 3 sts, skip next 2 sts) around, join, fasten off (66).

Rnd 6: Join orange with sl st in 2nd st, ch 3, dc in each of next 3 sts, 5 dc in next st, dc in next 4 sts, skip next 2 sts, (dc in next 4 sts, 5 dc in next st, dc in next 4 sts, skip next 2 sts) around, join, fasten off (78).

Rnd 7: Join ecru with sl st in 2nd st, ch 3, dc in next 4 sts, 5 dc in next st, dc in next 5 sts, skip next 2 sts, (dc in next 5 sts, 5 dc in next st, dc in next 5 sts, skip next 2 sts) around, join, fasten off (90).

Rnd 8: Join yellow with sl st in 2nd st, ch 3, dc in next 5 sts, 5 dc in next st, dc in next 6 sts, skip next 2 sts, (dc in next 6 sts, 5 dc in next st, dc in next 6 sts, skip next 2 sts) around, join, fasten off (102).

Rnd 9: Join orange with sl st in 2nd st, ch 3, dc in next 6 sts, 5 dc in next st, dc in next 7 sts, skip next 2 sts, (dc in next 7 sts, 5 dc in next st, dc in next 7 sts, skip next 2 sts) around, join, fasten off (114).

Edging
Holding Sides wrong sides together, matching sts, working through both thicknesses, join ecru with sc in first st, sc in next 8 sts, 3 sc in next st, sc in next st, **turn,** sl st in next st; for **hanging loop,** ch 10, skip next st, sl st in each of next 2 sts, **turn;** ch 1, 20 sc in next ch lp, sl st in next st on this rnd, sc in next 17 sts on last rnd, 3 sc in next st, (sc in next 18 sts, 3 sc in next st) 4 times, sc in last 9 sts, join with sl st in first sc, fasten off.

Cluster Flower Pot Holder

Finished Size:
9¾" square not including hanging loop.

Continued on next page

Chef's Choice

Continued from page 113

Materials:
- ★ Size-3 crochet cotton:
  - 150 yds. green
  - 55 yds. orange
  - 30 yds. yellow
- ★ E crochet hook or size needed to obtain gauge

Gauge:
5 dc = 1"; 5 dc rows = 2".

Skill Level:
Average

Pot Holder

Front
Rnd 1: With yellow, ch 2, 6 sc in 2nd ch from hook, join with sl st in first sc (6 sc).

NOTES: For **beginning double crochet cluster (beg dc-cl)**, ch 3, (yo, insert hook in same st, yo, draw lp through, yo, draw through 2 lps on hook) 2 times, yo, draw through all 3 lps on hook.

For **double crochet cluster (dc-cl)**, yo, insert hook in next st, yo, draw lp through, yo, draw through 2 lps on hook, (yo, insert hook in same st, yo, draw lp through, yo, draw through 2 lps on hook) 2 times, yo, draw through all 4 lps on hook.

Rnd 2: Beg dc-cl, ch 3, (dc-cl in next st, ch 3) around, join with sl st in top of beg dc-cl, fasten off (6 ch-3 sps).

NOTES: For **beginning treble crochet cluster (beg tr-cl)**, ch 4, *yo 2 times, insert hook in same sp, yo, draw lp through, (yo, draw through 2 lps on hook) 2 times; repeat from * 2 more times, yo, draw through all 4 lps on hook.

For **treble crochet cluster (tr-cl)**, yo 2 times, insert hook in next ch sp, yo, draw lp through, (yo, draw through 2 lps on hook) 2 times, *yo 2 times, insert hook in same sp, yo, draw lp through, (yo, draw through 2 lps on hook) 2 times; repeat from * 2 more times, yo, draw through all 5 lps on hook.

Rnd 3: Join orange with sl st in any ch sp, beg tr-cl, ch 3, tr-cl in same sp, ch 3, *(tr-cl, ch 3, tr-cl) in next ch sp, ch 3; repeat from * around, join with sl st in top of beg tr-cl, fasten off (12 ch-3 sps).

Rnd 4: Join green with sl st in first ch sp, ch 4, 2 tr in same sp, *[dc in next st, 3 hdc in next ch sp, sc in next st, 3 hdc in next ch sp, dc in next st], (3 tr, ch 2, 3 tr) in next ch sp; repeat from * 2 more times; repeat between [ ], 3 tr in same sp as first st; to **join**, ch 1, sc in top of ch-4 (60 sts, 4 ch-2 sps).

Rnd 5: Ch 3, dc around joining sc, *dc in each st across to next corner ch sp, (2 dc, ch 2, 2 dc) in next ch sp; repeat from * 2 more times, dc in each st across, 2 dc in same sp as first st, join as before (76 dc, 4 ch-2 sps).

Rnd 6: Ch 3, dc around joining sc, *[ch 1, skip next st, (dc in next st, ch 1, skip next st) across] to next corner ch sp, (2 dc, ch 2, 2 dc) in next ch sp; repeat from * 2 more times; repeat between [ ], 2 dc in same sp as first st, join (52 dc, 40 ch-1 sps, 4 ch-2 sps).

Rnd 7: Ch 3, dc around joining sc, *dc in each ch-1 sp and in each st across to next corner ch-2 sp, (2 dc, ch 2, 2 dc) in next ch-2 sp; repeat from * 2 more times, dc in each ch-1 sp and in each st across, 2 dc in same sp as first st, join (108 dc, 4 ch-2 sps).

Rnds 8-10: Repeat rnds 5-7, ending with 156 dc and 4 ch-2 sps in last rnd. At end of last rnd, fasten off.

Back
Rnd 1: With green, ch 4, sl st in first ch to form ring, ch 3, 2 dc in ring, (ch 2, 3 dc in ring) 3 times; to **join**, ch 1, sc in top of ch-3 (12 dc, 4 ch-2 sps).

Rnds 2-5: Ch 3, dc around joining sc, dc in each st around with (2 dc, ch 2, 2 dc) in each corner ch-2 sp, 2 dc in same sp as first st, join as before, ending with 76 dc and 4 ch-2 sps in last rnd. At end of last rnd, fasten off.

Rnd 6: Join yellow with sl st in first ch sp, ch 3, dc in same sp, dc in each st around with (2 dc, ch 2, 2 dc) in each corner ch sp, 2 dc in same sp as first st, join, fasten off (92 dc, 4 ch-2 sps).

Rnd 7: With green, repeat rnd 6, **do not** fasten off (108 dc, 4 ch-2 sps).

Rnd 8: Repeat rnd 2, fasten off (124 dc, 4 ch-2 sps).

Rnd 9: With orange, repeat rnd 6 (140 dc, 4 ch-2 sps).

Rnd 10: With green, repeat rnd 6 (156 dc, 4 ch-2 sps).

Edging
Rnd 1: Holding Front and Back wrong sides together, with Front facing you, matching sts, working through both thicknesses, join yellow with sc in any corner ch sp, 2 sc in same sp, sc in each st around with 3 sc in each corner ch sp, join with sl st in first sc, fasten off (168 sc).

Rnd 2: Join orange with sc in 4th st, (sc, ch 3, sc) in next st, *ch 3, dc in 3rd ch from hook, skip next 2 sts, (sc, ch 3, sc) in next st; repeat from * around to last 4 sts, sc in each of next 2 sts, 3 sc in next st, sc in next st, **turn**, sl st in next st; for **hanging loop**, ch 10; skip next st, sl st in each of next 2 sts, **turn**, ch 1, 20 sc in next ch-10 lp, sl st in next st, join, fasten off. ☆

Christmas Kitchen Set

Continued from page 109

Skill Level:

Average

Wreath Side (make 4)

Rnd 1: With variegated, ch 5, sl st in first ch to form ring, ch 3, 19 dc in ring, join with sl st in top of ch-3 (20 dc).

Rnd 2: Ch 3, 2 dc in next st, (dc in next st, 2 dc in next st) around, join, fasten off (30).

Rnd 3: Working this rnd in **front lps** only, join green with sc in first st, ch 3, (sc in next st, ch 3) around, join with sl st in first sc.

Rnd 4: Working in **back lps** of rnd 2, sl st in first st, ch 3, dc in next st, 2 dc in next st, (dc in each of next 2 sts, 2 dc in next st) around, join with sl st in top of ch-3, fasten off (40).

Rnd 5: Repeat rnd 3.

Rnd 6: Working in **back lps** of rnd 4, sl st in first st, ch 3, 2 dc in next st, (dc in next st, 2 dc in next st) around, join with sl st in top of ch-3, fasten off (60).

Pot Holder

Holding 2 Wreath Sides wrong sides together, matching sts, working through both thicknesses, join green with sc in first st, ch 3, (sc in next st, ch 3) around, join with sl st in first sc; for **hanging loop**, ch 12, sl st in same st, **turn**, ch 1, 20 sc in next ch lp, sl st in same st on Wreath, fasten off.

Finishing

For **berries**, sew 30 beads in clusters of 3 over front of Pot Holder as desired.

Cut 2 pieces of ribbon each 18" long. Tie each piece into a bow around one st on front of Pot Holder as shown in photo.

Towel Topper

Holding remaining 2 Wreath Sides wrong sides together, matching sts, working through both thicknesses, join green with sc in first st, (ch 3, sc in next st) across. Leaving 5½" opening for towel, fasten off.

Finishing

1: Cut hem and/or fringe off one end of towel. With sewing needle and thread, gather across cut end. Insert into open end of Towel Topper; sew opening closed.

2: For **berries**, sew 33 beads in clusters of 3 over front of Towel Topper as desired.

3: Cut remaining ribbon in half. Tie each piece into a bow around one st on front of Towel Topper as shown.

Hanging Loop

NOTE: For **single crochet front post (sc-fp,** see page 158) insert hook from front to back around post of next st, yo, draw lp through, yo, draw through both lps on hook.

Row 1: With back of Towel Topper facing you, working in 4 sts at center top of rnd 6 on Wreath, join green with sc-fp around post of first st, sc-fp around each of next 3 sts, turn (4 sc-fp).

Rows 2-6: Ch 2, hdc in each st across, turn.

Row 7: Ch 2, (yo, insert hook in next st, yo, draw lp through) 3 times, yo, draw through all 7 lps on hook, fasten off.

For **button**, sew jingle bell to center top front of Wreath using sp between center 2 sts on row 6 for buttonhole. ✩

Fancy Wreath Ornaments

Design by Nanette Seale

All-Buttoned Up

Finished Size:
3⅛" across.

Materials:
★ Small amount red size-10 bedspread cotton
★ 8 clear ⅜" flat buttons
★ 2" cabone ring
★ Craft glue or hot glue gun
★ No. 7 steel crochet hook or size needed to obtain gauge

Gauge:
Rnds 2 and 3 = ⅝".

Skill Level:
Average

Wreath

Rnd 1: Working around ring (see page 159), join with sc around ring, work 95 more sc around ring, join with sl st in first sc (96 sc).

Rnd 2: Ch 1, sc in each st around, join.

Rnd 3: Ch 3, (dc, ch 2, 2 dc) in same st, skip next 3 sts, *(2 dc, ch 2, 2 dc) in next st, skip next 3 sts; repeat from * around, join with sl st in top of ch-3, fasten off.

Glue buttons evenly spaced around rnd 1.

Ribbon Roses

Finished Size:
3⅛" across.

Materials:
★ Small amount red/white/green variegated size-10 bedspread cotton
★ 2 white and one red ⅝" satin ribbon roses
★ 2" cabone ring
★ Craft glue or hot glue gun
★ No. 7 steel crochet hook or size needed to obtain gauge

Gauge:
Rnds 2-4 = ⅝".

Skill Level:
Average

Wreath

Rnd 1: Working around ring (see page 159), join with sc around ring, work 94 more sc around ring, join with sl st in first sc (95 sc).

Rnd 2: Ch 1, sc in each st around, join.

Rnd 3: Ch 1, sc in first st, ch 5, skip next 4 sts, (sc in next st, ch 5, skip next 4 sts) around, join (19 ch-5 sps).

Rnd 4: Sl st in first ch sp, ch 1, 7 sc in same sp and in each ch sp around, join, fasten off.

Glue one red rose between rnds 1 and 2 and one white rose to each side of red rose.

Tiny Charms

Finished Size:
3" across.

Materials:
★ Small amount green size-10 bedspread cotton
★ ⅝" x ⅞" jewelled Christmas tree charm
★ ½" x ⅝" jewelled bell charm
★ 2" cabone ring
★ Craft glue or hot glue gun
★ No. 7 steel crochet hook or size needed to obtain gauge

Gauge:
Rnds 2 and 3 = ½".

Skill Level:
Average

Wreath

Rnd 1: Working around ring (see page 159), join with sc around ring, work 95 more sc around ring, join with sl st in first sc (96 sc).

Rnd 2: Ch 1, sc in each st around, join.

NOTE: For **cluster (cl)**, yo, insert hook in next st, yo, draw lp through, yo, draw through 2 lps on hook, (yo, insert hook in same st, yo, draw lp through, yo, draw through 2 lps on hook) 4 times,

Continued on next page

Fancy Wreath Ornaments

Continued from page 117

yo, draw through all 6 lps on hook.

Rnd 3: Ch 1, sc in first st, ch 3, skip next 2 sts, cl in next st, ch 3, skip next 2 sts, (sc in next st, ch 3, skip next 2 sts, cl in next st, ch 3, skip next 2 sts) around, join, fasten off.

Glue bell to top of rnds 1-3 of Wreath and Christmas tree to bottom of rnds 1 and 2.

White Christmas

Finished Size:
3⅜" across.

Materials:
- ★ Small amount white size-10 bedspread cotton
- ★ 10" metallic gold ⅛" satin ribbon
- ★ 2 metallic gold ½" ribbon roses
- ★ 2" cabone ring
- ★ Craft glue or hot glue gun
- ★ No. 7 steel crochet hook or size needed to obtain gauge

Gauge:
Rnds 2-4 = ¾".

Skill Level:
Average

Wreath

Rnd 1: Working around ring (see page 159), join with sc around ring, work 95 more sc around ring, join with sl st in first sc (96 sc).

Rnd 2: Ch 4, skip next st, (dc in next st, ch 1, skip next st) around, join with sl st in 3rd ch of ch-4 (48 dc, 48 ch-1 sps).

Rnd 3: Ch 1, sc in each st and in each ch-1 sp around, join with sl st in first sc (96 sc).

Rnd 4: Ch 1, sc in first st, skip next 2 sts, 5 dc in next st, skip next 2 sts, (sc in next st, skip next 2 sts, 5 dc in next st, skip next 2 sts) around, join, fasten off.

Weave ribbon through every 2 dc on rnd 2; glue ends together.

Glue ribbon roses to rnd 2.

Joined Rings

Finished Size:
3½" across.

Materials:
- ★ Size-10 bedspread cotton:
  50 yds. green

small amount red
- ★ Eight ⅝" cabone rings
- ★ No. 7 steel crochet hook or size needed to obtain gauge

Gauge:
2 sc rows = ¼".

Skill Level:
Average

Wreath

Rnd 1: For **first ring,** working around one cabone ring (see page 159), with green, join with sc around ring, work 26 more sc around ring, join with sl st in first sc (27 sc).

Rnd 1: For **next ring,** working around another cabone ring, with green, work 27 sc around ring, join with sl st in first sc (27 sc).

Row 2: Working in rows, (ch 2, skip next 2 sts, sc in next st) 4 times leaving remaining sts unworked, **do not** turn or fasten off.

Repeat next ring 5 more times for a total of 7 rings.

Rnd 1: For **last ring,** working around last cabone ring, with green, work 27 sc around ring, join with sl st in first sc (27 sc).

Row 2: Working in rows, (ch 2, skip next 2 sts, sc in next st) 4 times leaving remaining sts unworked; keeping row 2 of each ring to inside of Wreath, sl st in 16th st on first ring; working on first ring only, ch 2, skip next 2 sts, (sc in next st, ch 2, skip next 2 sts) 3 times, join with sl st in joining sl st of rnd 1 on 2nd ring, fasten off.

Inside Edging

Working around inside of Wreath, join green with sc in ch sp after any joining between Rings, 2 sc in each of next 2 ch sps, sc in ch sp before next joining, (sc in ch sp after next joining, 2 sc in each of next 2 ch sps, sc in ch sp before next joining) around, join with sl st in first sc, fasten off.

Outside Edging

Rnd 1: Working on outside of Wreath, join green with sc in st after any joining between Rings, ch 2, skip next st, (sc in next st, ch 2, skip next st) 6 times, *sc in st after next joining, ch 2, skip next st, (sc in next st, ch 2, skip next st) 6 times; repeat from * around, join with sl st in first sc.

Rnd 2: Sl st in first ch sp, ch 1, 2 sc in same sp, 2 sc in each ch sp around, join, fasten off.

For **trim,** with red, ch 115, fasten off. Weave through ch sps of rnd 1 on Outside Edging; tie ends into a bow.

Jingle Bells

Finished Size:
2 x 4¾".

Materials:
- ★ Small amount each red, white and green size-10 bedspread cotton
- ★ Three 1⅛" cabone rings
- ★ Three ⅜" brass jingle bells
- ★ Tapestry needle
- ★ No. 7 steel crochet hook or size needed to obtain gauge

Gauge:
3 sc rows = ⅜".

Skill Level:
Average

Ornament

Rnd 1: For **first ring,** working around ring (see page 159), with red, join with sc around ring, work 49 more sc around ring, join with sl st in first sc (50 sc).

Rnd 1: For **second ring,** working around next ring, with red, work 50 sc around ring, join with sl st in first sc (50 sc).

Row 2: Working in rows, (ch 2, skip next 2 sts, sc in next st) 8 times leaving remaining sts unworked, **do not** turn or fasten off.

Rnd 1: For **third ring,** working around last ring, with red, work 50 sc around ring, join with sl st in first sc (50 sc).

Row 2: Working in rows, (ch 2, skip next 2 sts, sc in next st) 16 times, ch 2, skip last st, sc in next unworked st on second ring, (ch 2, skip next 2 sts, sc in next st) 8 times, ch 2, sc in next unworked st on first ring, (ch 2, skip next 2 sts, sc in next st) 16 times, ch 2, skip last st, sc in joining sl st of rnd 1 on second ring, fasten off.

Edging

Rnd 1: Join white with sc in first ch sp after joining on 2nd ring, 2 sc in same sp, *(ch 1, 3 sc in next ch sp) 7 times, ch 1, skip next ch sp between joined Rings, 3 sc in next ch sp, (ch 1, 3 sc in next ch sp) 15 times, ch 1, skip next ch sp between joined Rings*, 3 sc in next ch sp; repeat between **, join with sl st in first sc, fasten off.

Rnd 2: Join green with sc in first ch sp, *(ch 2, skip next st, sc in next st, ch 2, skip next st, sc in next ch sp) 6 times, ch 2, skip next ch sp, sc in next ch sp; repeat between ( ) 14 more times, ch 2, skip next ch sp*, sc in next ch sp; repeat between **, join, fasten off.

Sew one jingle bell to top of rnd 1 on each Ring. ✿

Basket of Daisies

Design by
Patricia Hall

Finished Size:

Fits boutique-style tissue box.

Materials:

- ★ Worsted-weight yarn:
  2 oz. each brown and white
  small amount each yellow and green
- ★ Tapestry needle
- ★ G crochet hook or size needed to obtain gauge

Gauge:

4 dc = 1"; 2 dc rows = 1".

Skill Level:

Average

Cover

Top

Rnd 1: With green, ch 20, sl st in first ch to form ring, ch 1, 24 sc in ring, join with sl st in first sc (24 sc).

Rnd 2: Ch 3, dc in same st, ch 2, 2 dc in next st, dc in next 4 sts, (2 dc in next st, ch 2, 2 dc in next st, dc in next 4 sts) around, join with sl st in top of first ch-3 (32 dc, 4 ch sps).

Rnds 3-4: Ch 3, dc in each st around with (2 dc, ch 2, 2 dc) in each corner ch sp, join (48, 64). At end of last rnd, fasten off.

Sides

Rnd 1: With brown, ch 66, sl st in first ch to form ring, ch 3, dc in each ch around, join with sl st in top of ch-3 (66 dc).

NOTES: For **sc front post st (sc-fp,** see page 159), insert hook from front to back around post of next st, yo, draw lp through, complete as sc.

For **sc back post (sc-bp),** insert hook from back to front around post of next st, yo, draw lp through, complete as sc.

For **dc front post (dc-fp),** insert hook from front to back around post of next st, yo, draw lp through, complete as dc.

For **dc back post (dc-bp),** insert hook from back to front around post of next st, yo, draw lp through, complete as dc.

Rnds 2-4: Ch 1, sc-fp around first st, ch 2, dc-fp around each of next 2 sts, dc-bp around each of next 3 sts, (dc-fp around each of next 3 sts, dc-bp around each of next 3 sts) around, join with sl st in top of ch-2.

Rnds 5-8: Ch 1, sc-bp around first st, ch 2, dc-bp around each of next 2 sts, dc-fp around each of next 3 sts, (dc-bp around each of next 3 sts, dc-fp around each of next 3 sts) around, join.

Rnds 9-12: Repeat rnd 2. At end of last rnd, fasten off.

Rnd 13: Join green with sc in first st, sc in each st around, join with sl st in first sc.

Rnds 14-15: Ch 3, dc in each st around, join with sl st in top of ch-3.

Rnd 16: Ch 1, sc first 2 sts tog, sc in next 31 sts, sc next 2 sts tog, sc in last 31 sts, join with sl st in first sc, fasten off (64 sc).

Matching sts, with green, sew Top to Sides.

Flower (make 27)

Rnd 1: With yellow, ch 4, sl st in first ch to form ring, ch 1, 8 sc in ring, join with sl st in first sc, fasten off (8 sc).

NOTE: For **cluster (cl)**, *yo 2 times, insert hook in same st, yo, draw lp through, (yo, draw through 2 lps on hook) 2 times; repeat from *, yo, draw through all 3 lps on hook.

Rnd 2: Join white with sl st in any st, (ch 4, cl, ch 4, sl st) in same st, (sl st, ch 4, cl, ch 4, sl st) in each st around, join with sl st in first sl st, fasten off.

Leaf (make 8)

With green, ch 9, sc in 2nd ch from hook, hdc in next ch, dc in next 4 chs, hdc in next ch, sl st in last ch, fasten off.

Tack flowers over green section covering completely leaving tissue opening uncovered as shown in photo. Tack 2 Leaves to each Side below Flowers. ✪

Golden oak, warm walnut or glistening cherry
glow with a life of their own when dressed in the timeless
elegance of crocheted lace. Treat yourself to the
gracious décor of Doily Splendor.

Chapter Five

Doily Splendor

Dublin Garden

Design by
Dot Drake

Finished Size:
15" across.

Materials:
★ Size-10 bedspread cotton:
   200 yds. white
   125 yds. each lt. pink, dk. pink, lavender and lilac
★ No. 8 steel crochet hook or size needed to obtain gauge.

Gauge:
10 sts = 1"; rnds 1-8 of Small Flower = 2½" across. Rnds 1-3 of Center Flower = 1⅝" across. Center Flower is 6¾" across.

Skill Level:
Average

First Small Flower

Rnd 1: With dk. pink, ch 5, sl st in first ch to form ring, ch 1, 12 sc in ring, join with sl st in first sc (12 sc).

Rnd 2: Ch 1, sc in first st, ch 3, skip next st, (sc in next st, ch 3, skip next st) around, join, fasten off (6 ch-3 sps).

Rnd 3: For **petals,** join lt. pink with sc in any ch sp, (hdc, 3 dc, hdc, sc) in same sp, (sc, hdc, 3 dc, hdc, sc) in each ch sp around, join (6 petals).

Rnd 4: Ch 4, *sc in back bar (see page 159) of first sc on next petal, ch 4; repeat from * around, join with sl st in first ch of first ch-4.

Rnd 5: Sl st in first ch sp, ch 1, (sc, hdc, 5 dc, hdc, sc) in same sp and in each ch sp around, join with sl st in first sc.

Rnd 6: Ch 5, (sc in back bar of first sc on next petal, ch 5) around, join with sl st in first ch of first ch-5.

Rnd 7: Sl st in first ch sp, ch 1, (sc, hdc, 9 dc, hdc, sc) in same sp and in each ch sp around, join with sl st in first sc, fasten off.

NOTE: For **picot,** ch 3, sl st in 3rd ch from hook.

Rnd 8: Join dk. pink with sc in 2nd st, *[sc in next 4 sts, picot, (sc, picot) in each of next 2 sts, sc in next 4 sts, sl st in next sp between petals], sc in 2nd st of next petal; repeat from * 4 more times; repeat between [ ], join, fasten off.

Rnd 9: Join white with sc in 2nd picot, ch 7, skip next 2 sc, dc next sc and 3rd sc on next petal tog, ch 7, skip next picot, (sc in next picot, ch 7, skip next 2 sc, dc next sc and 3rd sc on next petal tog, ch 7, skip next picot) around, join, fasten off (12 ch-7 sps).

Second Small Flower

Rnds 1-8: Using lavender instead of dk. pink and lilac instead of lt. pink, repeat same rnds of First Small Flower.

Rnd 9: Join white with sc in 2nd picot; joining to last Small Flower, ch 3, sl st in 8th ch sp on other Flower, ch 3, skip next 2 sc on this Flower, dc next sc and 3rd sc on next petal tog, ch 3, sl st in next ch sp on other Flower, ch 3, skip next picot on this Flower, (sc in next picot, ch 7, skip next 2 sc, dc next sc and 3rd sc on next petal tog, ch 7, skip next picot) around, join, fasten off.

Third Small Flower

Rnds 1-8: Repeat same rnds of First Small Flower.

Rnd 9: Repeat same rnd of Second Small Flower. Repeat Second and Third Small Flowers 4 more times for a total of 11 Flowers.

Twelfth Small Flower

Rnds 1-8: Using lavender instead of dk. pink and lilac instead of lt. pink, repeat same rnds of First Small Flower.

Rnd 9: Join white with sc in 2nd picot; joining to last Small Flower, ch 3, sl st in 8th ch sp on other Flower, ch 3, skip next 2 sc on this Flower, dc next sc and 3rd sc on next petal tog, ch 3, sl st in next ch sp on other Flower, ch 3, skip next picot on this Flower, *(sc in next picot, ch 7, skip next 2 sc, dc next sc and 3rd sc on next petal tog, ch 7, skip next picot) 2 times*, sc in next picot; joining to First Small Flower, ch 3, sl st in 2nd ch sp on other Flower, ch 3, skip next 2 sc on this Flower, dc next and 3rd sc on next petal tog, ch 3, sl st in next ch sp on other Flower, ch 3, skip next picot on this Flower; repeat between **, join, fasten off.

Center Flower

Rnd 1: With dk. pink, ch 8, sl st in first ch to form ring, ch 1, 24 sc in ring, join with sl st in first sc, fasten off (24 sc).

Rnd 2: Join lavender with sl st in any st, ch 4, (dc in next st, ch 1) around, join with sl st in 3rd ch of ch-4, fasten off (24 dc, 24 ch-1 sps).

Rnd 3: Join white with sc in any st, sc in each ch sp and in each st around, join with sl st in first sc, fasten off (48 sc).

Rnd 4: Join dk. pink with sc in first st, sc in same st, ch 4, skip next 3 sts, (2 sc in next st, ch 4, skip next 3 sts) around, join, fasten off (12 ch-4 sps).

Rnd 5: For **petals,** join white with sc in any ch-4 sp, sc in same sp, ch 21, sc in 2nd ch from hook, sc in each ch across, 2 sc in same ch-4 sp, (2 sc in next ch-4 sp, ch 21, sc in 2nd ch from hook, sc in each ch across, 2 sc in same ch-4 sp) around, join (12 petals).

Rnd 6: Sl st in next st; (*working on opposite side of ch-20, sc in each of first 3 chs, hdc in next ch, dc in next ch, tr in next 12 chs, dc in next ch, hdc in next

Continued on page 131

True Blue

Design by
Karen Ferrer

Finished Size:
12¾" across.

Materials:
★ 180 yds. blue size-10 bedspread cotton
★ No. 8 steel crochet hook or size needed to obtain gauge

Gauge:
Rnds 1-4 = 2¼" across.

Skill Level:
Average

Doily

Rnd 1: Ch 6, sl st in first ch to form ring, ch 1, 12 sc in ring, join with sl st in first sc (12 sc).

Rnd 2: Ch 5, (dc in next st, ch 2) around, join with sl st in 3rd ch of ch-5 (12 dc, 12 ch-2 sps).

Rnd 3: Ch 2, hdc in same st, ch 3, skip next ch sp, (2 hdc in next st, ch 3, skip next ch sp) around, join with sl st in top of ch-2 (24 hdc, 12 ch-3 sps).

Rnd 4: Sl st in next st, sl st in each of next 2 chs, ch 2, hdc in same ch, ch 4, (2 hdc in 2nd ch of next ch-3 sp, ch 4) around, join.

Rnd 5: Sl st in next st, sl st in each of next 2 chs, ch 2, hdc in same ch, 2 hdc in next ch, ch 4, (2 hdc in 2nd ch of next ch-4 sp, 2 hdc in next ch, ch 4) around, join.

Rnd 6: Ch 3, dc in each of next 3 sts, 5 dc in next ch sp, (dc in next 4 sts, 5 dc in next ch sp) around, join with sl st in top of ch-3 (108 dc).

Rnd 7: Ch 3, dc in same st, ch 2, skip next 2 sts, (2 dc in next st, ch 2, skip next 2 sts) around, join.

Rnd 8: Ch 3, dc in same st, 2 dc in next st, ch 2, skip next ch sp, (2 dc in each of next 2 sts, ch 2, skip next ch sp) around, join.

Rnd 9: Sl st in next st, ch 3, dc in next st, ch 4, sc in 3rd ch from hook, ch 1, skip next ch sp and next st, (dc in each of next 2 sts, ch 4, sc in 3rd ch from hook, ch 1, skip next ch sp and next st) around, join.

Rnd 10: Ch 2, dc in next st, ch 4, sc in 3rd ch from hook, ch 1, skip next ch sp, (dc next 2 sts tog, ch 4, sc in 3rd ch from hook, ch 1, skip next ch sp) around, skip first ch-2, join with sl st in next dc.

Rnd 11: Ch 8, sc in 3rd ch from hook, ch 2, skip next ch sp, (dc in next st, ch 5, sc in 3rd ch from hook, ch 2, skip next ch sp) around, join with sl st in 3rd ch of ch-8.

Rnd 12: Ch 10, skip next ch sp, (tr in next st, ch 6, skip next ch sp) around, join with sl st in 4th ch of ch-10.

Rnd 13: Sl st in first ch sp, ch 3, (2 dc, ch 2, 3 dc) in same sp, ch 2, *(3 dc, ch 2, 3 dc) in next ch sp, ch 2; repeat from * around, join with sl st in top of ch-3.

Rnd 14: Sl st in each of next 2 sts, sl st in next ch sp, ch 3, dc in same sp, ch 3, (2 dc in next ch sp, ch 3) around, join.

Rnds 15-17: Sl st in next st, sl st in each of next 2 chs, ch 3, dc in same ch, ch 3, (2 dc in 2nd ch of next ch-3 sp, ch 3) around, join.

Rnd 18: Sl st in next st, sl st in each of next 2 chs, ch 3, dc in same ch, ch 6, hdc in 5th ch from hook, ch 1, (2 dc in 2nd ch of next ch-3 sp, ch 6, hdc in 5th ch from hook, ch 1) around, join, fasten off.★

Tralee Doily

Design by
Dot Drake

Finished Size:
18¼" square.

Materials:
★ 480 yds. white size-10 bedspread cotton
★ No. 8 steel crochet hook or size needed to obtain gauge

Gauge:
Rnds 1-7 of Flower Motif = 1¾" across. Rnds 1-4 of Center Motif = 2" across. Flower and Center Motifs are 4½" across.

Skill Level:
Advanced

First Flower Motif

Rnd 1: Ch 6, sl st in first ch to form ring, ch 1, 16 sc in ring, join with sl st in first sc (16 sc).

Rnd 2: Ch 1, sc in first st, ch 5, skip next 3 sts, (sc in next st, ch 5, skip next 3 sts) around, join (4 ch-5 sps).

Rnd 3: For **petals,** sl st in first ch sp, ch 1, (sc, hdc, 3 dc, hdc, sc, hdc, 3 dc, hdc, sc) in same sp and in each ch sp around, join (8 petals).

Rnd 4: Sl st in back bar (see page 159) of first sc on first petal, ch 3, (sl st in back bar of first sc on next petal, ch 3) around, join with sl st in first sl st (8 ch-3 sps).

Rnd 5: Sl st in first ch sp, ch 1, (sc, hdc, 3 dc, hdc, sc) in same sp and in each ch sp around, join with sl st in first sc.

Rnd 6: Sl st in back bar of first sc on first petal, ch 4, (sl st in back bar of first sc on next petal, ch 4) around, join with sl st in first sl st.

Rnd 7: Sl st in first ch sp, ch 1, (sc, hdc, 4 dc, hdc, sc) in same sp and in each ch sp around, join with sl st in first sc.

Rnd 8: Sl st in back bar of first sc, ch 6, skip first 2 petals, (sl st in back bar of first sc on next petal, ch 14, sl st in same st, ch 6, skip next 2 petals) 3 times, sl st in back bar of first sc on first petal, ch 14, join with sl st in first sl st (4 ch-6 sps, 4 ch-14 lps).

Rnd 9: Sl st in first ch-6 sp, ch 1, 6 sc in same sp, (2 sc, hdc, 17 dc, hdc, 2 sc) in next ch-14 lp, *6 sc in next ch-6 sp, (2 sc, hdc, 17 dc, hdc, 2 sc) in next ch-14 lp; repeat from * around, join with sl st in first sc (116 sts).

Rnd 10: Sl st in next 5 sts, *[sc in next st, ch 3, skip next 2 sts, (dc in next st, ch 2, skip next st) 4 times, (dc, ch 3, dc) in next st, (ch 2, skip next st, dc in next st) 4 times, ch 3, skip next 2 sts, sc in next st], sl st in next 6 sts; repeat from * 2 more times; repeat between [ ], join with sl st in joining sl st of last rnd (72 sts, 32 ch-2 sps, 12 ch-3 sps).

NOTES: For **cluster (cl),** (yo, insert hook in 3rd ch

from hook, yo, draw lp through, yo, draw through 2 lps on hook) 2 times, yo, draw through all 3 lps on hook.
For **picot,** ch 3, sl st in 3rd ch from hook.

Rnd 11: Sl st in each of next 2 sl sts; *[for **extension,** (ch 3, cl) 6 times; with top of last cl towards you, ch 5, cl, sl st in ch between 5th and 6th cls, (ch 3, cl) 5 times; with petals in center towards you, sl st in each of next 3 sl sts, 3 sc in next ch-3 sp, sc in next st, 2 sc in next ch-2 sp, (sc in next st, picot, 2 sc in next ch-2 sp) 3 times, sc in next st, (2 sc, picot, 2 sc) in next ch-3 sp, sc in next st, 2 sc in next ch-2 sp, (sc in next st, picot, 2 sc in next ch-2 sp) 3 times, sc in next st, 3 sc in next ch-3 sp], sl st in each of next 3 sl sts; repeat from * 2 more times; repeat between [ ], join, fasten off (4 extensions, 4 petals).

One-Side Joined Flower Motif
(make 6)

Rnds 1-10: Repeat same rnds of First Flower Motif.

NOTE: For **joining picot,** ch 1, sl st in corresponding picot on other Motif, ch 1, sl st in first ch-1.

Rnd 11: Sl st in each of next 2 sl sts; for **extension,** (ch 3, cl) 6 times; joining to corresponding Flower Motif (see Joining Diagram on page 130), sl st in tip of first extension on other Motif; with top of last cl on this Motif towards you, ch 5, cl, sl st in ch between 5th and 6th cls, (ch 3, cl) 5 times; with petals in center towards you, sl st in each of next 3 sl sts, 3 sc in next ch-3 sp, sc in next st, 2 sc in next ch-2 sp, (sc in next st, picot, 2 sc in next ch-2 sp) 3 times, sc in next st, (2 sc, work joining picot, 2 sc) in next ch-3 sp, sc in next st, 2 sc in next ch-2 sp, (sc in next st, picot, 2 sc in next ch-2 sp) 3 times, sc in next st, 3 sc in next ch-3 sp, sl st in each of next 3 sl sts, (ch 3, cl) 6 times, sl st in tip of next extension on other Motif; with top of last cl on this Motif towards you, ch 5, cl, sl st in ch between 5th and 6th cls, (ch 3, cl) 5 times; with petals in center towards you, sl st in each of next 3 sl sts, *[3 sc in next ch-3 sp, sc in next st, 2 sc in next ch-2 sp, (sc in next st, picot, 2 sc in next ch-2 sp) 3 times, sc in next st, (2 sc, picot, 2 sc) in next ch-3 sp, sc in next st, 2 sc in next ch-2 sp, (sc in next st, picot, 2 sc in next ch-2 sp) 3 times, sc in next st, 3 sc in next ch-3 sp, sl st in each of next 3 sl sts], (ch 3, cl) 6 times; with top of last cl towards you, ch 5, cl, sl st in ch between 5th and 6th cls, (ch 3, cl) 5 times; with petals in center towards you, sl st in each of next 3 sl sts; repeat from *; repeat between [ ], join, fasten off.

Two-Side Joined Flower Motif

Rnds 1-10: Repeat same rnds of First Flower Motif.

Rnd 11: Sl st in each of next 2 sl sts; for **extension,** (ch 3, cl) 6 times; joining to corresponding

Continued on next page

Tralee Doily

Continued from page 129

Flower Motif (see diagram on page 130), *sl st in tip of first extension on other Motif; with top of last cl on this Motif towards you, ch 5, cl, sl st in ch between 5th and 6th cls, (ch 3, cl) 5 times; with petals in center towards you, sl st in each of next 3 sl sts, 3 sc in next ch-3 sp, sc in next st, 2 sc in next ch-2 sp, (sc in next st, picot, 2 sc in next ch-2 sp) 3 times, sc in next st, (2 sc, work joining picot, 2 sc) in next ch-3 sp, sc in next st, 2 sc in next ch-2 sp, (sc in next st, picot, 2 sc in next ch-2 sp) 3 times, sc in next st, 3 sc in next ch-3 sp, sl st in each of next 3 sl sts, (ch 3, cl) 6 times, sl st in tip of next extension on other Motif; with top of last cl on this Motif towards you, ch 5, cl, sl st in ch between 5th and 6th cls, (ch 3, cl) 5 times; with petals in center towards you, sl st in each of next 3 sl sts, 3 sc in next ch-3 sp, sc in next st, 2 sc in next ch-2 sp, (sc in next st, picot, 2 sc in next ch-2 sp) 3 times, sc in next st, (2 sc, picot, 2 sc) in next ch-3 sp, sc in next st, 2 sc in next ch-2 sp, (sc in next st, picot, 2 sc in next ch-2 sp) 3 times, sc in next st, 3 sc in next ch-3 sp, sl st in each of next 3 sl sts*, (ch 3, cl) 6 times; joining to remaining 2 extensions of First Flower Motif; repeat between **, join, fasten off.

Center Motif

Rnd 1: Ch 6, sl st in first ch to form ring, ch 3, 15 dc in ring, join with sl st in top of ch-3 (16 dc).

Rnd 2: Ch 5, (dc in next st, ch 2) around, join with sl st in 3rd ch of ch-5 (16 dc, 16 ch-2 sps).

Rnd 3: Ch 1, sc in first st, (sc, picot, sc) in next ch sp, *sc in next st, (sc, picot, sc) in next ch sp; repeat from * around, join with sl st in first sc (48 sc).

Rnd 4: Ch 6, skip next 2 sts, (dc in next st, ch 3, skip next 2 sts) around, join with sl st in 3rd ch of ch-6 (16 dc, 16 ch-3 sps).

Rnd 5: For **petals,** sl st in first ch sp, ch 1, (sc, hdc, 3 dc, hdc, sc) in same sp and in each ch sp around, join with sl st in first sc (16 petals).

Rnd 6: Sl st in each of next 2 sts, ch 1, sc in next st, ch 5, (sc in 2nd dc of next petal, ch 5) around, join.

Rnd 7: Sl st in first ch sp, ch 1, (sc, hdc, 3 dc) in same sp, work joining picot in center bottom picot of second Flower Motif, *[(3 dc, hdc, sc) in same sp on this Motif, (sc, hdc, dc, picot, 5 dc, hdc, sc) in next ch sp, (sc, hdc, 3 dc) in next ch sp, ch 7, drop lp from hook, insert hook in 2nd dc after picot on last petal, draw dropped lp through, (sc, hdc, dc, picot, 5 dc, hdc, sc) in ch-7 sp just made, (3 dc, hdc, sc) in 2nd half of last ch-5 sp worked, (sc, hdc, 3 dc) in next ch-5 sp, ch 7, drop lp from hook, insert hook in 4th dc on last petal, draw dropped lp through, (sc, hdc, 3 dc) in ch-7 sp just made, ch 7, drop lp from

hook, insert hook in 2nd dc after picot on last petal, (sc, hdc, dc, picot, 2 dc) in ch-7 just made, ch 3, cl, ch 1, sl st in joining between next 3 extensions on Flower Motifs, ch 4, cl, sl st in bottom ch of first ch-3 on first cl, (3 dc, picot, hdc, sc) in next ch-7 sp, (3 dc, picot, hdc, sc) in 2nd half of next ch-7 sp and in 2nd half of next ch-5 sp], (sc, hdc, 3 dc) in next ch-5 sp, work joining picot in center bottom picot of next Flower Motif; repeat from * 2 more times; repeat between [ ], join, fasten off.

Border

Rnd 1: Join with sc in tip of extension on any corner, [◊(ch 4, dc in 4th ch from hook) 5 times, sc in center picot on next petal, (ch 4, dc in 4th ch from hook) 5 times, *sc in joining between next 2 extensions, (ch 4, dc in 4th ch from hook) 5 times, sc in center picot on next petal, (ch 4, dc in 4th ch from hook) 5 times; repeat from *◊, sc in tip of next extension]; repeat between [ ] 2 more times; repeat between ◊◊; join with sl st in first sc (120 ch-4 sps, 24 sc).

Rnd 2: Sl st in first ch sp, ch 1, 5 sc in same ch sp and in each ch sp around, join (120 5-sc groups).

Rnd 3: Sl st in next st, ch 1, sc in next st, *[(ch 5, sc in 3rd sc of next 5-sc group) 29 times, ch 3, (dc, ch 3, dc) in sp between last 5-sc group and next 5-sc group, ch 3], sc in 3rd sc of next 5-sc group; repeat from * 2 more times; repeat between [ ], join (29 ch-5 sps and 2 ch-3 sps across each side between corner ch-3 sps).

Rnd 4: Sl st in each of next 2 chs, ch 1, sc in same ch sp, picot, *ch 5, (sc in next ch-5 sp, picot, ch 5) across to ch-3 sp before next corner ch-3 sp, sc in next ch-3 sp, picot, ch 3, (dc, ch 3, dc) in 2nd

JOINING DIAGRAM

ch of next ch-3 sp, ch 3, sc in next ch-3 sp, picot; repeat from * around; to **join,** ch 2, dc in first sc.

Rnds 5-8: Ch 1, sc around joining dc, picot, *ch 5, (sc in next ch-5 sp, picot, ch 5) across to ch-3 sp before next corner ch-3 sp, sc in next ch-3 sp, picot, ch 3, (dc, ch 3, dc) in 2nd ch of next ch-3 sp, ch 3, sc in next ch-3 sp, picot; repeat from * around, join as before.

Rnd 9: Ch 1, sc around joining dc, *ch 5, (sc in next ch-5 sp, ch 5) across to ch-3 sp before next corner ch-3 sp, sc in next ch-3 sp, ch 3, (dc, ch 3, dc) in 2nd ch of next ch-3 sp, ch 3, sc in next ch-3 sp; repeat from * 3 more times, ch 5, join with sl st in first sc.

Rnd 10: Sl st in first ch-5 sp, ch 1, 6 sc in same sp, [*3 sc next ch-5 sp, ch 5, drop lp from hook, insert hook in 4th sc of last 6-sc group, draw dropped lp through, (3 sc, picot, 3 sc) in ch-5 sp just made, 3 sc in 2nd half of next ch-5 sp; repeat from * across to ch-3 sp before next corner ch-3 sp, 3 sc in next ch-3 sp, ch 5, drop lp from hook, insert hook in 4th sc of last 6-sc group, draw dropped lp through, (3 sc, picot, 3 sc) in ch-5 sp just made, 5 sc in next corner ch-3 sp, ch 7, drop lp from hook, insert hook in first sc of last 5-sc group, (4 sc, picot, 4 sc) in ch-7 sp just made, 3 sc in next ch-3 sp, 3 sc in next ch-5 sp, ch 5, drop lp from hook, insert hook in first sc of 3-sc group on last ch-3 sp, draw dropped lp through, (3 sc, picot, 3 sc) in ch-5 sp just made, 3 sc in 2nd half of next ch-5 sp]; repeat between [ ] around, sl st in each of first 3 sts, ch 5, drop lp from hook, insert hook in 4th sc of last 6-sc group, draw dropped lp through, (3 sc, picot, 3 sc) in ch-5 sp just made, join with sl st in next sc, fasten off. ☆

Dublin Garden

Continued from page 125

ch, sc in last ch, sc in end of next row, sc in next st, hdc in next st, dc in next st, tr in next 12 sts, dc in next st, hdc in next st, sc in each of next 3 sts*, sl st in next 4 sts) 11 times; repeat between **, sl st in each of last 2 sts, join with sl st in joining sl st of last rnd, fasten off.

Rnd 7: Join dk. pink with sc in first st of any petal, (*sc in next 19 sts, 3 sc in next st, sc in next 20 sts, working around sl sts, sc in sp between next two 2-sc groups on rnd before last*, sc in next sc on last rnd) 11 times; repeat between **, join, fasten off.

Rnd 8: Working inside ring of Small Flowers, for **joining rnd,** join white with sc in 2nd unworked ch sp of any Small Flower, ch 5, sc in 2nd sc of 3-sc group on tip of any petal on Center Flower, ch 5, sc in next ch sp on Small Flower, ch 6, tr next ch sp on this Flower and first unworked ch sp on next Small Flower tog, picot, ch 6, (sc in next ch sp, ch 5, sc in 2nd sc of 3-sc group on tip of next petal on Center Flower, ch 5, sc in next ch sp on Small Flower, ch 6, tr next ch sp on this Flower and first unworked ch sp on next Small Flower tog, picot, ch 6) around, join with sl st in first sc, fasten off.

Border

Rnd 1: Working in unworked ch sps on outer edge of Small Flowers, join white with sc in first unworked ch sp of any Small Flower, *picot, ch 9, (sc in next ch sp, picot, ch 9) 3 times, sc in next unworked ch sp on next Small Flower; repeat from *10 more times, (picot, ch 9, sc in next ch sp) 3 times, picot; to **join,** ch 5, tr in first sc (48 ch sps).

Rnd 2: Ch 1, sc around joining tr, picot, (ch 9, sc in next ch sp, picot) around, join as before.

Rnd 3: Ch 1, sc around joining tr, picot, *[ch 11, sl st in 7th ch from hook, (6 sc, picot, sc, ch 5, sl st in 5th ch from hook, sc, picot, 6 sc) in ch-7 lp, sl st in first sc of first 6-sc group on same lp, ch 4, sc in next ch-9 sp, picot, ch 5, tr in 5th ch of next ch-9 sp, picot, (ch 2, tr, picot) 4 times in same ch, ch 3, tr in 5th ch of next ch-9 sp, picot, (ch 2, tr, picot) 4 times in same ch, ch 5], sc in next ch-9 sp, picot; repeat from * 10 more times; repeat between [ ], join with sl st in first sc, fasten off. ☆

Set

Summer Garden Set

Design by
Jo Ann Maxwell

Runner

Finished Size:

10½" x 33".

Materials:

★ Size-10 bedspread cotton:
264 yds. assorted scrap colors - each Motif requires 8 yds. of Main Color (MC) and 4 yds. of Contrasting Color (CC)
225 yds. white
★ No. 5 steel crochet hook or size needed to obtain gauge

Gauge:

Rnds 1 and 2 of Motif = 1⅝" across. Each Motif is 4" across.

Skill Level:

Average

First Motif

Rnd 1: With MC, ch 4, sl st in first ch to form ring, ch 3, 23 dc in ring, join with sl st in top of ch-3, fasten off (24 dc).

NOTES: For **beginning cluster (beg cl)**, ch 3, (yo, insert hook in same st, yo, draw lp through, yo, draw through 2 lps on hook) 3 times, yo, draw through all 4 lps on hook.

For **cluster (cl)**, yo, insert hook in next st, yo, draw lp through, yo, draw through 2 lps on hook, (yo, insert hook in same st, yo, draw lp through, yo, draw through 2 lps on hook) 3 times, yo, draw through all 5 lps on hook.

Rnd 2: Join CC with sl st in any st, beg cl, ch 3, skip next st, (cl in next st, ch 3, skip next st) around, join with sl st in top of beg cl, fasten off (12 cls, 12 ch-3 sps).

Rnd 3: Join MC with sc in any st, dc in next ch sp, (ch 1, dc in same sp) 4 times, *sc in next st, dc in next ch sp, (ch 1, dc in same sp) 4 times; repeat from * around, join with sl st in first sc, fasten off.

Rnd 4: Join white with sc in 3rd dc of any 5-dc group, ch 7, (sc in 3rd dc of next 5-dc group, ch 7) around, join (12 ch-7 sps).

NOTE: For **shell**, (2 dc, ch 3, 2 dc) in 4th ch of next ch-7 sp.

Rnd 5: Ch 1, sc in first st, ch 4, shell, ch 4, (sc in next st, ch 4, shell, ch 4) around, join, fasten off.

One-Side Joined Motif

Rnds 1-4: Repeat same rnds of First Motif.

Rnd 5: Ch 1, sc in first st, ch 4, 2 dc in 4th ch of next ch-7 sp; joining to corresponding Motif (see Runner Joining Diagram on page 135), ch 1, sl st in 2nd ch of ch-3 sp on other Motif indicated on diagram, ch 1, 2 dc in same ch on this Motif, ch 4, sc in next st, ch 4, 2 dc in 4th ch of next ch-7 sp, ch 1, sl st in 2nd ch of next ch-3 sp on other Motif, ch 1, 2 dc in same ch on this Motif, ch 4, (sc in next st, ch 4, shell, ch 4) around, join, fasten off.

Two-Side Joined Motif

Rnds 1-4: Repeat same rnds of First Motif.

Rnd 5: Ch 1, sc in first st, ch 4, 2 dc in 4th ch of next ch-7 sp; joining to corresponding Motif, ch 1, sl st in 2nd ch of indicated ch-3 sp on other Motif, ch 1, 2 dc in same ch on this Motif, ch 4, sc in next st, ch 4, 2 dc in 4th ch of next ch-7 sp, ch 1, sl st in 2nd ch of next ch-3 sp on other Motif, ch 1, 2 dc in same ch on this Motif, ch 4, sc in next st, ch 4, 2 dc in 4th ch of next ch-7 sp; joining to next Motif, ch 1, sl st in 2nd ch of indicated ch-3 sp on other Motif, ch 1, 2 dc in same ch on this Motif, ch 4, sc in next st, ch 4, 2 dc in 4th ch of next ch-7 sp, ch 1, sl st in 2nd ch of next ch-3 sp on other Motif, ch 1, 2 dc in same ch on this Motif, ch 4, (sc in next st, ch 4, shell, ch 4) around, join, fasten off.

Three-Side Joined Motif

Rnds 1-4: Repeat same rnds of First Motif.

Rnd 5: Ch 1, sc in first st, ch 4, 2 dc in 4th ch of next ch-7 sp; joining to corresponding Motif, ch 1, sl st in 2nd ch of indicated ch-3 sp on other Motif, ch 1, 2 dc in same ch on this Motif, ch 4, sc in next st, ch 4, 2 dc in 4th ch of next ch-7 sp, ch 1, sl st in 2nd ch of next ch-3 sp on other Motif, ch 1, 2 dc in same ch on this Motif, ch 4, *sc in next st, ch 4, 2 dc in 4th ch of next ch-7 sp; joining to next Motif, ch 1, sl st in 2nd ch of indicated ch-3 sp on other Motif, ch 1, 2 dc in same ch on this Motif, ch 4, sc in next st, ch 4, 2 dc in 4th ch of next ch-7 sp, ch 1, sl st in 2nd ch of next ch-3 sp on other Motif, ch 1, 2 dc in same ch on this Motif, ch 4; repeat from *, (sc in next st, ch 4, shell, ch 4) around, join, fasten off.

Work Motifs according to Runner Joining Diagram.

Edging

Working around entire outer edge, join white with sl st in first dc of any unworked shell, ch 5, dc in next

Continued on next page

dc, ch 2, (dc, ch 2, dc) in next ch-3 sp, (ch 2, dc in next dc) 2 times, *dc in first dc of next unworked shell, ch 2, dc in next dc, ch 2, (dc, ch 2, dc) in next ch-3 sp, (ch 2, dc in next dc) 2 times; repeat from * around, join with sl st in 3rd ch of ch-5, fasten off.

Doily

Finished Size:
11¼" x 12½".

Materials:
★ Size-10 bedspread cotton:
84 yds. assorted scrap colors - each Motif requires 8 yds. of Main Color (MC) and 4 yds. of Contrasting Color (CC)
75 yds. white
★ No. 5 steel crochet hook or size needed to obtain gauge

Gauge:
Rnds 1 and 2 of Motif = 1⅝" across. Each Motif is 4" across.

Skill Level:
Average

Center Motif
Work same as Runner's First Motif on page 134.

One-Side Joined Motif
Rnds 1-4: Repeat same rnds of Runner's First Motif.

Rnd 5: Ch 1, sc in first st, ch 4, 2 dc in 4th ch of next ch-7 sp; joining to Center Motif (see Doily Joining Diagram), ch 1, sl st in 2nd ch of any ch-3 sp on other Motif, ch 1, 2 dc in same ch on this Motif, ch 4, sc in next st, ch 4, 2 dc in 4th ch of next ch-7 sp, ch 1, sl st in 2nd ch of next ch-3 sp on Center Motif, ch 1, 2 dc in same ch on this Motif, ch 4, (sc in next st, ch 4, shell, ch 4) around, join, fasten off.

Two-Side Joined Moitf
Rnds 1-4: Repeat same rnds of Runner's First Motif.

Rnd 5: Ch 1, sc in first st, ch 4, 2 dc in 4th ch of next ch-7 sp; joining to last Motif, ch 1, sl st in 2nd ch of corresponding ch-3 sp on other Motif, ch 1, 2 dc in same ch on this Motif, ch 4, sc in next st, ch 4, 2 dc in 4th ch of next ch-7 sp, ch 1, sl st in 2nd ch of next ch-3 sp on other Motif, ch 1, 2 dc in same

ch on this Motif, ch 4, sc in next st, ch 4, 2 dc in 4th ch of next ch-7 sp; joining to Center Motif, ch 1, sl st in 2nd ch of next unworked ch-3 sp on other Motif, ch 1, 2 dc in same ch on this Motif, ch 4, sc in next st, ch 4, 2 dc in 4th ch of next ch-7 sp, ch 1, sl st in 2nd ch of next ch-3 sp on Center Motif, ch 1, 2 dc in same ch on this Motif, ch 4, (sc in next st, ch 4, shell, ch 4) around, join, fasten off.
Repeat Two-Side Joined Motif 3 more times.

Three-Side Joined Motif
Rnds 1-4: Repeat same rnds of Runner's First Motif.
Rnd 5: Ch 1, sc in first st, ch 4, 2 dc in 4th ch of next ch-7 sp; joining to last Motif, *ch 1, sl st in 2nd ch of corresponding ch-3 sp on other Motif, ch 1, 2 dc in same ch on this Motif, ch 4, sc in next st, ch 4, 2 dc in 4th ch of next ch-7 sp, ch 1, sl st in 2nd ch of next ch-3 sp on other Motif, ch 1, 2 dc in same ch on this Motif, ch 4, sc in next st, ch 4*, 2 dc in 4th ch of next ch-7 sp; joining to Center Motif, ch 1, sl st in 2nd ch of next unworked ch-3 sp on other Motif, ch 1, 2 dc in same ch on this Motif, ch 4, sc in next st, ch 4, 2 dc in 4th ch of next ch-7 sp, ch 1, sl st in 2nd ch of next ch-3 sp on other Motif, ch 1, 2 dc in same ch on this Motif, ch 4, sc in next st, ch 4, 2 dc in 4th ch of next ch-7 sp; joining to first Motif; repeat between **, (sc in next st, ch 4, shell, ch 4) around, join, fasten off.

Edging
Work same as Runner's Edging on page 134. ✩

DOILY JOINING DIAGRAM

Center Motif

One-Side Joined Motif

Two-Side Joined Motif

Three-Side Joined Motif

RUNNER JOINING DIAGRAM

First Motif

One-Side Joined Motif

Three-Side Joined Motif

Two-Side Joined Motif

Pineapple Ring

Design by
Zelda Workman

Finished Size:
18" across.

Materials:
★ 350 yds. white size-10 bedspread cotton
★ No. 7 steel crochet hook or size needed to obtain gauge

Gauge:
Rnds 1-3 = 2" across.

Skill Level:
Average

Doily

Rnd 1: Ch 6, sl st in first ch to form ring, ch 4, (dc in ring, ch 1) 11 times, join with sl st in 3rd ch of ch-4 (12 dc, 12 ch-1 sps).

Rnd 2: Sl st in first ch sp, ch 5, (dc same sp and next ch sp tog, ch 2) 11 times, yo, insert hook in same sp, yo, draw lp through, yo, draw through 2 lps on hook, insert hook in 3rd ch of ch-5, yo, draw lp through, yo, draw through all 3 lps on hook.

Rnd 3: Sl st in first ch sp, ch 7, dc same sp and next ch sp tog, ch 4) 11 times, yo, insert hook in same sp, yo, draw lp through, yo, draw through 2 lps on hook, insert hook in 3rd ch of ch-7, yo, draw lp through, yo, draw through all 3 lps on hook.

Rnd 4: Ch 6, dc same st and next ch sp tog, ch 3, (dc same ch sp and next st tog, ch 3, dc same st and next ch sp tog, ch 3) 11 times, yo, insert hook in same sp, yo, draw lp through, yo, draw through 2 lps on hook, insert hook in 3rd ch of ch-6, yo, draw lp through, yo, draw through all 3 lps on hook (24 dc, 24 ch-3 sps).

Rnd 5: Repeat rnd 3.

NOTE: For **picot**, sl st in 5th ch from hook.

Rnd 6: Sl st in each of next 2 chs, ch 1, sc in same ch sp, ch 7, picot, ch 3, sc in next ch sp, (ch 7, sc in next ch sp, ch 7, picot, ch 3, sc in next ch sp) around; to **join,** ch 3, tr in first sc (12 picot lps, 12 ch-7 sps).

Rnd 7: Ch 1, sc around joining tr, ch 15, skip next picot lp, (sc in next ch-7 sp, ch 15, skip next picot lp) around, join with sl st in first sc.

Rnd 8: Sl st in first ch sp, ch 1, 15 sc in same sp, ch 5, (15 sc in next ch sp, ch 5) around, join.

Rnd 9: Sl st in next 6 sts, ch 4, 2 tr in same st, 5 tr in next st, 3 tr in next st, ch 5, (3 tr in 7th sc of next 15-sc group, 5 tr in next st, 3 tr in next st, ch 5) around, join with sl st in top of ch-4.

Rnd 10: Ch 5, tr in next tr, (ch 1, tr in next tr) 9 times, ch 2, *tr in next tr, (ch 1, tr in next tr) 10 times, ch 2; repeat from * around, join with sl st in 4th ch of ch-5.

Rnd 11: Sl st in first ch-1 sp, ch 1, sc in same sp, *[(ch 3, sc in next ch-1 sp) 9 times, ch 2, skip next ch-2 sp], sc in next ch-1 sp; repeat from * 10 more times; repeat between [ ], join with sl st in first sc.

Rnd 12: Sl st in first ch-3 sp, ch 1, sc in same sp, *[(ch 3, sc in next ch-3 sp) 8 times, ch 2, skip next ch-2 sp], sc in next ch-3 sp; repeat from * 10 more times; repeat between [ ], join.

Rnd 13: Sl st in first ch-3 sp, ch 1, sc in same sp, *[(ch 3, sc in next ch-3 sp) 7 times, ch 2, skip next ch-2 sp], sc in next ch-3 sp; repeat from * 10 more times; repeat between [ ], join.

Rnd 14: Sl st in first ch-3 sp, ch 1, sc in same sp, *[(ch 3, sc in next ch-3 sp) 6 times, ch 3, skip next ch-2 sp], sc in next ch-3 sp; repeat from * 10 more times; repeat between [ ], join.

Rnd 15: Sl st in first ch-3 sp, ch 1, sc in same sp, *[(ch 4, sc in next ch-3 sp) 5 times, ch 5, skip next ch-3 sp], sc in next ch-3 sp; repeat from * 10 more times; repeat between [ ], join.

Rnd 16: Sl st in first ch-4 sp, ch 1, sc in same sp, *[(ch 5, sc in next ch-4 sp) 4 times, ch 3, dc in 3rd ch of next ch-5 sp, ch 3], sc in next ch-4 sp; repeat from * 10 more times; repeat between [ ], join.

Rnd 17: Sl st in each of next 2 chs, ch 1, sc in same ch sp, *[(ch 5, sc in next ch-5 sp) 3 times, ch 3, skip next ch-3 sp, 3 dc in next st, ch 3, skip next ch-3 sp], sc in next ch-5 sp; repeat from * 10 more times; repeat between [ ], join.

Rnd 18: Sl st in each of next 2 chs, ch 1, sc in same ch sp, *[(ch 6, sc in next ch-5 sp) 2 times, ch 3, 3 dc in 3rd ch of next ch-3 sp, ch 2, 3 dc in first ch of next ch-3 sp, ch 3], sc in next ch-5 sp; repeat from * 10 more times; repeat between [ ], join.

Rnd 19: Sl st in each of next 2 chs, ch 1, sc in same ch sp, *[ch 7, sc in next ch-6 sp, ch 4, 3 dc in 3rd ch of next ch-3 sp, ch 2, 3 dc in next ch-2 sp, ch 2, 3 dc in first ch of next ch-3 sp, ch 4], sc in next ch-6 sp; repeat from * 10 more times; repeat between [ ], join.

Rnd 20: Sl st in each of next 3 chs, ch 1, sc in same ch sp, *[ch 6, 3 dc in 4th ch of next ch-4 sp, ch 2, (3 dc in next ch-2 sp, ch 2) 2 times, 3 dc in first ch of next ch-4 sp, ch 6], sc in next ch-7 sp; repeat

Continued on page 145

Christmas Tree Doily

Design by Dot Drake

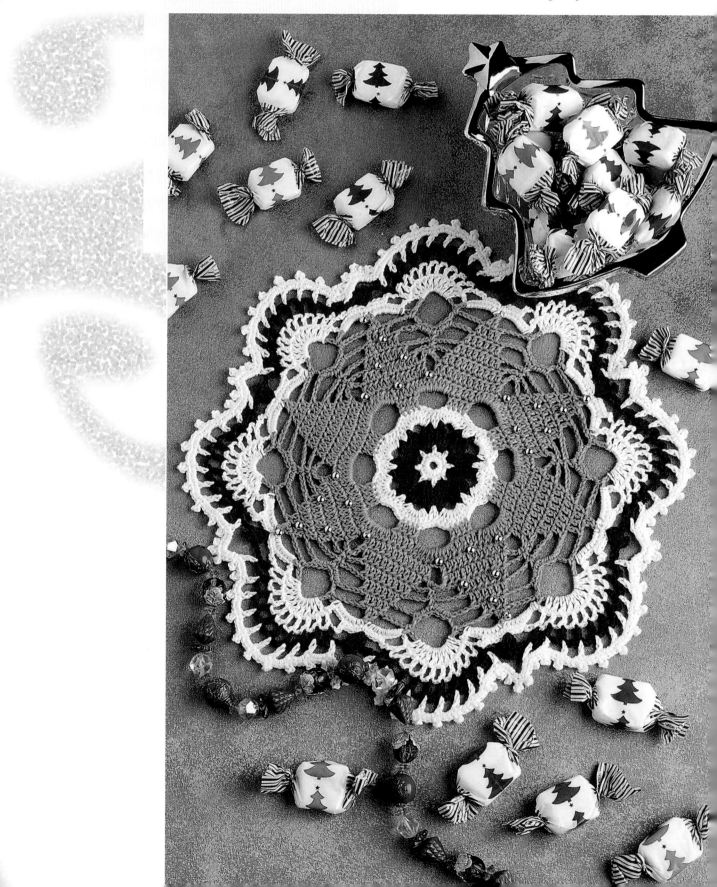

Finished Size:
10" across.

Materials:
★ Size-10 bedspread cotton:
  60 yds. each green and white
  30 yds. red
★ 28 gold 4-mm beads
★ Green sewing thread
★ Beading needle
★ No. 8 steel crochet hook or size needed to obtain gauge

Gauge:
Rnds 1-4 = 2½" across.

Skill Level:
Average

Doily

Rnd 1: With white, ch 6, sl st in first ch to form ring, ch 1, 16 sc in ring, join with sl st in first sc (16 sc).

Rnd 2: Ch 1, sc in first st, ch 3, skip next st, (sc in next st, ch 3, skip next st) around, join, fasten off (8 ch-3 sps).

NOTES: For **beginning cluster (beg cl),** ch 4, *yo 2 times, insert hook in same sp, yo, draw lp through, (yo, draw through 2 lps on hook) 2 times; repeat from *, yo, draw through all 3 lps on hook.

For **cluster (cl),** yo 2 times, insert hook in next ch sp, yo, draw lp through, (yo, draw through 2 lps on hook) 2 times, *yo 2 times, insert hook in same sp, yo, draw lp through, (yo, draw through 2 lps on hook) 2 times; repeat from *, yo, draw through all 4 lps on hook.

Rnd 3: Join red with sl st in any ch sp, beg cl, ch 5, cl in same sp, ch 1, *(cl, ch 5, cl) in next ch sp, ch 1; repeat from * around, join with sl st in top of beg cl, fasten off (8 ch-5 sps, 8 ch-1 sps).

Rnd 4: Join white with sl st in first ch-5 sp, ch 3, 7 dc in same sp, 2 dc in next ch-1 sp, (8 dc in next ch-5 sp, 2 dc in next ch-1 sp) around, join with sl st in top of ch-3, fasten off (80 dc).

Rnd 5: Join green with sl st in 3rd st, ch 3, dc in each of next 3 sts, ch 7, skip next 6 sts, (dc in next 4 sts, ch 7, skip next 6 sts) around, join (32 dc, 8 ch-7 sps).

Rnd 6: Ch 3, dc in each st and 10 dc in each ch sp around, join (112 dc).

Rnd 7: Ch 3, dc in next 7 sts, ch 5, skip next 2 sts, (dc in next 12 sts, ch 5, skip next 2 sts) 7 times,

dc in last 4 sts, join.

Rnd 8: Ch 3, dc in next 6 sts, skip next st, ch 3, sc in next ch sp, ch 3, skip next st, (dc in next 10 sts, ch 3, skip next st, sc in next ch sp, ch 3, skip next st) 7 times, dc in each of last 3 sts, join.

Rnd 9: Ch 3, dc in next 5 sts, (*ch 5, skip next ch sp, sc in next st, ch 5, skip next ch sp and next st*, dc in next 8 sts) 7 times; repeat between **, dc in each of last 2 sts, join.

Rnd 10: Ch 3, dc in next 4 sts, (*ch 7, skip next ch sp, sc in next st, ch 7, skip next ch sp and next st*, dc in next 6 sts) 7 times; repeat between **, dc in last st, join.

Rnd 11: Ch 3, dc in each of next 3 sts, (*ch 7, 3 sc in next ch sp, sc in next st, 3 sc in next ch sp, ch 7, skip next st*, dc in next 4 sts) 7 times; repeat between **, join.

Rnd 12: Sl st in next st, ch 2, dc in next st, (*ch 7, sc in next ch sp, ch 10, sc in next ch sp, ch 7, skip next st*, dc next 2 sts tog) 7 times; repeat between **, skip first ch-2, join with sl st in next dc, fasten off.

Rnd 13: Skip first ch-7 sp, join white with sl st in next ch-10 sp, ch 4, dc in same sp, (ch 1, dc in same sp) 8 times, ch 3, 9 sc in each of next 2 ch-7 sps, ch 3, *dc in next ch-10 sp, (ch 1, dc in same sp) 9 times, ch 3, 9 sc in each of next 2 ch-7 sps, ch 3; repeat from * around, join with sl st in 3rd ch of ch-4.

Rnd 14: Ch 5, dc in next dc, (ch 2, dc in next dc) 8 times, ch 3, skip next 4 sc, sc in next 9 sc, ch 3, *dc in next dc, (ch 2, dc in next dc) 9 times, ch 3, skip next 4 sc, sc in next 9 sc, ch 3; repeat from * around, join with sl st in 3rd ch of ch-5, fasten off.

NOTE: For **picot,** ch 3, sl st in top of last st made.

Rnd 15: Join red with sl st in first dc, ch 6, dc in next dc, (ch 3, dc in next dc) 8 times, ch 3, skip next 4 sc, (2 dc, picot, dc) in next st, ch 3, *dc in next dc, (ch 3, dc in next dc) 9 times, ch 3, skip next 4 sc, (2 dc, picot, dc) in next sc, ch 3; repeat from * around, join with sl st in 3rd ch of ch-6, fasten off.

Rnd 16: Join white with sl st in first dc, ch 6, dc in next dc, (ch 3, dc in next dc) 8 times, ch 6, skip next 2 ch-3 sps, *dc in next dc, (ch 3, dc in next dc) 9 times, ch 6, skip next 2 ch-3 sps; repeat from * around, join with sl st in 3rd ch of ch-6.

Rnd 17: Ch 1, sc in first st, picot, *[(3 sc in next ch-3 sp, sc in next st, picot) 9 times, (3 sc, picot, sc, ch 5, sl st in top of last st made, sc, picot, 3 sc) in next ch-6 sp], sc in next st, picot; repeat from * 6 more times; repeat between [ ], join with sl st in first sc, fasten off.

Sew beads around rnds 6, 8, 10 and 12 on every other tree as shown in photo.✩

Blushing Pineapple Rose

Design by
Jo Ann Maxwell

Finished Size:
13¾" across.

Materials:
★ Size-10 bedspread cotton:
150 yds. cream
30 yds. pink
★ No. 5 steel crochet hook or size needed to obtain gauge

Gauge:
Rnds 1-6 = 2" across.

Skill Level:
Average

Doily

Rnd 1: With pink, ch 4, sl st in first ch to form ring, ch 1, 8 sc in ring, join with sl st in first sc (8 sc).

Rnd 2: Ch 1, sc in first st, ch 2, (sc in next st, ch 2) around, join (8 ch-2 sps).

Rnd 3: For **petals**, sl st in first ch sp, ch 1, (sc, 5 dc, sc) in same sp and in each ch sp around, join (8 petals).

Rnd 4: Working behind petals, ch 1, sc in first st, ch 3, (sc in first sc on next petal, ch 3) around, join.

Rnd 5: Sl st in first ch sp, ch 1, (sc, 7 dc, sc) in same sp and in each ch sp around, join.

Rnd 6: Working behind petals, ch 1, sc in first st, ch 4, (sc in first sc on next petal, ch 4) around, join, fasten off.

Rnd 7: Join cream with sc in any ch sp, (9 dc, sc) in same sp, (sc, 9 dc, sc) in each ch sp around, join.

Rnd 8: Sl st in each of next 3 sts, ch 1, sc in same st, ch 5, skip next 3 sts, sc in next st, ch 5, skip next 6 sts, (sc in next st, ch 5, skip next 3 sts, sc in next st, ch 5, skip next 6 sts) around, join (16 ch-5 sps).

NOTES: For **beginning shell (beg shell)**, ch 3, (dc, ch 2, 2 dc) in same ch or ch sp.

For **shell**, (2 dc, ch 2, 2 dc) in next ch or ch sp.

Rnd 9: Sl st in each of next 3 chs, beg shell, ch 2, (shell in 3rd ch of next ch-5 sp, ch 2) around, join with sl st in top of ch-3.

Rnd 10: Sl st in next st, sl st in next ch sp, beg shell, ch 2, sc in next ch-2 sp, ch 2, (shell in ch sp of next shell, ch 2, sc in next ch-2 sp, ch 2) around, join.

Rnd 11: Sl st in next st, sl st in next ch sp, beg shell, ch 3, 7 dc in next shell, ch 3, (shell in next shell, ch 3, 7 dc in next shell, ch 3) around, join.

Rnd 12: Sl st in next st, sl st in next ch sp, beg shell, *[ch 3, sc in next ch-3 sp, dc in next dc, (ch 1, dc in next dc) 6 times, sc in next ch-3 sp, ch 3], shell in next shell; repeat from * 6 more times; repeat between [ ], join.

Rnd 13: Sl st in next st, sl st in next ch sp, ch 3, (dc, ch 2, 2 dc, ch 2, 2 dc) in same sp, *[ch 3, skip next ch-3 sp and next sc, (sc in next dc, ch 3) 7 times], (2 dc, ch 2, 2 dc, ch 2, 2 dc) in next shell; repeat from * 6 more times; repeat between [ ], join.

Rnd 14: Sl st in next st, sl st in next ch-2 sp, beg shell, *[ch 3, shell in next ch-2 sp, ch 3, skip next ch-3 sp, (sc in next ch-3 sp, ch 3) 6 times, skip next ch-3 sp], shell in next ch-2 sp; repeat from * 6 more times; repeat between [ ], join.

Rnd 15: Sl st in next st, sl st in next ch–2 sp, beg shell, *[ch 4, sc in next ch-3 sp, ch 4, shell in next shell, ch 3, skip next ch-3 sp, (sc in next ch-3 sp, ch 3) 5 times], shell in next shell; repeat from * 6 more times; repeat between [ ], join.

Rnd 16: Sl st in next st, sl st in next ch-2 sp, beg shell, *[ch 4, (sc in next ch-4 sp, ch 4) 2 times, shell in next shell, ch 3, skip next ch-3 sp, (sc in next ch-3 sp, ch 3) 4 times], shell in next shell; repeat from * 6 more times; repeat between [ ], join.

Rnd 17: Sl st in next st, sl st in next ch-2 sp, beg shell, *[ch 4, (sc in next ch-4 sp, ch 4) 3 times, shell in next shell, ch 3, skip next ch-3 sp, (sc in next ch-3 sp, ch 3) 3 times], shell in next shell; repeat from * 6 more times; repeat between [ ], join.

Rnd 18: Sl st in next st, sl st in next ch-2 sp, beg shell, *[ch 4, (sc in next ch-4 sp, ch 4) 4 times, shell in next shell, ch 3, skip next ch-3 sp, (sc in next ch-3 sp, ch 3) 2 times], shell in next shell; repeat from * 6 more times; repeat between [ ], join.

Rnd 19: Sl st in next st, sl st in next ch-2 sp, beg shell, *[ch 4, (sc in next ch-4 sp, ch 4) 5 times, shell in next shell, ch 3, skip next ch-3 sp, sc in next ch-3 sp, ch 3], shell in next shell; repeat from * 6 more times; repeat between [ ], join.

Rnd 20: Sl st in next st, sl st in next ch-2 sp, beg shell, *[ch 4, (sc in next ch-4 sp, ch 4) 6 times, shell in next shell, skip next 2 ch-3 sps], shell in next shell; repeat from * 6 more times; repeat between [ ], join.

Rnd 21: Sl st in next st, sl st in next ch-2 sp, ch 1, sc in same sp, ch 5, (sc in next ch-4 sp or in next shell, ch 5) around, join with sl st in first sc.

Rnd 22: Sl st in each of next 3 chs, beg shell, ch 3, sc in next ch-5 sp, ch 3, (shell in 3rd ch of next ch-5 sp, ch 3, sc in next ch-5 sp, ch 3) around, join with sl st in top of ch-3.

Rnd 23: Ch 5, dc in next dc, ch 2, (dc, ch 2, dc, ch 2, dc) in next ch-2 sp, (ch 2, dc in next dc) 2 times, skip next 2 ch-3 sps, *(dc in next dc, ch 2) 2 times, (dc, ch 2, dc, ch 2, dc) in next ch-2 sp, (ch 2, dc in next dc) 2 times, skip next 2 ch-3 sps; repeat from * around, join with sl st in 3rd ch of ch-5, fasten off.

Rnd 24: Join pink with sc in first dc, (ch 3, sc in next dc) 6 times, *sc in next dc, (ch 3, sc in next dc) 6 times; repeat from * around, join with sl st in first sc, fasten off.

Connermara Centerpiece

Design by
Dot Drake

Finished Size:
17" across.

Materials:
- ★ 480 yds. white size-10 bedspread cotton
- ★ No. 8 steel crochet hook or size needed to obtain gauge

Gauge:
Rnds 1-7 of Center = 2¾" across.

Skill Level:
Advanced

Center

Rnd 1: Ch 6, sl st in first ch to form ring, ch 1, 20 sc in ring, join with sl st in first sc (20 sc).

Rnd 2: Ch 4, (dc in next st, ch 1) around, join with sl st in 3rd ch of ch-4 (20 dc, 20 ch-1 sps).

Rnd 3: Ch 1, sc in each st and in each ch sp around, join with sl st in first sc (40 sc).

Rnd 4: Ch 1, sc in first st, ch 3, skip next st, (sc in next st, ch 3, skip next st) around, join (20 ch-3 sps).

Rnd 5: For **small petals,** sl st in first ch sp, ch 1, (sc, 3 dc, sc) in same sp and in each ch sp around, join (20 small petals).

Rnd 6: Working behind small petals, sl st in back bar (see page 159) of first sc on first petal, ch 3, (sl st in back bar of first sc on next petal, ch 3) around, join with sl st in first sl st (20 ch-3 sps).

Rnd 7: Sl st in first ch sp, ch 1, (sc, 4 dc, sc) in same sp and in each ch sp around, join with sl st in first sc.

Rnd 8: Repeat rnd 6.

Row 9: Working in rows; for **first large petal,** sl st in first ch sp, ch 1, 3 sc in same sp, ch 3, 3 sc in next ch sp leaving remaining ch sps unworked, turn (6 sc, 1 ch-3 sp).

Row 10: Ch 1, sc in first st, ch 3, skip next st, sc in next st, ch 3, sc in next ch sp, ch 3, sc in next st, ch 2, skip next st, dc in last st, turn (3 ch-3 sps, 1 ch-2 sp).

Rows 11-14: Ch 1, sc in first st, ch 3, skip next ch-2 sp, sc in next ch-3 sp, (ch 3, sc in next ch-3 sp) 2 times, ch 2, dc in last st, turn.

Row 15: Ch 3, skip next ch-2 sp, sc in next ch-3 sp, (ch 3, sc in next ch-3 sp) 2 times, turn (3 ch-3 sps).

Rows 16-17: Ch 3, sc in first ch sp, (ch 3, sc in next ch sp) 2 times, turn. At end of last row, **do not** turn, fasten off.

Row 9: For **second large petal,** join with sc in next unworked ch sp on rnd 8, 2 sc in same sp, ch 3, 3 sc in next ch sp leaving remaining ch sps unworked, turn (6 sc, 1 ch-3 sp).

Rows 10-17: Repeat same rows of first large petal.

Repeat second large petal 8 more times for a total of 10 large petals. At end of last large petal, **do not** fasten off.

Rnd 18: *Working in ends of rows, skip first row, 4 sc in next row, skip next row, 4 sc in each of next 2 rows, skip next row, 4 sc in next row, skip last 2 rows, sc in sp between large petals on rnd 8, skip first row on next large petal, 4 sc in next row, (skip next row, 4 sc in next row) 2 times, 4 sc in next row, skip last 2 rows, 4 sc in each of next 3 ch sps; repeat from * around, join with sl st in first sc (450 sc).

NOTE: For **picot,** ch 3, sl st in 3rd ch from hook.

Rnd 19: *Sl st in each st across to first sc of first 4-sc group on top of next large petal, ch 7, drop lp from hook, insert hook in 4th sc of 3rd 4-sc group on top of last large petal, draw dropped lp through, 3 sc in next ch-7 sp, (picot, 3 sc in same sp) 3 times; repeat from * 9 more times; sl st in each st across first large petal, join with sl st in joining sl st of last rnd, fasten off.

First Shamrock Motif

Rnd 1: *Ch 7, sl st in first ch to form ring; for **petal,** ch 1, (2 sc, 2 hdc, 13 dc, 2 hdc, 2 sc) in ring; repeat from * 2 more times, join with sl st in first sc on first petal (21 sts on each petal).

Rnd 2: Sl st in next 4 sts, ch 1, sc in same st, sc in next 12 sts, skip last 4 sts on this petal, skip first 4 sts on next petal, (sc in next 13 sts, skip last 4 sts on this petal, skip first 4 sts on next petal) 2 times, join with sl st in first sc (39 sc).

Rnd 3: Sl st in next st, ch 1, sc in same st, (ch 5, skip next st, sc in next st) 4 times, ch 5, skip next 3 sts, sc in next st, (ch 5, skip next st, sc in next st) 5 times, ch 5, skip next 3 sts, sc in next st, (ch 5, skip next st, sc in next st) 4 times, skip last 3 sts; to **join,** ch 2, dc in first sc (16 ch-5 sps).

Rnd 4: Ch 1, sc around joining dc, picot, (ch 5,

Continued on next page

Connermara Centerpiece

Continued from page 143

sc in next ch sp, picot) around, join as before.

Rnd 5: Ch 1, sc around joining dc, (ch 5, sc in next ch sp) around, join.

Rnd 6: Ch 1, sc around joining dc, picot, (ch 6, sc in next ch sp, picot) 2 times, ch 3, 4 dc in next ch sp; joining to Center, ch 1, sl st in center picot between any 2 large petals, ch 1, sl st in top of last dc on this Motif, 4 dc in same sp, ch 3, sc in next ch sp, picot, *[(ch 6, sc in next ch sp, picot) 2 times, ch 3, (4 dc, picot, 4 dc) in next ch sp, ch 3], sc in next ch sp, picot; repeat from *; repeat between [ ], join with sl st in first sc, fasten off.

First Rose Motif

Rnd 1: Ch 7, dc in 7th ch from hook, ch 3, (dc in same ch, ch 3) 4 times, join with sl st in 3rd ch of ch-6 (6 dc, 6 ch-3 sps).

Rnd 2: For **petals**, sl st in first ch sp, ch 1, (sc, hdc, 3 dc, hdc, sc) in same sp and in each ch sp around, join with sl st in first sc (6 petals).

Rnd 3: Sl st in back bar of first sc on first petal, ch 4, (sl st in back bar of first sc on next petal, ch 4) around, join with sl st in first sl st (6 ch-4 sps).

Rnd 4: Sl st in first ch sp, ch 1, (sc, hdc, 5 dc, hdc, sc) in same sp and in each ch sp around, join with sl st in first sc.

Rnd 5: Sl st in each of next 2 sts, ch 1, sc in same st, [*(ch 5, skip next st, sc in next st) 2 times, ch 5, skip next 4 sts, sc in next st; repeat from *, ch 5, skip next 3 sts, sc in next st], ch 5, skip next 4 sts, sc in next st; repeat between [ ], skip next 4 sts; to **join**, ch 2, dc in first sc (16 ch-5 sps).

Rnds 6-7: Repeat rnds 4 and 5 of First Shamrock Motif on page 143.

Rnd 8: Ch 1, sc around joining dc, picot, (ch 6, sc in next ch sp, picot) 2 times, ch 3, 4 dc in next ch sp; joining to last Shamrock Motif, ch 1, sl st in corresponding picot between 4-dc groups after last joined picot between 4-dc groups, ch 1, sl st in top of last dc on this Motif, 4 dc in same sp, ch 3, sc in next ch sp, ch 1, sl st in next picot on other Motif, ch 1, sl st in top of last sc on this Motif, (ch 6, sc in next ch sp, picot) 2 times, ch 3, 4 dc in next ch sp; joining to Center, ch 1, sl st in center picot between next large petals, ch 1, sl st in top of last dc on this Motif, 4 dc in same sp, ch 3, *sc in next ch sp, picot, (ch 6, sc in next ch sp, picot) 2 times, ch 3, (4 dc, picot, 4 dc) in next ch sp, ch 3; repeat from * around, join with sl st in first sc, fasten off.

Second Shamrock Motif

Rnds 1-5: Repeat same rnds of First Shamrock Motif.

Rnd 6: Joining to side of last Rose Motif, repeat rnd 8 of First Rose Motif.

Repeat First Rose Motif and Second Shamrock Motif 3 more times for a total of 9 Motifs.

Last Rose Motif

Rnds 1-5: Repeat same rnds of First Rose Motif.

Rnds 6-7: Repeat rnds 4 and 5 of First Shamrock Motif.

Rnd 8: Ch 1, sc around joining dc, picot, (ch 6, sc in next ch sp, picot) 2 times, ch 3, 4 dc in next ch sp; joining to last Shamrock Motif, ch 1, sl st in corresponding picot between 4-dc groups on other Motif, ch 1, sl st in top of last dc on this Motif, 4 dc in same sp, ch 3, sc in next ch sp, ch 1, sl st in next picot on other Motif, ch 1, sl st in top of last sc on this Motif, (ch 6, sc in next ch sp, picot) 2 times, ch 3, 4 dc in next ch sp; joining to Center, ch 1, sl st in center picot between next large petals, ch 1, sl st in top of last dc on this Motif, 4 dc in same sp, ch 3, *sc in next ch sp, (picot, ch 6, sc in next ch sp) 2 times; joining to First Shamrock Motif, ch 1, sl st in corresponding picot on other Motif, ch 1, sl st in top of same sc on this Motif, ch 3, 4 dc in next ch sp, ch 1, sl st in next picot between 4-dc groups on First Shamrock Motif, ch 1, sl st in top of last dc on this Motif, 4 dc in same sp, ch 3, sc in next ch sp, picot, (ch 6, sc in next ch sp, picot) 2 times, ch 3, (4 dc, picot, 4 dc) in next ch sp, ch 3, join with sl st in first sc, fasten off.

Small Shamrock

Rnd 1: For **petals**, (ch 6, sl st in first ch to form ring, ch 1, 13 sc in ring) 3 times, join with sl st in first sc on first petal (13 sc on each petal).

Rnd 2: Working in space between Motifs and Center, sl st in next 4 sts, dc in picot before any joined picot on Center, sl st in each of next 3 sts on this petal, dc in next unworked picot on next Motif, sl st in last 5 sts on this petal, sl st in first 5 sts on next petal, dc in next unworked picot on same Motif, sl st in each of next 3 sts on this petal, dc in next unworked picot on next Motif, sl st in last 5 sts on this petal, sl st in first 5 sts on next petal, dc in next unworked picot on same Motif, sl st in each of next 3 sts on this petal, dc in next unworked picot on Center, sl st in last 5 sts on this petal, join with sl st in joining sl st of last rnd, fasten off.

Repeat Small Shamrock in each sp between Motifs and Center for a total of 10 Shamrocks.

Edging

Rnd 1: Working around outer edge, join with sc in ch-3 sp before any unworked picot between 4-dc groups on top of any Motif, ch 5, *[sc in next picot,

ch 5, (sc in next ch-3 sp or ch-5 sp, ch 5) 4 times, sc in next joining, ch 5], (sc in next ch-3 sp or ch-5 sp, ch 5) 4 times; repeat from * 8 more times; repeat between [ ], (sc in next ch-3 sp or ch-5 sp, ch 5) 3 times, join with sl st in first sc (100 ch-5 sps).

Rnd 2: Sl st in first ch sp, ch 1, 8 sc in same sp, *•ch 5, drop lp from hook, insert hook in 2nd sc of last 8-sc group, draw dropped lp through, (4 sc, picot, 4 sc) in next ch sp, 7 sc in next ch sp on rnd 1, ch 5, drop lp from hook, insert hook in first sc of 7-sc group, draw dropped lp through, 4 sc in next ch-5 sp, ch 5, drop lp from hook, insert hook in 2nd sc after last picot made, draw dropped lp through, 3 sc in next ch sp, (picot, 3 sc in same sp) 3 times, (sc, picot, 3 sc) in 2nd half of next ch sp, sc in same sp on this rnd as last 7-sc group•, 8 sc in next ch sp on rnd 1*; repeat between **, [◊5 sc in each of next 2 ch sps, 4 sc in next ch sp, ch 6, drop lp from hook, insert hook in 5th sc of last 8-sc group, draw dropped lp through, 3 sc in next ch sp, (picot, 3 sc in same sp) 3 times, 4 sc in 2nd half of last worked ch sp on rnd 1, 8 sc in next ch sp◊; repeat between ** 3 more times]; repeat between [ ] 8 more times; repeat between ◊◊; repeat between ••, join, fasten off. ☆

Pineapple Ring

Continued from page 137

from * 10 more times; repeat between [ ], join.

Rnd 21: Sl st in next 6 chs, ch 3, 2 dc in same ch, *[ch 2, (3 dc in next ch-2 sp, ch 2) 3 times, 3 dc in first ch of next ch-6 sp, ch 9], 3 dc in 6th ch of next ch-6 sp; repeat from * 10 more times; repeat between [ ], join with sl st in top of ch-3.

Rnd 22: Sl st in each of next 2 sts, sl st in next ch-2 sp, ch 3, 2 dc in same sp, ch 2, (3 dc in next ch-2 sp, ch 2) 3 times, *[3 dc in first ch of next ch-9 sp, ch 4, sc in same ch-9 sp, ch 4, 3 dc in 9th ch of same ch-9 sp, ch 2], (3 dc in next ch-2 sp, ch 2) 4 times; repeat from * 10 more times; repeat between [ ], join.

Rnd 23: Sl st in each of next 2 sts, sl st in next ch-2 sp, ch 3, 2 dc in same sp, ch 2, (3 dc in next ch-2 sp, ch 2) 3 times, *[3 dc in first ch of next ch-4 sp, ch 2, 3 dc in 4th ch of next ch-4 sp, ch 2], (3 dc in next ch-2 sp, ch 2) 5 times; repeat from * 10 more times; repeat between [ ], 3 dc in last ch-2 sp, ch 2, join.

Rnd 24: Sl st in each of next 2 sts, sl st in next ch-2 sp, ch 3, 2 dc in same sp, ch 2, (3 dc in next ch-2 sp, ch 2) around, join.

Rnd 25: Sl st in each of next 2 sts, sl st in next ch-2 sp, ch 3, 2 dc in same sp, ch 3, (3 dc in next ch-2 sp, ch 3) around, join.

Rnd 26: Sl st in next st, ch 6, dc same st and 2nd ch of next ch-3 sp tog, ch 3, (dc same ch and 2nd dc of next 3-dc group tog, ch 3, dc same dc and 2nd ch of next ch-3 sp tog, ch 3) around, yo, insert hook in same ch, yo, draw lp through, yo, draw through 2 lps on hook, insert hook in 3rd ch of ch-6, yo, draw lp through, yo, draw through all 3 lps on hook.

Rnds 27-28: Sl st in each of next 2 chs, ch 6, (dc same ch and 2nd ch of next ch-3 sp tog, ch 3) around, yo, insert hook in same ch, yo, draw lp through, yo, draw through 2 lps on hook, insert hook in 3rd ch of ch-6, yo, draw lp through, yo, draw through all 3 lps on hook.

Rnd 29: Sl st in first ch sp, ch 1, sc in same sp, ch 6, skip next ch sp, (sc in next ch sp, ch 6, skip next ch sp) around, join with sl st in first sc, fasten off. ☆

Floral Squares

Design by
Dot Drake

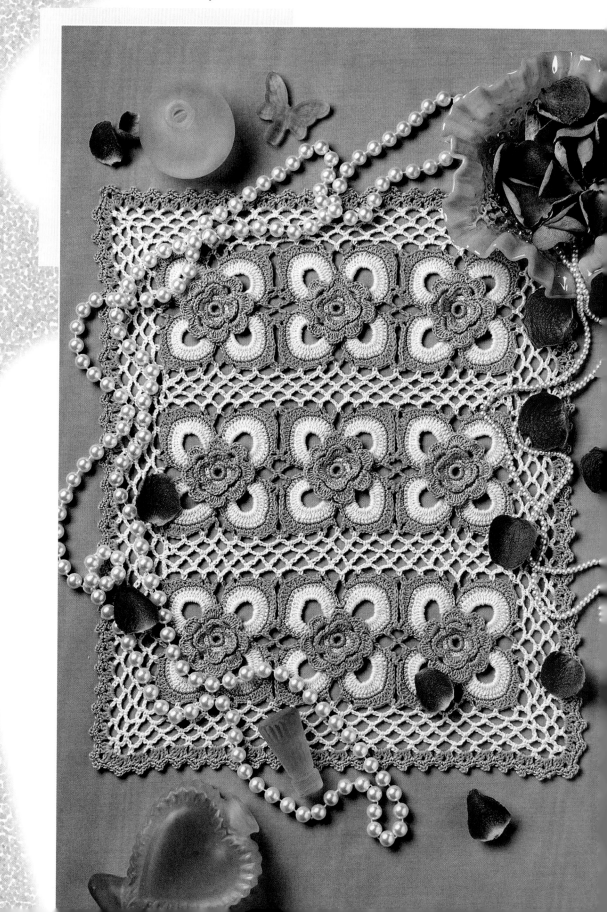

Finished Size:

12½" x 14½".

Materials:

★ 150 yds. each ecru, rose, yellow and green size-10 bedspread cotton

★ No. 8 steel crochet hook or size needed to obtain gauge

Gauge:

Rnds 1-5 of Motif = 1¾" across. Each Motif is 3⅛" square.

Skill Level:

Advanced

First Strip

First Motif

Rnd 1: With rose, ch 7, sl st in first ch to form ring, ch 1, 16 sc in ring, join with sl st in first sc (16 sc).

Rnd 2: Ch 1, sc in first st, ch 5, skip next 3 sts, (sc in next st, ch 5, skip next 3 sts) around, join (4 ch-5 sps).

Rnd 3: For **petals**, sl st in first ch sp, ch 1, (sc, hdc, 5 dc, hdc, sc) in same sp and in each ch sp around, join (4 petals).

Rnd 4: Working behind petals, ch 1, sl st in back bar of first dc (see illustration) on first petal, ch 5, sl st in back bar of 5th dc on same petal, ch 5, (sl st in back bar of first dc on next petal, ch 5, sl st in back bar of 5th dc on same petal, ch 5) around, join with sl st in first sl st (8 ch-5 sps).

Rnd 5: Repeat rnd 3, fasten off (8 petals).

BACK BAR

Rnd 6: Working behind petals, join yellow with sl st in first sl st on rnd 4, *[ch 17, sl st in 17th ch from hook to form ring, (sl st, ch 1, 2 sc, 3 hdc, 26 dc, 3 hdc, 2 sc) in ring, sc in each of next 3 skipped sts on rnd 1], sl st in next sl st on rnd 4; repeat from * 2 more times; repeat between [ ], join with sl st in first sl st, fasten off (156 sts not counting sl sts).

Rnd 7: Join rose with sc in 6th st, sc in next 25 sts, ch 2, skip next 13 sts, (sc in next 26 sts, ch 2, skip next 13 sts) around, join, fasten off (104 sts, 4 ch-2 sps).

Rnd 8: Join green with sc in 4th st, sc in each of next 2 sts, (*ch 4, sc in each of next 3 sts, hdc in next st, dc in each of next 2 sts, 2 dc in next st, ch 4, sl st in top of last st made, 2 dc in next st, dc in each of next 2 sts, hdc in next st, sc in each of next 3 sts, ch 4, sc in each of next 3 sts, ch 5, skip next 3 sts, next ch-2 sp and next 3 sts*, sc in each of next 3 sts) 3 times; repeat between **, join, fasten off.

Second Motif

Rnds 1-7: Repeat same rnds of First Motif.

Rnd 8: Join green with sc in 4th st, sc in each of next 2 sts, ch 4, sc in each of next 3 sts, hdc in next st, dc in each of next 2 sts, 2 dc in next st; joining to side of last Motif made, ch 2, sc in corresponding ch-4 sp on other Motif, ch 2, sl st in top of last st made on this Motif, 2 dc in next st, dc in each of next 2 sts, hdc in next st, sc in each of next 3 sts, ch 2, sc in next ch-4 sp on other Motif, ch 2, sc in each of next 3 sts on this Motif, ch 2, sc in next ch-5 sp on other Motif, ch 2, skip next 3 sts, next ch-2 sp and next 3 sts on this Motif, sc in each of next 3 sts, ch 2, sc in next ch-4 sp on other Motif, ch 2, sc in each of next 3 sts on this Motif, hdc in next st, dc in each of next 2 sts, 2 dc in next st, ch 2, sc in next ch-4 sp on other Motif, ch 2, sl st in top of last st made on this Motif, 2 dc in next st, dc in each of next 2 sts, hdc in next st, sc in each of next 3 sts, ch 4, sc in each of next 3 sts, ch 5, skip next 3 sts, next ch-2 sp and next 3 sts, (sc in each of next 3 sts, ch 4, sc in each of next 3 sts, hdc in next st, dc in each of next 2 sts, 2 dc in next st, ch 4, sl st in top of last st made, 2 dc in next st, dc in each of next 2 sts, hdc in next st, sc in each of next 3 sts, ch 4, sc in each of next 3 sts, ch 5, skip next 3 sts, next ch-2 sp and next 3 sts) around, join, fasten off.

Repeat Second Motif one more time for a total of 3 Motifs.

Edging

Row 1: Working across one long edge, join ecru with sc in center ch-4 sp on corner petal before one long edge, (*ch 5, skip next 4 sts, sc in next st, ch 5, sc in next ch-4 sp, ch 5, sc in next ch-5 sp, ch 5, sc in next ch-4 sp, ch 5, skip next 3 sts, sc in next st, ch 5*, sc in next joining sc between Motifs) 2 times; repeat between **, sc in last ch-4 sp, turn (18 ch-5 sps).

Row 2: Ch 5, sc in first ch sp, (ch 5, sc in next ch sp) across, ch 2, dc in last st, fasten off (18 ch-5 sps, 1 ch-2 sp).

Second Strip

First & Second Motifs

Work same as First Strip First and Second Motifs.

Edging on First Side

Row 1: Repeat same row of First Strip Edging.

Row 2: Joining to row 2 of Edging on First Strip, ch 2, sc in first dc on other Strip, ch 2, sc in first ch sp on this Strip, (ch 2, sc in next ch-5 sp on other Strip, ch 2, sc in next ch sp on this Strip) across, ch 2, sc in last ch-5 sp on other Motif, dc in last st on this Strip, fasten off.

Continued on next page

Floral Squares

Continued from page 147

Edging on Second Side

Working across other long edge, work same as First Strip Edging on page 147.

Third Strip

First & Second Motifs

Work same as First Strip First and Second Motifs on page 147.

Edging

Row 1: Repeat same row of First Strip Edging.

Row 2: Joining to row 2 of unjoined Edging on Second Strip, ch 2, sc in first dc on other Strip, ch 2, sc in first ch sp on this Strip, (ch 2, sc in next ch-5 sp on other Strip, ch 2, sc in next ch sp on this Strip) across, ch 2, sc in last ch-5 sp on other Motif, dc in last st on this Strip, fasten off.

Border

Rnd 1: Working around entire outer edge, join ecru with sl st in center ch sp on corner petal before one short end, ch 8, dc in same sp, ◊ch 5, skip next 3 sts, sc in next st, ch 5, (sc in next ch sp, ch 5) 3 times, skip next 4 sts, sc in next st, ch 5, *sc in next joining sc between Motifs, ch 5, skip next 3 sts, sc in next st, ch 5, (sc in next ch sp, ch 5) 3 times, skip next 4 sts, sc in next st, ch 5; repeat from *, (dc, ch 5, dc) in next corner ch sp, ch 5, skip next 3 sts, sc in next st, ch 5, (sc in next ch sp, ch 5) 3 times, skip next 4 sts, sc in next st, [ch 5, sc in next ch sp, ch 5, sc in next joining sc, ch 5, sc in next ch sp, ch 5, skip next 3 sts, sc in next st, ch 5, (sc in next ch sp, ch 5) 3 times, skip next 4 sts, sc in next st]; repeat between [ ]◊, ch 5, (dc, ch 5, dc) in next corner ch sp; repeat between ◊◊; to **join**, ch 2, dc in 3rd ch of ch-8 (84 ch-5 sps).

Rnd 2: Ch 1, sc around joining dc, ch 5, (sc, ch 5, sc) in next corner ch sp, *ch 5, (sc in next ch sp, ch 5) across to next corner ch sp, (sc, ch 5, sc) in next corner ch sp; repeat from * 2 more times, (ch 5, sc in next ch sp) across; to **join**, ch 2, dc in first sc.

Rnd 3: Ch 1, sc around joining dc, ch 5, sc in next ch sp, ch 5, (dc, ch 5, dc) in next corner ch sp, *ch 5, (sc in next ch sp, ch 5) across to next corner ch sp, (dc, ch 5, dc) in next corner ch sp; repeat from * 2 more times, (ch 5, sc in next ch sp) across, join as before.

Rnd 4: Ch 1, sc around joining dc, ch 5, (sc in next ch sp, ch 5) 2 times, (sc, ch 5, sc) in next corner ch sp, *ch 5, (sc in next ch sp, ch 5) across to next corner ch sp, (sc, ch 5, sc) in next corner ch sp; repeat from * 2 more times, (ch 5, sc in next ch sp) across, join.

Rnd 5: Ch 1, sc around joining dc, *ch 5, (sc in next ch sp, ch 5) across to next corner ch sp, (sc, ch 5, sc) in next corner ch sp; repeat from * 3 more times, ch 5, (sc in next ch sp, ch 5) across, join with sl st in first sc, fasten off.

Rnd 6: Join green with sl st in any corner ch sp, ch 3, (2 dc, ch 3, 3 dc) in same sp, (2 dc, ch 2, 2 dc) in each ch sp around with (3 dc, ch 3, 3 dc) in each corner ch sp, join with sl st in top of ch-3, fasten off.

Rnd 7: Join rose with sc in any corner ch-3 sp, [◊(ch 3, sc in same sp) 2 times, ch 1, sc in sp between next 3-dc group and next 2-dc group, ch 1, (sc, ch 3, sc) in next ch-2 sp, *ch 1, sc in sp between next two 2-dc groups, ch 1, (sc, ch 3, sc) in next ch-2 sp; repeat from * across to next corner ch-3 sp, ch 1, sc in sp between next 2-dc group and next 3-dc group, ch 1◊, sc in next ch-3 sp]; repeat between [ ] 2 more times; repeat between ◊◊, join with sl st in first sc, fasten off.✿

Rosslare Doily

Design by
Dot Drake

Rosslare Doily

Continued from page 149

Finished Size:

12½" across.

Materials:

★ Size-10 bedspread cotton:
180 yds. white
90 yds. aqua
★ No. 8 steel crochet hook or size needed to obtain gauge

Gauge:

Rnds 1-5 of Center = 2⅛" across. Each Flower is 2" across.

Skill Level:

Advanced

Center

Rnd 1: With white, ch 10, sl st in first ch to form ring, ch 1, 24 sc in ring, join with sl st in first sc (24 sc).

Rnd 2: Working this rnd in **front lps** only, ch 1, sc in first st, ch 3, skip next st, (sc in next st, ch 3, skip next st) around, join (12 ch-3 sps).

Rnd 3: For **petals,** sl st in first ch sp, ch 1, (sc, hdc, 2 dc, hdc, sc) in same sp and in each ch sp around, join (12 petals).

Rnd 4: Sl st in back bar (see page 159) of first sc on first petal, ch 4, (sl st in back bar of first sc on next petal, ch 4) around, join with sl st in first sl st (12 ch-4 sps).

Rnd 5: Sl st in first ch sp, ch 1, (sc, hdc, 3 dc, hdc, sc) in same sp and in each ch sp around, join with sl st in first sc.

Rnd 6: Ch 2; working behind petals, in **back lps** of rnd 1, sl st in first st, ch 3, dc in each st around, join with sl st in top of ch-3 (24 dc).

Rnd 7: Ch 1, sc in first st, ch 16, (sc in each of next 2 sts, ch 16) around to last st, sc in last st, join with sl st in first sc (12 ch-16 lps).

Rnd 8: Sl st in first ch lp, ch 1, (6 sc, hdc, 17 dc, hdc, 6 sc) in same lp and in each ch lp around, join, fasten off (31 sts on each ch lp).

Rnd 9: Join white with sc in 10th st, *[ch 2, skip next st, (dc in next st, ch 2, skip next st) 2 times, (dc, ch 3, dc) in next st, ch 2, skip next st, (dc in next st, ch 2, skip next st) 2 times, sc in next st, skip next 18 sts], sc in next st; repeat from * 10 more times; repeat between [ ], join (96 sts, 72 ch-2 sps, 12 ch-3 sps).

NOTE: For **picot,** ch 3, sl st in 3rd ch from hook.

Rnd 10: Sl st in next ch-2 sp, ch 1, sc in same sp, *[sc in next st, (2 sc in next ch-2 sp, sc in next st) 2 times, (2 sc, picot, 2 sc) in next ch-3 sp, sc in next st, (2 sc in next ch-2 sp, sc in next st) 2 times, sc in next ch-2 sp, skip next 2 sts], sc in next ch-2 sp; repeat from * 10 more times; repeat between [ ], join, fasten off (240 sc, 12 picots).

Rnd 11: Join aqua with sl st in 6th st after any picot, ch 3, tr in 6th st before next picot, (ch 5, dc in 5th ch from hook) 3 times, *tr 6th st after next picot and 5th st before next picot tog, (ch 5, dc in 5th ch from hook) 3 times; repeat from * around, skip first ch-3, join with sl st in next tr (36 ch-4 sps).

Rnd 12: Sl st in first ch sp, ch 1, sc in same sp, picot, (ch 5, sc in next ch sp, picot) around; to **join,** ch 2, dc in first sc.

Rnds 13-14: Ch 1, sc around joining dc, picot, (ch 5, sc in next ch sp, picot) around, join as before. At end of last rnd, **do not** fasten off. Set aside.

First Flower

Rnd 1: With white, ch 5, sl st in first ch to form ring, ch 1, 12 sc in ring, join with sl st in first sc (12 sc).

Rnd 2: Ch 1, sc in first st, ch 4, skip next st, (sc in next st, ch 4, skip next st) around, join (6 ch-4 sps).

Rnd 3: For **petals,** sl st in first ch sp, ch 1, (sc, hdc, 5 dc, hdc, sc) in same sp and in each ch sp around, join (6 petals).

Rnd 4: Sl st in back bar of first sc on first petal, ch 5, (sl st in back bar of first sc on next petal, ch 5) around, join with sl st in first sl st (6 ch-5 sps).

Rnd 5: Sl st in first ch sp, ch 1, (sc, hdc, 4 dc) in same sp; joining to last rnd of Center, ch 1, sl st in first ch sp on Center, ch 1, sl st in top of last dc made, (3 dc, hdc, sc) in same sp on this Flower, (sc, hdc, 4 dc) in next ch sp, ch 1, sl st in next ch sp on Center, ch 1, sl st in top of last dc made, (3 dc, hdc, sc) in same sp on this Flower, (sc, hdc, 4 dc, picot, 3 dc, hdc, sc) in each ch sp around, join with sl st in first sc, fasten off.

Next Flower

Rnds 1-4: Repeat same rnds of First Flower.

Rnd 5: Sl st in first ch sp, ch 1, (sc, hdc, 4 dc) in same sp, joining to side of last Flower, ch 1, sl st in picot on first petal after joined petals, ch 1, sl st in top of last dc made, (3 dc, hdc, sc) in same sp on this Flower, (sc, hdc, 4 dc) in next ch sp; joining to last rnd of Center, skip next unworked ch sp, *ch 1, sl st in next ch sp on Center, ch 1, sl st in top of last dc made, (3 dc, hdc, sc) in same sp on this Flower*, (sc, hdc, 4 dc) in next ch sp; repeat between **, (sc, hdc, 4 dc, picot, 3 dc, hdc, sc) in each ch sp around, join with sl st in first sc, fasten off.

Repeat Next Flower 9 more times.

Last Flower

Rnds 1-4: Repeat same rnds of First Flower.

Rnd 5: Sl st in first ch sp, ch 1, (sc, hdc, 4 dc) in

Continued on next page

same sp, joining to side of last Flower, ch 1, sl st in picot of first petal after joined petal, ch 1, sl st in top of last dc made, (3 dc, hdc, sc) in same sp on this Flower, (sc, hdc, 4 dc) in next ch sp; joining to last rnd of Center, skip next unworked ch sp, *ch 1, sl st in next ch sp on Center, ch 1, sl st in top of last dc made, (3 dc, hdc, sc) in same sp on this Flower*, (sc, hdc, 4 dc) in next ch sp; repeat between **, (sc, hdc, 4 dc) in next ch sp, joining to side of First Flower, ch 1, sl st in picot on petal before joined petals, ch 1, sl st in top of last dc made, (3 dc, hdc, sc) in same sp on this Flower, (sc, hdc, 4 dc, picot, 3 dc, hdc, sc) in each ch sp around, join with sl st in first sc, fasten off.

Remainder of Center

Rnds 15-17: Working behind Flowers, ch 1, sc around joining dc, picot, (ch 6, sc in next ch sp, picot) around; to **join,** ch 3, dc in first sc.

Rnds 18-20: Ch 1, sc around joining dc, picot, (ch 7, sc in next ch sp, picot) around; to **join,** ch 4, dc in first sc.

Rnd 21: Ch 1, sc around joining dc, picot, ch 4, sc in first unworked picot on adjoining Flower, ch 4, sc in next ch sp on Center, picot, ch 4, sc in next unworked picot on Flower, ch 4, sc in next ch sp on Flower, picot, (ch 7, sc in next ch sp, picot, ch 4, sc in first unworked picot on next Flower, ch 4, sc in

next ch sp on Center, picot, ch 4, sc in next unworked picot on Flower, ch 4, sc in next ch sp on Center, picot) around; to **join,** ch 3, tr in first sc.

Rnd 22: Ch 7, sl st in 3rd ch from hook, *[(ch 2, tr around joining tr, picot) 3 times, ch 5, (sc in next ch-4 sp, picot, ch 5) 4 times], tr in 4th ch of next ch-7 sp, picot; repeat from * 10 more times; repeat between [ ], join with sl st in 4th ch of ch-7, fasten off (60 ch-5 sps, 36 ch-2 sps).

Block if necessary.

Edging

Rnd 1: Join white with sc in sp between 2 unworked petals on any Flower, ch 20, (sc in sp between 2 unworked petals on next Flower, ch 20) around, join with sl st in first sc (12 ch-20 sps).

Rnd 2: Sl st in first ch-20 sp, ch 1, 34 sc in same sp, *[turn, sc in each of first 2 sc, ch 2, skip next 2 sts, (dc in next st, ch 2, skip next 2 sts) 9 times, sc in each of next 2 sts, sl st in last st, **turn,** sl st in each of next 2 sts, 2 sc in next ch-2 sp, (sc, hdc, dc, hdc, sc) in next 5 ch-2 sps, **turn,** ch 8, sl st in sp between 10th and 11th sts, **turn,** (7 sc, picot, 7 sc) in next ch-8 sp, (sc, hdc, dc, hdc, sc) in each of next 3 ch-2 sps, 2 sc in next ch-2 sp, sl st in each of last 2 sts], 34 sc in next ch-20 sp; repeat from * 10 more times; repeat between [ ], join with sl st in first sc, fasten off. ☆

"Follow Your Heart" Doily

Design by
Karen Robison

Finished Size:
18½" across.

Materials:
★ Size-10 bedspread cotton — 275 yds. white; No. 10 steel crochet hook or size needed to obtain gauge.

Gauge:
Rnds 1-5 = 3¾" across.

NOTE: For cluster (cl), yo, insert hook in next ch, st or sp, yo, draw lp through, yo, draw through 2 lps on hook, (yo, insert hook in same sp, yo, draw lp through, yo, draw through 2 lps on hook) 2 times, yo, draw through all 4 lps on hook.

For beginning cluster (beg cl), ch 2, (insert hook in same st or sp, yo, draw lp through, yo, draw through 2 lps on hook) 2 times, yo, draw through all 3 lps on hook.

Skill Level:
Average

Doily

Rnd 1: Ch 4, yo, insert hook in 4th ch from hook, yo, draw lp through, yo, draw through 2 lps on hook, yo, insert hook in same ch, yo, draw lp through, yo, draw through 2 lps on hook, yo, draw through all 3 lps on hook (first cl made), ch 2, (cl in same ch, ch 2) 5 times, join with sl st in top of first cl (6 cls, 6 ch-2 sps).

Rnd 2: Sl st in next ch, beg cl, ch 3, cl in next ch, ch 3, skip next cl, *(cl in next ch, ch 3) 2 times, skip next cl; repeat from * around, join with sl st in top of beg cl (12 cls, 12 ch-3 sps).

Rnd 3: Ch 1, sc in first st, ch 1, (sc, ch 5, sc) in 2nd ch of next ch-3 sp, ch 1, *sc in next cl, ch 1, (sc, ch 5, sc) in 2nd ch of next ch-3 sp, ch 1; repeat from * around, join with sl st in first sc, fasten off.

Rnd 4: Join with sc in 3rd ch of first ch-5 sp, ch 5, (sc in 3rd ch of next ch-5 sp, ch 5) around, join.

Rnd 5: Ch 1, sc in first st, ch 3, (sc, ch 5, sc) in 3rd ch of next ch-5 sp, ch 3, *sc in next st, ch 3, (sc, ch 5, sc) in 3rd ch of next ch-5 sp, ch 3; repeat from * around, join, fasten off (24 ch-3 sps, 12 ch-5 sps).

Rnd 6: Join with sl st in first ch-5 sp, beg cl, ch 1, cl in same sp, ch 3, 9 dc in next ch-5 sp, ch 3, *(cl, ch 1, cl) in next ch-5 sp, ch 3, 9 dc in next ch-5 sp, ch 3; repeat from * around, join with sl st in top of beg cl (54 dc, 12 cls, 12 ch-3 sps, 6 ch-1 sps).

Rnd 7: Sl st in first ch-1 sp, beg cl, ch 2, cl in same sp, *[ch 3, skip next ch-3 sp, cl in next st, (ch 1, cl in next st) 8 times, ch 3, skip next ch-3 sp], (cl, ch 2, cl) in next ch-1 sp; repeat from * 4 more times; repeat between [ ], join (66 ch sps).

Rnd 8: Sl st in first ch-2 sp, beg cl, ch 3, cl in same sp, *[ch 3, skip next ch-3 sp, cl in next ch-1 sp, (ch 1, cl in next ch-1 sp) 7 times, ch 3, skip next ch-3 sp], (cl, ch 3, cl) in next ch-2 sp; repeat from * 4 more times; repeat between [ ], join (60).

Rnd 9: Sl st in first ch-3 sp, beg cl, (ch 3, cl in same sp) 2 times, *[ch 3, skip next ch-3 sp, cl in next ch-1 sp, (ch 1, cl in next ch-1 sp) 6 times, ch 3, skip next ch-3 sp], (cl, ch 3, cl, ch 3, cl) in next ch-3 sp; repeat from * 4 more times; repeat between [ ], join.

Rnd 10: Sl st in first ch-3 sp, beg cl, ch 3, cl in same sp, *[ch 5, (cl, ch 3, cl) in next ch-3 sp, ch 3, skip next ch-3 sp, cl in next ch-1 sp, (ch 1, cl in next ch-1 sp) 5 times, ch 3, skip next ch-3 sp], (cl, ch 3, cl) in next ch-3 sp; repeat from * 4 more times; repeat between [ ], join.

Rnd 11: Sl st in first ch-3 sp, beg cl, ch 3, cl in same sp, *[ch 5, dc in 3rd ch of next ch-5 sp, ch 5, (cl, ch 3, cl) in next ch-3 sp, ch 3, skip next ch-3 sp, cl in next ch-1 sp, (ch 1, cl in next ch-1 sp) 4 times, ch 3, skip next ch-3 sp], (cl, ch 3, cl) in next ch-3 sp; repeat from * 4 more times; repeat between [ ], join.

Rnd 12: Sl st in first ch-3 sp, beg cl, ch 3, cl in same sp, *[ch 5, (dc in 3rd ch of ch-5, ch 5) 2 times, (cl, ch 3, cl) in next ch-3 sp, ch 3, skip next ch-3 sp, cl in next ch-1 sp, (ch 1, cl in next ch-1 sp) 3 times, ch 3, skip next ch-3 sp], (cl, ch 3, cl) in next ch-3 sp; repeat from * 4 more times; repeat between [ ], join.

Rnd 13: Sl st in first ch-3 sp, beg cl, ch 3, cl in same sp, *[ch 5, dc in 3rd ch of next ch-5 sp, ch 5, cl in 3rd ch of next ch-5 sp, ch 5, dc in 3rd ch of next ch-5 sp, ch 5, (cl, ch 3, cl) in next ch-3 sp, ch 3, skip next ch-3 sp, cl in next ch-1 sp, (ch 1, cl in next ch-1 sp) 2 times, ch 3, skip next ch-3 sp], (cl, ch 3, cl) in next ch-3 sp; repeat from * 4 more times; repeat between [ ], join.

Rnd 14: Sl st in first ch-3 sp, beg cl, ch 3, cl in same sp, *[ch 5, dc in 3rd ch of next ch-5 sp, ch 5, cl in 5th ch of next ch-5 sp, ch 1, cl in next cl, ch 1, cl in first ch of next ch-5 sp, ch 5, dc in 3rd ch of next ch-5 sp, ch 5, (cl, ch 3, cl) in next ch-3 sp, ch 3, skip next ch-3 sp, cl in next ch-1 sp, ch 1, cl in next ch-1 sp, ch 3, skip next ch-3 sp], (cl, ch 3, cl) in next ch-3 sp; repeat from * 4 more times; repeat between [ ], join (66).

Rnd 15: Sl st in first ch-3 sp, beg cl, ch 3, cl in same sp, *[ch 5, dc in 3rd ch of next ch-5 sp, ch 5, cl in 5th ch of next ch-5 sp, ch 1, cl in next ch-1 sp, ch 1, cl in next cl, ch 1, cl in next ch-1 sp, ch 1, cl in first ch of next ch-5 sp, ch 5, dc in 3rd ch of next ch-5 sp, ch 5, (cl, ch 3, cl) in next ch-3 sp, ch 3, skip next ch-3 sp, cl in next ch-1 sp, ch 3, skip next ch-3 sp], (cl, ch 3, cl) in next ch-3 sp; repeat from * 4 more times; repeat between [ ], join (72).

Rnd 16: Sl st in first ch-3 sp, beg cl, ch 3, cl in same sp, *[(ch 5, dc in 3rd ch of next ch-5 sp) 2 times, ch 3, cl in 5th ch of same ch-5 sp, ch 1, (cl in

Continued on page 155

Flower Coaster Doily

Design by
Judy Teague Treece

Finished Size:
5¼" across.

Materials:
★Size-10 bedspread cotton — 40 yds. each red and white; No. 6 steel crochet hook or size needed to obtain gauge.

Gauge:
Rnds 1-4 = 2½" across.

Skill Level:
Average

Coaster/Doily

Rnd 1: With red, ch 5, sl st in first ch to form ring, ch 1, 6 sc in ring, join with sl st in first sc (6 sc).

Rnd 2: Ch 5, (tr in same st, ch 1) 2 times, (tr, ch 1) 3 times in each st around, join with sl st in 4th ch of ch-5 (18 tr, 18 ch sps).

Rnd 3: Sl st in first ch sp, ch 1, sc in same sp, ch 4, (sc in next ch sp, ch 4) around, join with sl st in first sc (18 sc, 18 ch sps).

Rnd 4: Sl st in first ch sp, ch 5, (tr, ch 2, tr, ch 1, tr) in same sp, ch 2, sc in next ch sp, ch 2, *(tr, ch 1, tr, ch 2, tr, ch 1, tr) in next ch sp, ch 2, sc in next ch sp, ch 2; repeat from * around, join with

sl st in 4th ch of ch-5, fasten off (27 ch-2 sps, 18 ch-1 sps).

Rnd 5: Join white with sl st in first ch-2 sp, ch 5, (tr, ch 1, tr, ch 2, tr, ch 1, tr, ch 1, tr) in same sp, ch 2, skip next 2 ch-2 sps, *(tr, ch 1, tr, ch 1, tr, ch 2, tr, ch 1, tr, ch 1, tr) in next ch-2 sp, ch 2, skip next 2 ch-2 sps; repeat from * around, join (18 ch-2 sps).

Rnd 6: Sl st in next ch-1 sp, (sl st in next st, sl st in next ch sp) 2 times, ch 5, tr in same sp, (ch 1, tr in same sp) 3 times, ch 3, sc in next ch-2 sp, ch 3, *tr in next ch-2 sp, (ch 1, tr in same sp) 4 times, ch 3, sc in next ch-2 sp, ch 3; repeat from * around, join, fasten off.

Rnd 7: Join red with sl st in center st of any 5-tr group, ch 5, (tr, ch 1, tr, ch 2, tr, ch 1, tr, ch 1, tr) in same sp, ch 8, skip next 2 ch-3 sps, *(tr, ch 1, tr, ch 1, tr, ch 2, tr, ch 1, tr, ch 1, tr) in center st of next 5-tr group, ch 8, skip next 2 ch-3 sps; repeat from * around, join.

Rnd 8: Sl st in first ch-1 sp, ch 1, (sc, ch 2, sc) in same sp, [◊*ch 1, (sc, ch 2, sc) in next ch sp; repeat from * 3 more times, ch 4; working over next ch-8 sp, (sc, ch 2, sc) in next ch-3 sp on rnd before last, ch 4; working around same ch-8 sp, (sc, ch 2, sc) in next ch-3 sp on rnd before last, ch 4◊, (sc, ch 2, sc) in next ch-1 sp]; repeat between [ ] 7 more times; repeat between ◊◊, join with sl st in first sc, fasten off.☆

"Follow Your Heart" Doily

Continued from page 153

next ch-1 sp, ch 1) 2 times, cl in next cl, ch 1, (cl in next ch-1 sp, ch 1) 2 times, cl in first ch of next ch-5 sp, ch 3, dc in 3rd ch of same ch-5 sp, ch 5, dc in 3rd ch of next ch-5 sp, ch 5, (cl, ch 3, cl) in next ch-3 sp, ch 3, skip next ch-3 sp, sc in next cl, ch 3, skip next ch-3 sp], (cl, ch 3, cl) in next ch-3 sp; repeat from * 4 more times; repeat between [ ], join (96).

Rnd 17: Sl st in first ch-3 sp, beg cl, ch 3, cl in same sp, *[ch 5, (dc in 3rd ch of next ch-5 sp, ch 5) 2 times, cl in 3rd ch of next ch-3 sp, (ch 1, cl in next ch-1 sp) 3 times, ch 3, (cl in next ch-1 sp, ch 1) 3 times, cl in first ch of next ch-3 sp, ch 5, (dc in 3rd ch of next ch-5 sp, ch 5) 2 times (cl, ch 3, cl) in next ch-3 sp, skip next 2 ch-3 sps], (cl, ch 3, cl) in next ch-3 sp; repeat from * 4 more times; repeat between [ ], join (36 ch-5 sps, 36 ch-1 sps, 18 ch-3 sps).

Rnd 18: Sl st in first ch-3 sp, ch 8, *[(dc in 3rd ch of next ch-5 sp, ch 5) 3 times, cl in next 4 cls skipping ch-1 sps in between, ch 3, dc in 3rd ch of next ch-3 sp, ch 3, cl in next 4 cls skipping ch-1 sps in between, ch 5, (dc in 3rd ch of next ch-5 sp, ch 5) 3 times], (dc in next ch-3 sp, ch 5) 2 times; repeat from * 4 more times; repeat between [ ], dc in last

ch-3 sp; to join, ch 2, dc in 3rd ch of ch-8 (54 ch-5 sps, 12 ch-3 sps).

Rnd 19: Ch 8, (dc in 3rd ch of next ch-5 sp, ch 5) 4 times; [◊for decrease (dec), *yo, insert hook in next cl, yo, draw lp through, yo, draw through 2 lps on hook, yo, insert hook in same st, yo, draw lp through, yo, draw through 2 lps on hook; repeat from * 3 more times, yo, draw through all 9 lps on hook, ch 3, (dc in 2nd ch of next ch-3 sp, ch 3) 2 times, dec◊, ch 5, (dc in 3rd ch of next ch-5 sp, ch 5) 9 times]; repeat between [ ] 4 more times; repeat between ◊◊, (ch 5, dc in 3rd ch of next ch-5 sp) 4 times, join as before (78 ch sps).

Rnd 20: Ch 8, dc in 3rd ch of next ch-5 sp, (ch 5, dc in 3rd ch of next ch-5 sp or in 2nd ch of next ch-3 sp) around, join.

Rnd 21: Ch 8, (dc in 3rd ch of next ch-5 sp, ch 5) around, join with sl st in 3rd ch of ch-8.

Rnd 22: Beg cl, ch 3, cl in same st, ch 1, *(cl, ch 3, cl) in next st, ch 1; repeat from * around, join with sl st in top of beg cl.

Rnd 23: Sl st in first ch-3 sp, ch 1, (2 sc, ch 3, 2 sc) in same sp, ch 2, sl st in next ch-1 sp, ch 2, *(2 sc, ch 3, 2 sc) in next ch-3 sp, ch 2, sl st in next ch-1 sp, ch 2; repeat from * around, join with sl st in first sc, fasten off.☆

General Instructions

Yarn & Hooks

Always use the weight of yarn specified in the pattern so you can be assured of achieving the proper gauge. It is best to purchase extra of each color needed to allow for differences in tension and dyes.

The hook size stated in the pattern is to be used as a guide. Always work a swatch of the stitch pattern with the suggested hook size. If you find your gauge is smaller or larger than what is specified, choose a different size hook.

Gauge

Gauge is measured by counting the number of rows or stitches per inch. Each of the patterns featured in this book will have a gauge listed. Gauge for some small motifs or flowers is given as an overall measurement. Proper gauge must be attained for the project to come out the size stated, and to prevent ruffling and puckering.

Make a swatch in the stitch indicated in the gauge section of the instructions. Lay the swatch flat and measure the stitches. If you have more stitches per inch than specified in the pattern, your gauge is too tight and you need a larger hook. Fewer stitches per inch indicates a gauge that is too loose. In this case, choose a smaller hook size. Next, check the number of rows. If necessary, adjust your row gauge slightly by pulling the loops down a little tighter on your hook, or by pulling the loops up slightly to extend them.

Once you've attained the proper gauge, you're ready to start your project. Remember to check your gauge periodically to avoid problems later.

Pattern Repeat Symbols

Written crochet instructions typically include symbols such as parentheses, asterisks and brackets. In some patterns a diamond or bullet (dot) may be added.

( ) Parentheses enclose instructions which are to be worked again later or the number of times indicated after the parentheses. For example, "(2 dc in next st, skip next st) 5 times" means to follow the instructions within the parentheses a total of five times. If no number appears after the parentheses, you will be instructed when to repeat further into the pattern. Parentheses may also be used to enclose a group of stitches which should be worked in one space or stitch. For example, "(2 dc, ch 2, 2 dc) in next st" means to work all the stitches within the parentheses in the next stitch.

* Asterisks may be used alone or in pairs, usually in combination with parentheses. If used in pairs, the instructions enclosed within asterisks will be followed by instructions for repeating. These repeat instructions may appear later in the pattern or immediately after the last asterisk. For example, "*Dc in next 4 sts, (2 dc, ch 2, 2 dc) in corner sp*, dc in next 4 sts; repeat between ** 2 more times" means to work through the instructions up to the word "repeat," then repeat only the instructions that are enclosed within the asterisks twice.

If used alone an asterisk marks the beginning of instructions which are to be repeated. Work through the instruc-

tions from the beginning, then repeat only the portion after the * up to the word "repeat"; then follow any remaining instructions. If a number of times is given, work through the instructions one time, repeat the number of times stated, then follow the remainder of the instructions.

[ ] Brackets, ◊ diamonds and • bullets are used in the same manner as asterisks. Follow the specific instructions given when repeating.

Finishing

Patterns that require assembly will suggest a tapestry needle in the materials. This should be a #16, #18 or #26 blunt-tipped tapestry needle. When stitching pieces together, be careful to keep the seams flat so pieces do not pucker.

Hiding loose ends is never a fun task, but if done correctly, may mean the difference between an item looking great for years or one that quickly shows signs of wear. Always leave 6-8" of yarn when beginning or ending. Thread the loose end into your tapestry needle and carefully weave through the back of several stitches. Then, weave in the opposite direction, going through different strands. Gently pull the end and clip, allowing the end to pull up under the stitches.

If your project needs blocking, a light steam pressing works well. Lay your project on a large table or on the floor, depending on the size, shaping and smoothing by hand as much as possible. Adjust your steam iron to the permanent press setting, then hold slightly above the stitches, allowing the steam to penetrate the thread. Do not rest the iron on the item. Gently pull and smooth the stitches into shape, spray lightly with starch and allow to dry completely.

Stiffening

There are many liquid products on the market made specifically for stiffening doilies and other soft items. For best results, carefully read the manufacturer's instructions on the product you select before beginning.

Forms for shaping can be many things. Styrofoam® shapes and plastic margarine tubs work well for items such as bowls and baskets. Glass or plastic drinking glasses are used for vase-type items. If you cannot find an item with the dimensions given in the pattern to use as a form, any similarly sized item can be shaped by adding layers of plastic wrap. Place the dry crochet piece over the form to check the fit, remembering that it will stretch when wet.

For shaping flat pieces, corrugated cardboard, Styrofoam® or a cutting board designed for sewing may be used. Be sure to cover all surfaces of forms or blocking board with clear plastic wrap, securing with cellophane tape.

If you have not used fabric stiffener before, you may wish to practice on a small swatch before stiffening the actual item. For proper saturation when using conventional stiffeners, work liquid thoroughly into the crochet piece and let stand for about 15 minutes. Then, squeeze out excess stiffener and blot with paper towels. Continue to blot while shaping to remove as much stiffener as possible. Stretch over form, shape and pin with rust-proof pins; allow to dry, then unpin.

Skill Level Requirements:

Easy — Requires knowledge of basic skills only; great for beginners or anyone who wants quick results.

Average — Requires some experience; very comfortable for accomplished stitchers, yet suitable for beginners wishing to expand their abilities.

Advanced — Requires a high level of skill in all areas; average stitchers may find some areas of these patterns difficult, though still workable.

Challenging — Requires advanced skills in both technique and comprehension, as well as a daring spirit; some areas may present difficulty for even the most accomplished stitchers.

For More Information

Sometimes even the most experienced needlecrafters can find themselves having trouble following instructions. If you have difficulty completing your project, write to:

Wishes & Wonders Editors
The Needlecraft Shop
23 Old Pecan Road
Big Sandy, Texas 75755

Acknowledgments

Our sincerest thanks and appreciation goes to the following manufacturers for generously providing their product for use in the following projects:

AD TECH
Pagent Queen — Crafty Magic Melt Glue

CARON INTERNATIONAL
Christmas Kitchen Set — Victorian Gold Christmas
Rosebud Ripple — Dazzleaire

COATS & CLARK
Baby's Bric-a-Brac — Red Heart Baby Sport
Basket of Sunflowers Coasters — Red Heart Classic
Chef's Choice — Speed Cro-Sheen
Connermara Centerpiece — Anchor
Crazy Patch — Red Heart Super Saver
Darling Dress — Red Heart Baby Sport
Diamond Bride — Red Heart Classic
Dublin Garden — Knit-Cro-Sheen
1800's Day Outfit — South Maid
Fancy Wreath Ornaments — South Maid
Floral Square — Knit-Cro-Sheen
Flower Coaster Doily — Knit-Cro-Sheen
Hearts & Flowers — Red Heart Super Saver
Hidden Secrets — Red Heart Classic
Holiday Lace Over — Red Heart Super Saver
Miss Daisy — Red Heart Baby Sport
Mr. Bumble — Red Heart Classic
Ocean Waves — Red Heart Classic
Pagent Queen — Knit-Cro-Sheen
Peach's Playdress — Red Heart Classic
Pineapple Ring — South Maid
Razz-Ma-Taz Afghan — Red Heart Classic
Summer Cherry Picnic — Red Heart Super Saver
Sunny Side Up — Red Heart Super Saver
Tralee Doily — Knit-Cro-Sheen
True Blue — Knit-Cro-Sheen

DMC
"Follow Your Heart" Doily — Traditions
Pagent Queen — Embroidery floss
Rosslare Doily — Cebelia

ELMORE PISGAH
Petunia Pigihoof — Lily's Sugar'n Cream
Summer Accessories — Lily's Sugar'n Cream

FAIRFIELD PROCESSING
Diamond Bride — Polyester fiberfill
Mr. Bumble — Polyester fiberfill
Pagent Queen — Polyester fiberfill
Poinsettia Pillow — Soft Touch pillow

FIBRE CRAFT
Diamond Bride — Oval gemstones

LION BRAND
Cuddle Babies — Jaimie
Girl's Night Out — Chenille Sensations
Milan Chenille Strips — Chenille Sensations
Starlight — Wool Ease
Wonderfully Warm — Homespun

OFFRAY
Pagent Queen — Wire-edged ribbon

SYNDEE
Pagent Queen — 11½" fashion doll

WRIGHTS
Pagent Queen — Gold pleated trim

Photography
Models: Natalie Smith, Jessica Staggs, Lois Ballance, Caleb Traylor, Kristina Woodlief, Laura Simcik, Victoria Ashley

Stitch Guide

Basic Stitches

Front Loop (a)/Back Loop (b)
(front lp/back lp)

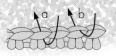

Chain (ch)
Yo, draw hook through lp.

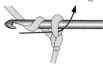

Slip Stitch (sl st)
Insert hook in st, yo, draw through st and lp on hook.

Single Crochet (sc)
Insert hook in st (a), yo, draw lp through, yo, draw through both lps on hook (b).

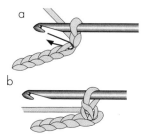

Half Double Crochet (hdc)
Yo, insert hook in st (a), yo, draw lp through (b), yo, draw through all 3 lps on hook (c).

a

b

c

Double Crochet (dc)
Yo, insert hook in st (a), yo, draw lp through (b), (yo, draw through 2 lps on hook) 2 times (c and d).

a

b

c

d

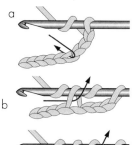

Treble Crochet (tr)
Yo 2 times, insert hook in st, yo, draw lp through, (yo, draw through 2 lps on hook) 3 times.

Final Step

Double Treble Crochet (dtr)
Yo 3 times, insert hook in st, yo, draw lp through, (yo, draw through 2 lps on hook) 4 times.

Final Step

Triple Treble Crochet (ttr)
Yo 4 times, insert hook in st, yo, draw lp through, (yo, draw through 2 lps on hook) 5 times.

Final Step

Changing Colors

Single Crochet Color Change
(sc color change)
Drop first color; yo with 2nd color, draw through last 2 lps of st.

Double Crochet Color Change
(dc color change)
Drop first color; yo with 2nd color, draw through last 2 lps of st.

Standard Stitch Abbreviations

ch(s)	chain(s)
dc	double crochet
dtr	double treble crochet
hdc	half double crochet
lp(s)	loop(s)
rnd(s)	round(s)
sc	single crochet
sl st	slip stitch
sp(s)	space(s)
st(s)	stitch(es)
tog	together
tr	treble crochet
tr tr	triple treble crochet
yo	yarn over

Decreasing

Single Crochet next 2 stitches together
(sc next 2 sts tog)
Draw up lp in each of next 2 sts, yo, draw through all 3 lps on hook.

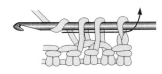

Half Double Crochet next 2 stitches together
(hdc next 2 sts tog)
(Yo, insert hook in next st, yo, draw lp through) 2 times, yo, draw through all 5 lps on hook.

Double Crochet next 2 stitches together
(dc next 2 sts tog)
(Yo, insert hook in next st, yo, draw lp through, yo, draw through 2 lps on hook) 2 times, yo, draw through all 3 lps on hook.

Special Stitches

Front Post/Back Post Stitches
(fp/bp)
Yo, insert hook from front to back (a) or back to front (b) around post of st on indicated row; complete as stated in pattern.

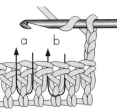
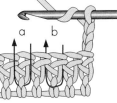

Afghan Knit Stitch

Knit #1

Knit #2

Knit #3

Knit #4

Reverse Single Crochet
(reverse sc)
Working from left to right, insert hook in next st to the right (a), yo, draw through st, complete as sc (b).

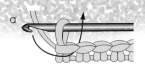
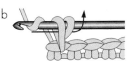

Sc Over Ring

Whipstitch
is used to join two or more pieces together.

The patterns in this book are written using American crochet stitch terminology. For our international customers, hook sizes, stitches and yarn definitions should be converted as follows:

US	= UK
sl st (slip stitch)	= sc (single crochet)
sc (single crochet)	= dc (double crochet)
hdc (half double crochet)	= htr (half treble crochet)
dc (double crochet)	= tr (treble crochet)
tr (treble crochet)	= dtr (double treble crochet)
dtr (double treble crochet)	= ttr (triple treble crochet)
skip	= miss

Thread/Yarns
Bedspread Weight	= No.10 Cotton or Virtuoso
Sport Weight	= 4 Ply or thin DK
Worsted Weight	= Thick DK or Aran

Measurements
1"	=	2.54 cm
1 yd.	=	.9144 m
1 oz.	=	28.35 g

But, as with all patterns, test your gauge (tension) to be sure.

Crochet Hooks
Metric	US
.60mm	14
.75mm	12
1.00mm	10
1.50mm	6
1.75mm	5
2.00mm	B/1
2.50mm	C/2
3.00mm	D/3
3.50mm	E/4
4.00mm	F/5
4.50mm	G/6
5.00mm	H/8
5.50mm	I/9
6.00mm	J/10

Embroidery Stitches

Backstitch

Back Bar of sc

Straight Stitch

French Knot

Stitch Guide
159

Index